Collecting
SylvaC Pottery

Stella M. Ashbrook

Francis Joseph
ISBN 1-870703-12-3

Acknowledgements

A collecting field as vast as Sylvac takes a lot of compiling and without the generosity of a number of people I wouldn't be finished today. I spent a great deal of time at libraries and surfing the internet and the great deal of interesting information seemed endless.

My thanks go to Kath Day, a long-standing employee of Sylvac who was extremely kind to let us photograph her collection as well as aid us with information and facts about Sylvac. Her unreserved enthusiasm inspired me throughout writing this book, and her memories of Sylvac and the factory gave us an insight into the day to day workings of this very popular manufacturer of its time.

I would like to thank Hanley City Library for their assistance, Barbara Baker for her contacts, the collectors for their handy hints and my Publisher Francis Salmon for his full support throughout.

Also I must thank my husband Robert for his tolerance, my family and friends for their encouragement, which have given constantly from start to finish - and if they didn't know about Sylvac before the compiling of this handbook, they sure do now!

© 2000 Francis Joseph Publications

ISBN 1-870703-72-3

Published by Francis Joseph,
5 Southbrook Mews, London SE12 8LG

Photography: Trevor Leek with additional photographs from collectors.

Typesetting by E J Folkard Print Services, 199 Station Road, Crayford, Kent DA1 3QF

Front cover photograph: 1380 Fox Terrier

Contents

About the Author

Upon leaving school, Stella engrossed herself in the vast arena of antiques and collectables and it became not only a hobby,but developed into a very interesting and fruitful career.

Working as an Auctioneer and Valuer for ten years with distinctive auction hoiuses, she gained invaluable experience within the fine art and antique industry, specialising in ceramics and glassware. Her work as an auctioneer has also been beneficial in raising funds for Charity, and her support of Marie Curie Cancer Care has raised several thousands of pounds.

Stella is married to Robert and they live in Shropshire with their baby daughter Madelaine. From here they successfully run collect2invest.com, an Internet site for collectors, providing unbiased advice to all on collectables and antiques

Stella's enthusiasm and knowledge of collectables has brought further writing for *Style Magazine* as well as Francis Joseph Publications.

Sylvac is just one of her many interests and here she endeavours to share her knowledge and experience on this most popular of subjects. There will be others to follow in this series.

Where it all Started – an Introduction

The Sylvan works ceased trading in 1982 and all the records relating to styles and dates of production etc, were destroyed. This hasn't stopped avid collectors from gaining as much information as possible over recent years, and piece by piece the general picture has been put together. There are still models however that haven't been recorded and these are avidly sought by collectors. If you have a colourway or a unique piece of Sylvac, it could be worth a small fortune.

The factory was founded in 1894 by William Shaw and William Copestake and given the company name of Shaw & Copestake. William Copestake however left the partnership half way through the first year and in 1895 Mr Richard Hull became William Shaw's partner in the Business. Their partnership grew in strength and over the forty years of producing decorative wares (and what was known as "fancies") Richard Hull was to have a major influence.

In 1935 Richard Junior joined the company and in 1936 the business became a Limited. With the input of Richard Hull Junior and William Shaw business continued strongly. In 1938 Thomas Lawrence (Longton Ltd) Falcon Pottery was acquired, due to a connection between the daughter and her marriage to Richard Hull. These two factories operated independently of each other for nineteen years until a suitable factory was built on land opposite the old Shaw and Copestake Factory.

These new premises brought the gradual merger of the two businesses and by 1964 the Falcon Mark was ceased. Following the voluntary liquidation of Shaw and Copestake in 1982 the premises and equipment were purchased by the North Midlands Co-Operative Society and from there leased to a workers co-operative society known as Longton Ceramics. Eighteen months later the united co-operative society took over and ran it under the Crown Winsor name. This was not to be a successful venture and they only managed five months of production before liquidation. The premises are now owned by Portmeirion Potteries Ltd who in 1991 began to operate from there. Every piece of Sylvac stock was sold off, and among them even some of the display pieces which command high prices today.

The Backbone of the Business

The Founders
Mr William Shaw and Mr Copestake a partnership, in business only for a few months. William Shaw was in his twenties when he joined forces with Mr Copestake and there is little information about his partner's short term at the factory. His name however was never was erased from use within the company and so Copestake's name remained throughout.

The Opportunity
In the same year as the company was founded, one door closed as another door opened. In walked Richard Hull who had had many experiences within the pottery trade - particularly overseas. Richard Hull was undoubtedly a huge asset to the Company. He was responsible for the development of the export business, a side that was to lead the way for the Companie's future success.

A Family Affair
Richard Hull Junior had the passion and foresight at a very young age to work along side his father so his goals could be achieved. He worked his way up the ladder and achieved great recognition of his business sense and unbelievable drive. His father passed away in 1935 and Richard junior became the new partner with William Shaw. His business acumen and knowledge of commercially sound wares proved to be very productive. The connection with the Falcon Pottery was his marriage to Eilleen Grundy, daughter of John Grundy, managing director of the Thomas Lawrence Falcon Pottery. This union proved to be a successful family affair and all members of the family became involved - even Mrs Hull was known to help out now and again in the business.

Directors
Mr Dennis was an innovative character who had a great deal of time and energy for the Shaw and Copestake Company. He was a friend of the Hull family and so therefore took over the late Mr Grundy's shares to become a director of Thomas Lawrence, Falcon Pottery in 1938 and from there onto the Board of Directors of Shaw and Copestake.

Mr Dennis had a lot to do with the building of the new Sylvan Works and ensured it was developed with modern equipment and methods for the twentieth century.

Designers and Modellers

A strong group of talented people made up the Sylvac Team throughout the years:

Reginald Thompson
Joined the Company in 1917 and became the decorating manager in 1922 at the tender age of nineteen. His outstanding artistic talent was the backbone of Sylvac and he continued to model as well as design up until his retirement in 1978.

Otakar Steinburger
Freelance Czechoslovakian modeler and designer of the 1930s. His most prolific of

pieces was "Mac" the Scottie Dog model numbers 1205-1209.

George Mathews
Joined the company in 1966 having replaced John Lawson as Reginald Thompsons assistant. He developed his own style of modeling animals, ornamental wares and tableware. He was made redundant when the company went into liquidation.

John Lawson
Worked under the supervision of Reginald Thompson and Stephen Czarnota around the early 1960s period. In that time he involved himself in modeling numerous wares including animals. He emigrated to America in 1966.

Stephen Czarnota
Hungarian Modeler who joined the Company in the late 1950s. The long faced dogs, caricature studies and comical wares were his specialty and are wares which are extremely collectable today. He left the Company in 1966 to explore the freedom of design elsewhere.

The Animal Range

As with all collecting fields the wider the range available over time, the more interesting the search for obscure models. Sylvac is no exception and its wide range of animals varies from the wild animals, like lions, elephants, camels and giraffes, to domestic animals like ducks cats and toitoises!

A cross section of designs appeal to tastes at their time of production, particularly from the 1930s through to the 1960s. Fo example, there are amusing figures, among them model no. 1238 which is an Elephant standing on one leg with his trunk raised and his arms out - he's wearing football kit! Another group are the Chimpanzee model no's. 96, 97, 98, all modeled seated and one looks like he's thumbing for a lift.

The amusing range that were produced around the post war period had increasing interest from abroad and due to marketing and production techniques the export sales proved to be 30% of production. It is these unusual models which flew overseas that are highly sought after now, and not only are they a rarity in auction houses but when seen at the collectors fairs dictate high price tags.

Rabbits – The Most Popular Range

The robust models of varying sizes and colours caught the eye of 1930s society and because of their undeniable cuteness proceeded to sell right up until 1975. The rabbit range seems to have been the most popular, appealing too young and old, and as such is a collecting field in its own right.

They came to be produced because while in France Mr Richard Hull had come across a similar model and knew immediately they could be commercially sound. Richard Hull went ahead with this brain-storm even though comments from his partner could have deterred his intentions. They were produced in all colours and glazes, the most common being the green glaze because it proved the most popular at the time of production. The glazes on the rabbits were matt until they discontinued it and experimented with a gloss finish around the 1970s period.

The shapes of the various models include crouching rabbits which were made in two sets and began production in the 1940s. They were modeled as three with their ears up and three with their ears down. There was also a small crouching bunny, model no: 1497, this was modeled with one ear up and one down. The lop eared rabbits which came into production in the late 1930s also had a variation, with the earlier models looking to one side and the later models looking straight ahead. These also were decorated with vibrant shades of orange, mustard and purple.

Included in this popular range of rabbits was Harry the Hare, numbered 1265, 1298, 1299, 1300. This design was registered in 1936 and records show number 1298 being produced until 1970 in shades of fawn and green, turquoise and matt yellow. The other models ceased production by 1940 and hence the rarity of them and the high secondary market prices.

Later models of rabbits from the 1950s onwards have been recorded and include upright comical characters and a large crouching rabbit, no2955. As well as the individual models there were also all the decorative wares which had rabbits modeled in or on them, including ashtrays, vases, wall plaques, bookends etc. The next range however came about in 1975 and was designed by George Mathews. They were modelled as lop eared rabbits in a fawn matt glaze. They stayed in production until 1982.

The range of rabbits proved to be a success that was not only popular throughout production but has continued in these later years to draw in new and old collectors alike. The curtain was drawn on the rabbit line by a children's rabbit money box, no5658. It was modelled clutching a carrot, with both ears bent down. Modelled by George Mathews in 1981, it does make you wonder if it should have had a caption "What's up?", on it, as it was only a year later that the Company went into liquidation.

Dogs, Pooches, Puppies and Pal's

Over two hundred dog figures were produced and nearly every breed was represented in one form or another. Prior to the Second World War when business was buoyant and competition fierce, Shaw and Copestake had produced approximately forty models.

Mr Richard Hull, who had connections in France, installed a French modeller initially to design the figures. The terriers proved to be the most sought after and continued to be saleable throughout all the business years. One of the most popular of the novelty dogs is known as the "Toothache" Dog. Modelled by Reginald Thompson, this is a seated dog with a bandage around his cheek, glazed in a fawn matt finish and produced up until the 1970s. The larger example is very sought after and dictates a high price if at a fair or auction.

One of the most elusive of all is what is known as the 'Mac' Dogs. These were produced in five sizes and designed by Otakar Steinburger who was a London based modeller from Czechoslovakia. This model was in the form of a seated Scottie Dog holding a golf ball. This could explain why the model has such national and international appeal - golf memorbillia is a collecting phenomenon in its own right.

Included in the range were decorative items that were adorned with a dog figure - whether it be a vase or an ashtray. Novelty dogs with expression by Stephen Czarnota are very collectable and to a collector of Sylvac a must in the range.

Have you a Gnome in your Garden or a Pixie in Your Plant Pots?

Each to their own I say. And if your hobby is collecting Gnomes then good luck! A Sylvac gnome in a collection is a great asset. Several models were produced in a cellulose glaze from the 1930s up until the 1960s. The largest of the gnomes is 16 inches high and the smallest 4½ inches high. Because of the glaze they were prone to damage from the elements and therefore few have survived the rigors of our temperamental weather.

Various models were discontinued over the thirty years. They were modelled lying down, seated holding a banjo and deep in thought, as well as having the usual decorative use on planters, vases, bulb pots etc. One of the rarest is a gnome on a toadstool, no2158, is there one in your Garden?

Pixies made on a smaller scale than the gnomes prove every bit as commercial. With their elfin character being modelled on flowerpots, wheelbarrows, toadstools etc, they were also combined with rabbits and tucked in simulated trunk bases hiding in the nooks and crannies. They were finished in both matt and gloss glazes. The pixies are endearing models and could be a collection on their own.

The Little Fancies!

Everyone houses some small ornament or other in their home and if your pleasure is small novelty wares then Sylvac would be the collectable for you.

During the 1930s until closure in 1982, wares could be bought in all shapes and sizes, from small bowls with rabbits, pixies and gnomes seated on the rims, to a coconut vase surmounted by two monkeys.

The *House in the Glen* range of wares was available with a pixie or a rabbit and the posy vases were modelled, as houses, in the form of mushrooms or toadstools. Along the same lines are the Woodland range which had the bases in the form of a tree stump and then squirrels, rabbits and deer applied. The *Squirrel* range comprised of planters and vases and the main decoration is the large tail of the squirrel, which forms the vase or the posy trough.

Another range which proved popular was the *Toadstool* vase number 707 which could have a Gnome, Pixie, Dog or Rabbit perched on its base. The majority of animals can be discovered in the Sylvac range. Some of the rarer pieces take the form of cats with corkscrew tails, Harry the Hare, Dumbo the Elephant, Standing Mule, and any of the Tinies which only stand 1½ inches high, and are modelled as a dog, duck, cat, rabbit or mouse.

So whether it's a miniature vase, a posy trough, a gnome or a pixie there is bound to be a piece that appeals to a new collector.

Character Jugs and Toby Jugs

Through ceramic history the form of full-length studies or head and shoulders has been used in the modelling of jugs. The 18th Century saw Toby Jugs modelled by Ralph Wood, and in the 19th Century numerous Staffordshire potters were modeling "Snuff Takers", "Lord Howe" and other Toby Jugs. The 20th century saw a revival with Royal Doulton, Beswick and Sadler producing the most noteable toby and character jugs, but Sylvac was no exception.

The majority of Sylvac's Toby and Character jug range came about in the 1960s. They purchased moulds for the jugs from Longton New Art Pottery Co. Ltd, who traded under the name of Kelsboro Ware. These models today still cause heated debates whether they are genuine Sylvac models. Sylvac did model some of their own jugsthough, and these were produced from the 1940s through to the late 1960s. Early examples can be seen in matt glazes while later models would be hand-painted.

Figures

In the early 1930s when fashion dictated female figurines were the best ornaments to embellish mantle pieces, Sylvac, although not a major contender in figural production, still produced a range which proved popular for many years.

The earlier figures of dancing ladies in cellulose glaze are relatively hard to find on the secondary market, and collectors so far have found only three examples. Styles of past eras were also copied and the *Country Craft Range* is obviously in the style of earlier staffordshire figures from the 19th Century. One of the most interesting figures is the Seated Red Indian Chief, model no: 1033, its an interesting piece and does make you ponder on the inspiration behind it at the time of design.

Advertising Wares

It has been noted that it was the industrial revolution in the mid 19th century which brought about the creation of advertising through ceramic products.

The manufacturing capabilities increased in the late 19th Century and therefore goods required wider marketing.

Sylvac like most Potteries enjoyed the production of advertising wares. The most common of all Sylvac advertising wares was in fact ashtrays. Two produced for the Lesney Toy Company, in the form of a sand buggy and aeroplane in 1973, are favorites today, as well as ashtrays with die-cast models mounted onto them in various forms. The more common wares are however the ones that bare breweries names.

The Leyland Lorry Ashtray model number 5404 was made in 1977 and is quite rare on the secondary market.

Jugs, Tankards, and Vehicles seemed to be the mainstay of promotional wares.

Tablewares

The range is vast and although there are numerous collectors for the tablewares, prices are kept low because of the quantity in which wares were produced. The most sought after tableware's would be the earlier pieces, which are modelled with matt novelties, such as the cruets with dogs heads as finials or the novelty face sauce pots that have comical expressions on jars that would hold "Pickled Cabbage", "Coleslaw" and "Tatare Sauce" etc.

The honey pots are widely collected as there are many different varieties and shapes. Again the matt variety with comical finial prove the most popular. With the demand for nostalgia the "Teddy Nursery" Range has increased in value. The baby's plate, cups, plates and egg cups, decorated with teddies in action came into production in the 1960s and proved very popular, it now appeals to collectors of nursery wares as well as to Sylvac collectors.

The other range - *Zooline Nursery wares* , which were decorated with comical wild animals like giraffes, monkeys and camels riding in a train, also proved popular in its time, the most novel being the egg cup holder which was in the form of a train.

One of the last ranges of tableware to be produced was the *Tudor Cottage Range.*

Patterns on Decorative Wares and Tablewares

Agincourt mottled
Alpine
Alton
Apple blossom embossed apple blossom
Appolo
Aqua fish
Assyria incised geometric griffins
Aurora slip-trail glazed pattern
Autumn embossed tree in autumn shades
Autumn chintz sprays of flora on white ground
Autumn leaves embossed leaves in autumn tints
Bacchanti
Bamboo - bamboo shoots
Banana leaf banana leaves
Begonia begonias
Belgravia tendrils
Blue tit tree stumps and birds
Bracken bracken
Brazil dark brown with green leaf
Cactus cactus
Canton fancy bird and flora, embossed pattern
Cavalier hand-painted on embossed pattern, later lithographed.
Cavalier new lithographed pattern
Chequers checks
Chesterfield angular plain shapes and colours
Churnet
Chrys
Classic vertical bands
Coral coral
Cordon-brun kitchen implements
Cornflower embossed cornflowers
Countryside lithographed country scenes
Croft embossed cottages
Dahlia flower heads, embossed
Dolphin dolphins
Duotone two tones on simplistic shapes
Egyptian eastern scenes
Etruscan graduated cylindrical petals
Evening Fantasy

Fern fern leaves, embossed
Fleur
Flora flower heads, embossed
Florence
Fuschia trailing embossed Fuschia
Giant Panda panda in bamboo or trunk base
Gossamer incised flora sprays
Glost
Gronant landscape
Harmony embossed swirls
Harvest Poppy wild poppies
Harvest Time wheatsheafs and mice
Heather & Thistle heather's and thistles
High Tide Waves
Hodnet floral spray
Hollington horizontal ribbed and knops
Holly Berry Leaves and Berries
House in Glen pixie or rabbit in toadstool base
Hyacinth Leaf hyacinth leaf, embossed
Indian Tree flowering Indian tree
Ivy Ware green, fawn, white, embossed ivy leaves
Lace cactus
Laronde plain, vertical bands
Lattice lattice work, embossed
Lily simplistically modelled
Limegrove floral sprays on white ground
Lincoln incised geometric flora
Linton
Looped graduated loops
Magnolia shaped as magnolia leaves
Manhatten
Maple embossed leaves, shaded on ribbed ground
Marina shell decoration
Medway pebble dash glaze
Milady embossed floral sprays
Milton
Misty Morn blue hand-painted or lithographed
Modus
Monaco bouquet of flora

Mosaic patterns of small squares
Moselle embossed with cupid and leaf design
Nautilus shell shaped
New Shell wicker effect, wavy base, pastel shades
New Style Flora incised and encrusted pattern
Nuleef large leaves
Oak embossed oak leaves
Oakwood
Olympus garlands of embossed flora
Opelle
Oslo
Palestine
Palm palm trees
Pebble pebble decorated
Pisces fish shaped
Plume lilac, stone, yellow, feathers embossed in contrasting shades
Primrose Primroses
Privet embossed privet
Raphique 1950s design, vertical lines in white on red, green, black or yellow
Rhapsody classical embossed pattern
Riverside reeds and swan
Rope ribbed overlapping rope
Rose rose sprays
Sablon floral sprays on black
Seahorse embossed seahorses
Shell wicker effect, pastel shades
Slymcraft white & black simplistic shapes
Solo green or white pod shaped.
Spectrum undulating shapes
Starway
Summer Reverie leaves on beige matt ground
Sycamore leaves embossed
Tapestry
Teddy Nusery teddies having fun
Texture --
Totem geometric incised pattern
Trentham
Tristan

Tudor
Tudor Cottage embossed cottage ware
Vine fruits and vine leaves and grapes
Vintage embossed pattern, urn shapes
Wall Pattern wall effect
Wild Duck embossed, 2 ducks flying over bull rushes
Woodland deer, mice, squirrels, rabbits on tree bases
Wyka wicker basket effect
Zooline animals in train

The Key to Production and Technique Developments

- Initially a design sketch, which would be made in detail with the correct measurements.

- The design would then go to the boardroom for discussion with all heads of department.

- The modeller would make a clay model and this would also go under discussion and all aspects of the production process would be finalised.

- The block mould is made. A specialist would be used for this process, forming an original block of plaster of paris, from which all other moulds would be made.

- All the earthenware consisted of china clay, flint, stone and ball clay. The moulds would be assembled and the clay poured into the plaster moulds and left to stand for an hour. This enabled water to be absorbed, forming a clay skin next to the plaster.

- After that hour the moulds would be opened and the surplus clay would be poured out. The cast would then be removed an the item would then be ready for other parts like legs and arms to be applied. They would also fettle the seams, ensuring a smooth finish.

- The firing of the figures took place in bottle ovens or gas kilns, and temperatures rose to 1160 degrees centigrade.

- The decorating department applied detail on shading and features. Then it went on to the dipping and glazing department. Once they had been dipped with the relevant colour it was back into the oven again.

- Once fired the next stop would be the packaging department where they were sorted for shops and overseas destinations.

Fakes and Reproductions

Over recent years the interest in Sylvac has increased dramatically as prices have been exposed on national newspapers, collecting magazines and TV shows. When demand is high for wares its not unusual to see them copied or faked - the rarer the piece or collectable model, the more likely a fake would be made as it then would be worth taking the risk.

Fakes have been identified on the market place and it's always sensible to record your finds with all the information on the unscrupulous wares so in twenty or so years they can be identified by future collectors.

What has already been discovered is unusual coloured and finished pieces on a range of jugs including the model 1969 Gnome and Mushroom Jug, model 1318 Rabbit Jug, model 1960 Stork Jug, model 1380 Terrier, models 1026.1027,1028 the Snub nosed

Rabbits and model 1959 the Squirrel and Acorn Jug. This information came to light through the Sylvac Collectors Club run by Mike and Derry Collins; they have been inundated with collectors querying various models.

IMPORTANT FACTS TO LOOK OUT FOR:
• The quality is inferior, and detail is poor.

• Fakes have much brighter enamels, or are in a totally different colourway to an original.

• The Glaze is inconsistent and either coagulates into groves or the foot rims or has very little glaze applied at all.

• Fakes may be smaller in size but it has only been noted as yet that this is marginal and on first glance possibly missed.

• The Sylvac stamp to the base isn't impressed with the usual back stamp; it looks more handwritten than uniformed.

Not from the publisher:

Over the last few years Norman Williams, a potter in Stoke on Trent has acquired a number of Sylvac moulds, and taken up the dormant trade name of Sylvac. Unfortunately, he deems it necessary to imitate the old Sylvac items as closely as possible, thus causing confusion among collectors. If you see items for sale that are below the normal prices that are achieved on the market or at local auctions, they are probably from him, and they do not have the investment potential of the original Sylvac, so beware. Norman Williams has done the same with the very good name of Crown Devon, and you can see that mark on garish looking items made by him, which some traders try to sell on as original. If you suspect any trader or auction house of passing on these items as original, we suggest you contact your local trading standards office immediately.

Marks and Backstamps

The "catchy" name of Sylvac came about when Richard decided to change the Trade name to keep in line with competition and as their name Sylvan was already in use by another pottery he changed the "N" to a "C" which stood for Copestake, and christened it SYLVAC.

• The earlier Daisy Mark was changed in 1935 to incorporate the new Sylvac name.

• Following on was a standard impressed mark that could be used on the bases of all wares.

• The 1980s saw the "Sylvac Ceramics" mark used for a short period.

Impressed marks

Impressed marks

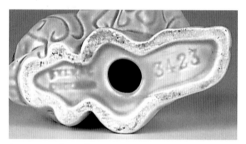

Impressed marks

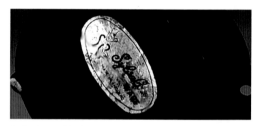

Label applied

Backstamp and Label

Long Neck Cats Model No: 3457   *Long Neck Cats Model No: 3457*

Caricature Cat Model No:5298, No:5299, No:5300

Two "Tinies" Scared Cats Model No:1400

Scared Cat Model No:1046

Sitting Cat Model No:3167

Laughing Cat with Bow Tie Model No:843

Caricature Cat Model No:2549

Siamese Cat Model No:5107

Scared Cats Model No's:1046, Tiny Scared Cats No's 1400

Scared Cats Model No:1046

Kitten in Ball of Wool Vase Model No: 3168

Puss In Shoe Model No:992

Crouching Cat Model No:1333

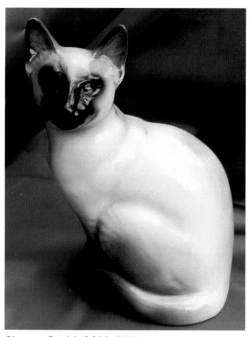

Siamese Cat Model No:5111

Chimney With Cat Model No:2425

Spaniel Dog Model No:114

Spaniel Dog Model No:115, Mongrel Puppy Model No:2974

Dachshund Dog Model No:3078

Basset Hound Dog Model No:3561, Spainiel Dog Model No:18

Dog Model No:2951, Dog Model No:2950

Liqueur Dog

Corgi Dog Model No:3128, Corgi Model No:5321

Shetland Sheepdog Model No:5023

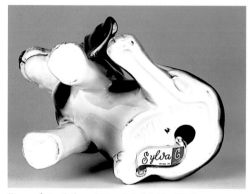

Base of Dachshund Dog Model No:3078

Spanial Dog Model No:5076, Cairn Terrier Dog Model No:3447

St Bernard Dog Model No:5320, Alsatian Dog Model No:5112

Brooch (Horse)Model No:5525, Pendant (Retriever Dog)Model No:5517

Poodle Dog Model No:5031, Poodel Model No:2962

Spanial Dog Model No:115, Spanial Dog Matt

Scottie Dog Model No:147

"Toby" Toothache Dog Model No:3183

Terrier Dog Model No:1378, Terrier Dog Model No:1378

Long Haired Cat Model No:5262, Seated Cat

Afgan Hound Dog Model No:5108, Collie Dog Model No:5000

Great Dane Dog Model No:5258, Pug Dog Model No:3552, St Bernard Dog Model No:5320

Boston Terrier Dog, Whippet Model No:5260

Scottie Dog Model No:1261, Scottie Dog Model No:1245

Sammy Dog Model No:1246, No:1247

Terrier Dog Model No:1380

Top Hat with Kitten Model No:1484

Sealyham Puppy Dog Model No:3177

Corgi Dog Sitting Model No:3128

Terrier Dog Standing Model No:1121

Small Scottie Dog Ashtray

"Funnie" Old English Sheepdog, Model No:3423

*Terrier Dog Sitting Model No:1379, Two "Tinies"
Terriers, Model No:1400*

Kittens in a Basket Model No:1296

Bunny Model No: 1046   *"Harry" The Hare Model No:1298*

Bunny Model No: 1026, 1065

"Harry" The Hare, Model No:1298

Acorn Jug with Squirrel (made in 2 sizes) Model No:1115, 1195

"Tiny" Mouse Model No:1400

Hare Model No:3120

Flower Jug with Stork Handle Model No:1138

Bookend Model No:1546 with Lop Eared Rabbit Model No:1509

Rope Vase Model No: 1307

House in the Glen Posy Model No:4890

Basket Posy with Pixie Model No:2276

Beige Mushroom and Pixie Jug Model No: 1969

Mr Sylvac Ashtray Model No: 3542, without lettering

Mr Sylvac Ashtray Model No: 3542, with lettering

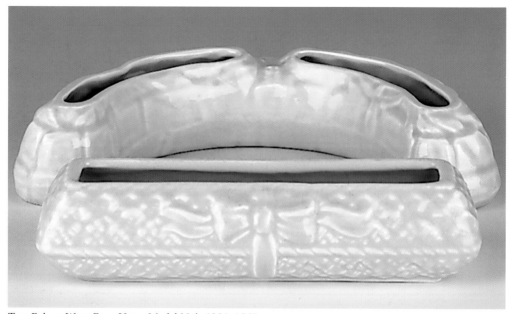

Two Falcon Ware Posy Vases Model No's:1984, 1965

Bull Model No: 3930. (Prestige Range)

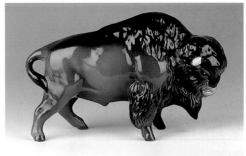

Bison Model No: 4732

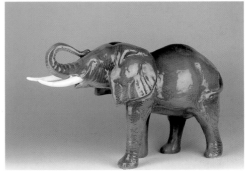

Buffalo Model No: 4733

Elephant Model No:68

Horseradish Face Pot Model No:5048

Beetroot Face Pot Model No:5127, Model No:4553

Pineapple Pot Model No:4583

Crimson Pot Model No:4585

Bread Sauce Face Pot Model No:4557

Pickled Cabbage Face Pot Model No:4755

Chutney Face Pot Model No:4753

Cucumber Face Pot Model No:4565

Onion Face Pot Model No:5126

Coleslaw Face Pot Model No:4750

Tartare Sauce Face Pot Model No:4915

Cavalier Range Tankard 5333 and Falcon Ware Beaker No: 308

Tea Bag Holder Cane Ware Range, Model No: 5038

Cavalier Tankard Model No 5328.

Queen Elizabeth II Silver Jubilee Wares

Denture Mosiac Range Pot and Cover Model No: 4965

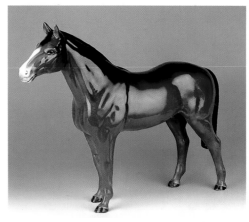

Hunter Horse Model No:3180

Squirrel Model No: 5211, (Prestige Range)

Horse Model No: 3180

Galloway Bull

Penquin Stooping Model No:131

Giraffe Model No:5234

Woodland Range Tree Vase With Squirrel Model No:4233

Stalking Fox Model No:1424

Fox Model No:5209 (Prestige Range)

Farleys Rusks Piggy Bank

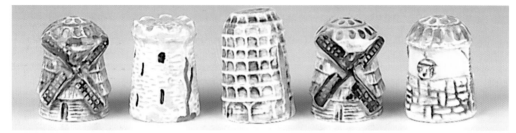

Thimbles: Windmill No:5058, Castle No:5053, Pisa No:5057, Windmill No:5058, Wishing Well No:5060

Stained Glass Vase, Lincoln Range

Rabbit Skiing Model No 28

Chicks on Nest Egg Cup Holder Model No:5466

Thimbles: Pig, Clown No.5059 and Lion

Gnome Model No: 1024, Gnome Model No: 962, Gnome Model No: 1024

Leyland Lorry Ashtray Model No: 5404

Rabbit Model No: 5658, Bloodhound Model No: 5130, Frog Model No: 5097

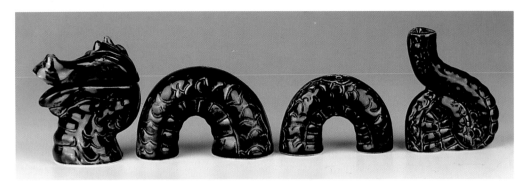

Sea Monster Cruet Set Model No: 5468

Sylvac Tablewares

Dolphin Range Posy Trough Model No:5190

Charles and Diana Commemorative China

Football Mug Model No:4721, Age of Chivalry Tankard Model No:4245, Golf Ball Mug Model No:4719

Charles and Diana Commemorative Tankard

Horse Dealer Character Jug Model No:5200

Mr Pickwick Character Jug Model No:4431, Mr Pickwick Character Jug Model No:4432

*Leprechaun Toby Jug
Model No: 4495,
Henry VIII Character
Jug Model No: 4488*

*Gaffer Character Jugs
Model No's: 4415 &
4416*

Santa Claus Character Jug Model No:4426, Santa Claus Character Jug Model No:4428

Cabby Character Jug Model No: 4467, Fisherman Model No: Mr Wolfe Model No:4459, William Shakespeare Model No: 4474, Sam Weller Model No: 4440, Tony Weller Model No: 4436, Gaffer Model No: 4416, Welsh Lady Model No: 4477

Grenadier Guardsman Character Jug Model No: 4494, Uncle Sam Model No: 2888, Yeoman of the Guard Model No: 4489

Maid Marion Character Jug, Model No:5117

Falstaff Character Jug, Model No:4479, Old Toby Model No:4404

"Hamish", John Grant Promotional Toby Jugs

Hunting Tankard

Falcon Ware Bowl incised decoration

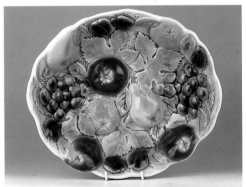

Vine Range Fruit Bowl

Clock

Misty Morn Jardiniere Model No:199

Riverside Range Vase Model No:4277

Sablon Vase Model No:752, Sablon Vase Gloss Glaze

Counter Top Sylvac Promotional Display TV

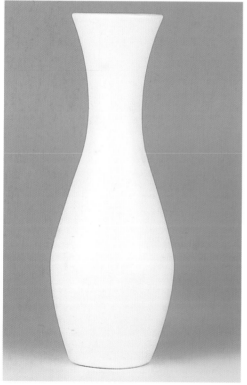

Sylmcraft Vase Model No:3047

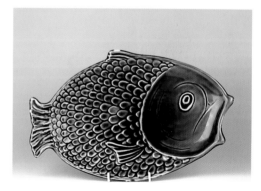

Pisces Fish Plate Model No:4685

Hollyberry Preserve Pot Model No:4530, Hollyberry Tray Model No:4399, Hollyberry Small Tray Model No:4634

Football Money Box

World Cup Football 1980 Tankards

Limegrove Pattern Milk Jug and Sugar Bowl Model No's: 3204 and 2977

Marina Plant Pot Model No:4201

Teapot Stand Model No:5428

Croft Range Teapot Model No:4809

4834 Croft Ware Teapot

Printed marks to Croft Ware Teapot

Croft Ware Salad Plate Model No:4811

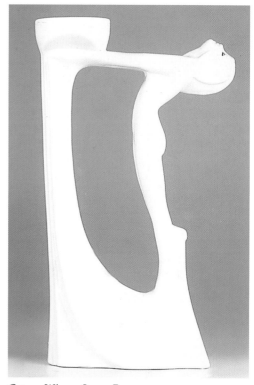

Crown Winsor Lamp Base

English Rose Jug Model No:5411, Sugar Bowl Model No:5410

Sylvac Card

Sylvac Ashtray

Irish Cauldron Jug Model No:1134

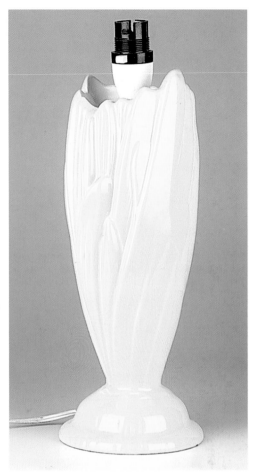

Hyacinth Lampbase Model No:2453

A Blue Rabbit - not Sylvac

Harrods Van (Crown Winsor)

Two advertising ashtrays

Gold Lustre Cup,
Fishing Tankard
Model No:4727

Three Horse and Foal Martingales, Model No:5583

Price Guide

Early numbers are predominantly Falcon Ware numbers up to and around model numbers 760's, its not unusual to see Falcon Ware marks to Sylvac's early wares.

Model No	Model	Size Inches	Market Value		Notes
Birds					
52	Two Ducks		£50-£80	$75-$130	
54	Eagle		£50-£80	$75-$130	
59	Pelican		£40-£60	$60-$100	
130	Penguin		£20-£30	$30-$50	
131	Penguin		£20-£30	$30-$50	
132	Penguin		£20-£30	$30-$50	
137	Bird		£15-£20	$20-$35	
138	Swallow		£15-£20	$20-$35	
591	Penguin Bowl	4	£25-£30	$35-$50	
700	Kingfisher Bird (to match Bowl 436)		£50-£80	$75-$130	
733	Pelican & Rock Vase	8	£40-£60	$60-$100	
787	Flying Duck Flower Holder	6	£15-£20	$20-$35	
793	Swan		£20-£30	$30-$50	
794	Swan		£15-£20	$20-$35	
795	Swan		£50-£80	$75-$130	
850	Bird on Tree Stump		£30-£50	$45-$80	
1082	Penguin	6	£50-£80	$75-$130	
1156	Boy Duck (goes with 1157)	5¾	£100-£150	$150-$245	
1180	Caricature of Chicken		£80-£120	$120-$200	
1290	Eagle	4	£100-£200	$150-$330	
1328	Wookpecker	4	£50-£80	$75-$130	
1330	Kingfisher	4	£40-£60	$60-$100	
1331	Bird	6¼	£40-£60	$60-$100	
1349	Seagull	3	£40-£80	$60-$130	
1350	Seagull	4	£60-£80	$90-$130	
1351	Seagull	5	£80-£120	$120-$200	
1357	Seagull	2¼	£30-£50	$45-$80	
1360	Flying Duck	12L	£80-£120	$120-$200	
1375	Duck	3	£80-£120	$120-$200	
1376	Bird	3	£80-£120	$120-$200	
1377	Pigeon	4	£80-£120	$120-$200	
1466	Chameleon on Branch	7L	£80-£120	$120-$200	
1492	Duck	5	£100-£200	$150-$330	
1498	Duck	3¼	£50-£80	$75-$130	
1499	Duck	4¼	£60-£80	$90-$130	
1681	Duck		£80-£120	$120-$200	
1682	Duck		£100-£150	$150-$245	
1683	Duck		£150-£200	$220-$330	
2397	Baby Duck		£40-£60	$60-$100	
2398	Baby Duck with Wings		£40-£60	$60-$100	
2443	Owl		£40-£60	$60-$100	
2444	Stork		£40-£60	$60-$100	
2632	Starling Bird		£20-£30	$30-$50	
2758	Owl		£20-£30	$30-$50	
2782	Swan		£10-£20	$15-$35	
2810	Swan on Stand		£15-£25	$20-$40	
3115	Duckling	2	£20-£30	$30-$50	
3117	Duckling	2	£30-£50	$45-$80	
3146	Cockerel		£30-£50	$45-$80	
3162	Grebe to go in bowl	4½	£30-£50	$45-$80	
3339	Osprey Prestige Bird	9½	£60-£100	$90-$165	
3393	Duck	5½	£40-£60	$60-$100	

Birds

Model No	Model	Size Inches	Market Value		Notes
3583	Penguin		£20-£30	$30-$50	
3585	Toucan Bird		£20-£30	$30-$50	
3755	Bird	4	£20-£30	$30-$50	
3789	Stork	9	£30-£50	$45-$80	
3790	Stork	6	£25-£30	$35-$50	
4798	Bird		£30-£50	$45-$80	
4930	Swan		£20-£30	$30-$50	
5040	Eagle		£80-£120	$120-$200	
5119	Mallard Duck	7½	£30-£50	$45-$80	
5120	Golden Eye Duck	6L	£30-£50	$45-$80	
5121	Gosling		£20-£30	$30-$50	
5122	Shoveller Duck	7½L	£30-£50	$45-$80	
5123	Tufted Duck		£30-£50	$45-$80	
5287	Eagle	8	£30-£50	$45-$80	

Bowls, Dishes & Plant Pots

Model No	Model	Size Inches	Market Value		Notes
122	Bowl		£8-£12	$10-$20	
169	Shell Dish		£40-£60	$60-$100	
183	Plant Pot		£30-£40	$45-$65	
198	Misty Morn/Rosslyn Plant Pot	6¾	£15-£20	$20-$35	
199	Misty Morn/Rosslyn Plant Pot	7	£15-£20	$20-$35	
251	Bowl		£5-£8	$5-$15	
252	Sanora/Dovedale/Rosslyn Bowl	12	£15-£20	$20-$35	
256	Leaf Dish	10D	£10-£20	$15-$35	
259	Sanora/Misty Morn/Rosslyn Bowl	12	£15-£20	$20-$35	
262	Plant Pot	6	£30-£50	$45-$80	
277	Springbok Bowl		£20-£30	$30-$50	
281	Hat Vase	11	£30-£50	$45-$80	
287	Bowl	10	£10-£20	$15-$35	
290	Sugar Leaf Bowl		£5-£8	$5-$15	
315	Plant Pot	6	£15-£20	$20-$35	
343	Hydrangea Fruit Bowl		£10-£20	$15-$35	
362	Plant Pot	4	£20-£30	$30-$50	
365	Plant Pot/Vase	12¾	£25-£30	$35-$50	
368	Bulb Bowl		£10-£20	$15-$35	
377	Sanora Bowl		£10-£20	$15-$35	
378	Sanora Bowl		£10-£20	$15-$35	
379	Sanora Bowl		£10-£20	$15-$35	
392	Bowl		£8-£12	$10-$20	
396	Bowl		£8-£12	$10-$20	
404	Plant Pot	7	£20-£40	$30-$65	
410	Pot		£10-£20	$15-$35	
411	Pot		£8-£12	$10-$20	
413	Fruit Bowl	12¼L	£12-£18	$15-$30	
415	Vine Patterned Bowl	11¼L	£12-£18	$15-$30	
436	Kingfisher Bowl	9D	£20-£30	$30-$50	
437	Bowl		£5-£8	$5-$15	
447	Bowl		£5-£8	$5-$15	
468	Frog & Lizard Bowl		£30-£50	$45-$80	
469	Frog & Lizard Bowl	8	£30-£50	$45-$80	
471	Diamond Shaped Bowl	10¼	£10-£20	$15-$35	
473	Bowl With Owl	7	£25-£30	$35-$50	
479	Sydney Range Bowl		£10-£20	$15-$35	
485	Bowl with Spout	5	£10-£20	$15-$35	
488	Triangular Bowl	4	£10-£15	$15-$25	
489	Bowl	8¾	£15-£20	$20-$35	
492	Rose Bowl	6¾	£12-£18	$15-$30	
493	Bowl	11	£15-£20	$20-$35	
493	Bowl	11	£15-£20	$20-$35	
498	Bowl		£8-£12	$10-$20	
500	Sydney Range Fruit Bowl		£12-£18	$15-$30	
504	Bowl		£8-£12	$10-$20	
505	Bowl		£8-£12	$10-$20	

Model No	Model	Size Inches	Market Value		Notes
508	Bowl		£10-£15	$15-$25	
547	Green/Blue Budgie Bowl	13	£30-£50	$45-$80	
550	Iceberg/Penguin Bulb Pot		£20-£30	$30-$50	
557	Bowl Fluted	3	£10-£15	$15-$25	
559	Rose Bowl	6	£10-£20	$15-$35	
566	Rose Bowl	5D	£20-£30	$30-$50	
568	Green Bunny Bowl	2	£20-£30	$30-$50	
569	Wild Duck Bowl	4¼	£15-£20	$20-$35	
575	Rose Bowl	8	£30-£40	$45-$65	
580	Plant Pot	4	£10-£15	$15-$25	
586	Bowl as a Barrel with Green Dog	3	£25-£30	$35-$50	
589	Bowl	4D	£20-£30	$30-$50	
590	Bowl		£8-£12	$10-$20	
592	Bowl		£8-£12	$10-$20	
597	Bowl		£8-£12	$10-$20	
598	Bulb Bowl		£8-£12	$10-$20	
601	Flower Pot	5D	£20-£30	$30-$50	
603	Plant Pot	6	£15-£20	$20-$35	
617	Plant Pot	7	£15-£20	$20-$35	
631	Classic Range Bowl	6D	£8-£12	$10-$20	
631	Bowl	7D	£20-£30	$30-$50	
636	Bowl	11¾L	£10-£20	$15-$35	
638	Duotone Bowl		£8-£12	$10-$20	
639	Duotone Bowl		£8-£12	$10-$20	
646	Classic Range Pot	5	£10-£20	$15-$35	
647	Classic Range Pot	4	£8-£12	$10-$20	
649	Classic Range Bowl	8D	£12-£18	$15-$30	
655	Pot		£5-£8	$5-$15	
657	Bowl		£8-£12	$10-$20	
663	Bowl		£5-£8	$5-$15	
680	Bowl with Bird	8	£20-£30	$30-$50	
690	Plant Pot with Couple in Garden	5	£15-£20	$20-$35	
693	Plant Pot with Couple in Garden		£20-£30	$30-$50	
694	Bowl	5	£10-£20	$15-$35	
695	Bowl		£10-£15	$15-$25	
701	Swallow Bowl		£12-£18	$15-$30	
702	Golden Crested Grebe Bowl		£40-£60	$60-$100	
704	Pot With Couple In Garden	5¾	£12-£18	$15-$30	
705	Bowl		£10-£15	$15-$25	
706	Bowl		£10-£15	$15-$25	
711	Bowl with Marigold	11¼D	£15-£20	$20-$35	
714	Plant Pot with Couple in Garden	6	£15-£30	$20-$50	
715	Plant Pot with Couple in Garden	8D	£18-£25	$25-$40	
718	Plant Pot with Couple in Garden	6¼	£15-£20	$20-$35	
722	Bowl with Fairy Scene	11	£15-£20	$20-$35	
726	Bowl with Garden Scene	9	£15-£20	$20-$35	
727	Small Dish		£5-£8	$5-$15	
728	Rose Bowl with Couple in Garden	6	£15-£30	$20-$50	
735	Cacti Pot		£8-£12	$10-$20	
736	Cacti Pot		£8-£12	$10-$20	
737	Cacti Pot		£8-£12	$10-$20	
738	Cacti Pot		£8-£12	$10-$20	
742	Cactus/Floral Pot		£10-£15	$15-$25	
747	Monkey Bowl		£30-£50	$45-$80	
759	Shell Range Pot		£15-£20	$20-$35	
786	Wild Duck Bowl	9D	£30-£40	$45-$65	
791	Wild Duck Bowl		£20-£30	$30-$50	
792	Wild Duck Plant Pot	9D	£18-£25	$25-$40	
812	Wild Duck Plant Pot	7D	£15-£20	$20-$35	
857	Tree Trunk Rose Bowl		£20-£30	$30-$50	
892	Plant Pot	6	£20-£30	$30-$50	
915	Harvest Poppy Plant Pot	8	£15-£25	$20-$40	
918	Harvest Poppy Rose Bowl	5	£10-£20	$15-$35	
938	Palestine Rose Bowl		£15-£20	$20-$35	

Bowls, Dishes & Plant Pots

Model No	Model	Size Inches	Market Value		Notes
940	Palestine Plant Pot	7D	£20-£30	$30-$50	
943	Palestine Bowl	11D	£25-£50	$35-$80	
955	Bowl		£15-£20	$20-$35	
958	Cornflower Rose Bowl	6	£15-£20	$20-$35	
965	Cornflower Rose Bowl		£15-£20	$20-$35	
970	Cornflower Bowl	6	£12-£18	$15-$30	
985	Plant Pot		£15-£20	$20-$35	
1019	Plant Pot		£20-£30	$30-$50	
1068	Flower Centre Bowl	10	£20-£30	$30-$50	
1069	Bowl		£15-£20	$20-$35	
1111	Bacchanti Flower Pot		£30-£50	$45-$80	
1136	Bowl		£8-£12	$10-$20	
1140	Bowl	2	£10-£20	$15-$35	
1168	Oval Dish	2	£15-£20	$20-$35	
1178	Flower Pot	8¾D	£20-£30	$30-$50	
1188	Ribbed Dish	5	£10-£15	$15-$25	
1199	Oval Dish		£10-£20	$15-$35	
1211	Bowl	2¾	£5-£10	$5-$15	
1214	Flower Pot	7D	£20-£30	$30-$50	
1215	Flower Pot	9¾	£10-£15	$15-$25	
1267	Flower Pot	8D	£15-£20	$20-$35	
1268	Flower Pot	9D	£18-£25	$25-$40	
1269	Flower Pot	10D	£20-£30	$30-$50	
1278	Shell Fruit Bowl	11D	£25-£30	$35-$50	
1279	Shell Flower Trough	12L	£15-£20	$20-$35	
1282	Shell Flower Pot	8D	£20-£30	$30-$50	
1283	Shell Flower Pot	9D	£25-£35	$35-$55	
1323	Pot		£8-£10	$10-$15	
1329	Falcon Bird		£40-£60	$60-$100	
1358	Plant Pot	8¼	£10-£20	$15-$35	
1368	Bowl and Cover	4¼	£15-£20	$20-$35	
1448	Bowl	5	£8-£12	$10-$20	
1514	Frog Plant Pot Holder		£40-£60	$60-$100	
1541	Bowl	3D	£10-£15	$15-$25	
1542	Bowl	4D	£10-£15	$15-$25	
1561	Flower Dish	4¼D	£5-£10	$5-$15	
1565	Oval Bowl	5	£8-£12	$10-$20	
1635	Plant Pot		£10-£20	$15-$35	
1653	Bowl	5	£10-£20	$15-$35	
1714	Bowl		£5-£10	$5-$15	
1738	Bowl	8D	£10-£15	$15-$25	
1754	Bowl		£5-£10	$5-$15	
1760	Bowl & Cover		£10-£15	$15-$25	
1767	Dragon Dish	13L	£70-£100	$105-$165	
1774	Cavalier Bowl		£15-£20	$20-$35	
1783	Oval Bowl	4	£8-£12	$10-$20	
1813	Neptune Bowl	2¼	£5-£10	$5-$15	
1821	Powder Bowl		£20-£30	$30-$50	
1822	Floral Dish	5L	£10-£20	$15-$35	
1823	Bowl	4D	£10-£15	$15-$25	
1826	Rose Bowl with Trellis	5	£10-£20	$15-$35	
1827	Bowl	3	£8-£12	$10-$20	
1830	Bowl	8L	£8-£12	$10-$20	
1848	Bowl	3D	£10-£15	$15-$25	
1851	Wild Duck Bowl	8L	£20-£30	$30-$50	
1852	Wild Duck Bowl	8L	£20-£30	$30-$50	
1860	Wild Duck Dond Shape Bowl	9L	£15-£20	$20-$35	
1910	Flower Shaped Dish	4D	£8-£12	$10-$20	
1919	Floral Dish	7¾D	£20-£30	$30-$50	
1920	Floral Dish	5D	£20-£25	$30-$40	
1921	Floral Dish	7D	£25-£30	$35-$50	
1923	Plant Pot	2	£5-£8	$5-$15	
1924	Ribbed Bowl	3D	£8-£10	$10-$15	
1933	Flower Shaped Dish		£10-£15	$15-$25	

Model No	Model	Size Inches	Market Value		Notes
1934	Flower Shaped Dish		£10-£15	$15-$25	
1935	Log Tray		£10-£15	$15-$25	
1939	Hobnail Bowl		£8-£12	$10-$20	
1955	Flower Shaped Dish		£8-£12	$10-$20	
2001	Shell Dish with Flora		£10-£15	$15-$25	
2002	Bowl		£5-£10	$5-$15	
2004	Bowl		£5-£10	$5-$15	
2027	Ivyleaf Bowl	5¼L	£10-£15	$15-$25	
2028	Bowl		£8-£12	$10-$20	
2035	Ivyleaf Bowl	9L	£12-£15	$15-$25	
2041	Bowl		£8-£12	$10-$20	
2043	Ivyleaf Plant Pot	4	£10-£15	$15-$25	
2047	Ivyleaf Plant Pot	5	£15-£20	$20-$35	
2048	Mushroom Bowl		£10-£15	$15-$25	
2069	Ivyleaf Bowl with Rabbit or Dog	4¾	£40-£60	$60-$100	
2090	Ivyleaf Bowl	4	£15-£20	$20-$35	
2097	Chrys Bowl	4	£8-£12	$10-$20	
2098	Chrys Bowl	9L	£15-£20	$20-$35	
2099	Chrys Pot	4¼	£10-£15	$15-$25	
2100	Chrys Pot	5¼	£15-£20	$20-$35	
2108	Chrys Basket	3¼	£15-£20	$20-$35	
2109	Chrys Basket	4	£22-£28	$30-$45	
2112	Seagull Bowl	10½W	£40-£60	$60-$100	
2114	Autumn Bowl		£30-£50	$45-$80	
2115	Autumn Plant Pot		£30-£50	$45-$80	
2119	Seagull Basket	7½	£60-£100	$90-$165	
2128	Shell Shaped Dish		£10-£15	$15-$25	
2129	Rope Plant Pot	5¾	£10-£15	$15-$25	
2134	Bowl	6L	£12-£18	$15-$30	
2135	Bowl		£5-£8	$5-$15	
2141	Bowl		£5-£10	$5-$15	
2143	Bowl		£5-£8	$5-$15	
2145	Bowl		£5-£8	$5-$15	
2146	Bowl		£5-£8	$5-$15	
2148	Bowl		£10-£15	$15-$25	
2150	Rope Plant Pot	7¾	£8-£12	$10-$20	
2153	Bowl		£5-£10	$5-$15	
2160	Rope Plant Pot Holder		£10-£12	$15-$20	
2166	Thistle Bowl	3½	£8-£12	$10-$20	
2167	Plant Pot	7L	£8-£12	$10-$20	
2171	Raphique Plant Pot		£10-£12	$15-$20	
2182	Raphique Bowl		£10-£15	$15-$25	
2183	Bowl		£8-£12	$10-$20	
2190	Raphique Bowl		£5-£10	$5-$15	
2191	Raphique Bowl		£8-£12	$10-$20	
2200	Small Bowl		£5-£10	$5-$15	
2204	Pot		£5-£8	$5-$15	
2209	Cactus Plant Pot		£12-£18	$15-$30	
2213	Raphique Bowl	7L	£8-£12	$10-$20	
2216	Bowl		£8-£12	$10-$20	
2228	Plant Pot Circle Design		£12-£18	$15-$30	
2229	Plant Pot Circle Design		£12-£18	$15-$30	
2230	Pot	4½	£5-£8	$5-$15	
2236	Bowl with Circle Design	10½L	£12-£18	$15-$30	
2239	Bowl		£5-£8	$5-$15	
2240	Bowl		£5-£8	$5-$15	
2242	Bowl		£5-£8	$5-$15	
2248	Cactus Plant Pot		£20-£30	$30-$50	
2249	Cactus Bowl	7½L	£20-£30	$30-$50	
2253	Pot		£5-£8	$5-$15	
2256	Bowl		£8-£12	$10-$20	
2259	Shell Bowl	12L	£15-£20	$20-$35	
2270	Lace Plant Pot Holder		£18-£25	$25-$40	
2279	Bowl		£8-£12	$10-$20	

Bowls, Dishes & Plant Pots

Model No	Model	Size Inches	Market Value		Notes
2290	Lace Bowl	6	£10-£20	$15-$35	
2294	Lace Flower Pot	6½	£12-£18	$15-$30	
2301	Lace Plant Pot	10¾	£8-£12	$10-$20	
2307	Bowl		£8-£12	$10-$20	
2315	Floral Dish	5L	£8-£12	$10-$20	
2316	Floral Bowl		£12-£18	$15-$30	
2317	Floral Bowl		£12-£18	$15-$30	
2318	Floral Bowl		£12-£18	$15-$30	
2325	Small Dish		£5-£8	$5-$15	
2333	Nuleef Bowl/Vase	7½	£10-£15	$15-$25	
2360	Nuleef Plant Pot Holder		£12-£18	$15-$30	
2361	Nuleef Bowl		£8-£12	$10-$20	
2362	Nuleef Bowl	4D	£5-£8	$5-$15	
2365	Bowl		£5-£8	$5-$15	
2367	Nuleef Bowl		£18-£25	$25-$40	
2371	Bowl		£5-£8	$5-$15	
2378	Bucket Shaped Pot	5¾	£8-£12	$10-$20	
2380	Bowl		£8-£10	$10-$15	
2381	Bowl		£5-£8	$5-$15	
2387	Bowl		£8-£12	$10-$20	
2388	Bucket Shaped Pot		£10-£15	$15-$25	
2389	Nuleef Plant Pot	6¼	£20-£30	$30-$50	
2393	Bowl		£5-£10	$5-$15	
2399	Bowl		£8-£12	$10-$20	
2405	Plume Bowl	13L	£8-£12	$10-$20	
2414	Bowl		£8-£12	$10-$20	
2415	Bowl		£8-£12	$10-$20	
2416	Bowl		£8-£12	$10-$20	
2417	Bowl		£8-£12	$10-$20	
2450	Pot		£5-£8	$5-$15	
2454	Bowl		£5-£8	$5-$15	
2458	Bowl		£5-£8	$5-$15	
2461	Jewel Plant Pot Holder	5¾	£12-£18	$15-$30	
2465	Moselle Cherub Centre Bowl	9	£40-£60	$60-$100	
2474	Moselle Bowl	11½L	£30-£50	$45-$80	
2479	Bowl		£8-£12	$10-$20	
2481	Bowl		£5-£8	$5-$15	
2482	Hyacinth Oval Bowl	7¾	£8-£12	$10-$20	
2483	Hyacinth Plant Pot Holder	5	£10-£15	$15-$25	
2485	Hyacinth Oval Bowl	11½L	£10-£15	$15-$25	
2489	Hyacinth Plant Pot Holder	6	£12-£18	$15-$30	
2491	Lilac Bowl		£8-£12	$10-$20	
2498	Floral Bowl		£8-£12	$10-$20	
2499	Floral Bowl		£10-£15	$15-$25	
2500	Floral Bowl		£12-£18	$15-$30	
2507	Squirrel Bowl	6¾	£20-£30	$30-$50	
2512	Squirrel Plant Pot Holder	8½D	£20-£30	$30-$50	
2513	Leaf Bowl		£5-£8	$5-$15	
2526	Bowl		£5-£8	$5-$15	
2527	Pot		£5-£8	$5-$15	
2535	Bowl	4½	£8-£12	$10-$20	
2541	Bowl		£8-£12	$10-$20	
2542	Bowl		£8-£12	$10-$20	
2546	Laronde Plant Pot Holder	6½	£12-£18	$15-$30	
2551	Jewel Plant Pot Holder	6½	£8-£12	$10-$20	
2556	Kitchen Bowl		£5-£8	$5-$15	
2558	Plant Pot Holder		£8-£12	$10-$20	
2559	Jewel Plant Pot	4	£8-£12	$10-$20	
2567	Laronde Flower Pot Holder	4¼	£8-£12	$10-$20	
2568	Laronde Flower Pot Holder	5¾	£10-£15	$15-$25	
2569	Bowl		£5-£8	$5-$15	
2578	Bowl		£5-£8	$5-$15	
2600	Squirrel Plant Pot Holder	19D	£10-£15	$15-$25	
2601	Gondola Bowl		£30-£50	$45-$80	

Model No	Model	Size Inches	Market Value		Notes
2601	Gondola Bowl with Floral		£40-£60	$60-$100	
2606	Bowl		£8-£12	$10-$20	
2610	Laronde Bowl		£5-£8	$5-$15	
2613	Laronde Bowl	14L	£8-£12	$10-$20	
2622	Bowl		£5-£8	$5-$15	
2625	Moselle Cherub Centre Bowl	14L	£80-£120	$120-$200	
2629	Bowl		£8-£12	$10-$20	
2630	Bowl		£8-£12	$10-$20	
2636	Laronde Bowl	11D	£12-£18	$15-$30	
2638	Laronde Bowl	10½	£8-£12	$10-$20	
2673	Bowl		£8-£12	$10-$20	
2690	House Bowl		£8-£12	$10-$20	
2691	Bowl		£5-£8	$5-$15	
2696	Bowl And Stand	8½L	£12-£18	$15-$30	
2701	Bowl		£5-£8	$5-$15	
2704	Plant Pot Holder	2	£8-£12	$10-$20	
2707	Jewel Bowl	15L	£10-£20	$15-$35	
2708	Jewel Bowl/Vase	5½	£8-£12	$10-$20	
2714	Plant Pot Holder	7¼	£10-£20	$15-$35	
2729	Moselle Cherub Bowl	6½L	£10-£20	$15-$35	
2733	Bowl		£5-£8	$5-$15	
2734	Bowl		£5-£8	$5-$15	
2735	Bowl		£5-£8	$5-$15	
2740	Bamboo Bowl		£8-£12	$10-$20	*
2742	Bamboo Flower Pot Holder		£12-£18	$15-$30	
2744	Plant Pot Holder		£8-£12	$10-$20	
2747	Bamboo Plant Holder		£8-£12	$10-$20	
2768	Bowl	8D	£10-£20	$15-$35	
2769	Pot		£5-£8	$5-$15	
2784	Basket Weave Bowl	6	£8-£12	$10-$20	
2785	Plant Pot Holder	6½	£10-£15	$15-$25	
2787	Bowl		£5-£8	$5-$15	
2790	Plant Pot Holder	5¾	£8-£12	$10-$20	
2796	Plant Pot Holder	4¼	£8-£12	$10-$20	
2802	Trellis Plant Pot	5½	£8-£12	$10-$20	
2804	Bowl	8½	£8-£12	$10-$20	
2805	Bowl		£8-£12	$10-$20	
2808	Pot		£8-£12	$10-$20	
2812	Corinthus Bowl on Foot	15½	£8-£12	$10-$20	
2814	Corinthus Bowl	7	£8-£12	$10-$20	
2823	Bowl		£8-£12	$10-$20	
2825	Pot		£5-£8	$5-$15	
2828	Corinthus Bowl	10½	£12-£18	$15-$30	
2830	Cone Plant Pot Holder		£8-£12	$10-$20	
2835	Cone Bowl		£8-£12	$10-$20	
2843	Trellis Trough	14½	£10-£15	$15-$25	
2849	Pot		£5-£8	$5-$15	
2854	Bowl		£8-£12	$10-$20	
2862	Gondola Candle Holder Bowl	5¼	£20-£30	$30-$50	
2873	Bowl		£5-£10	$5-$15	
2877	Apple Blossom Plant Pot Holder	6¾	£15-£20	$20-$35	
2878	Apple Blossom Plant Pot Holder		£12-£18	$15-$30	
2882	Apple Blossom Bowl	7L	£12-£18	$15-$30	
2883	Apple Blossom Bowl	10¼L	£15-£20	$20-$35	
2884	Apple Blossom Bowl	14L	£18-£25	$25-$40	
2889	Trough		£8-£12	$10-$20	
2890	Twin Handled Bowl		£8-£12	$10-$20	
2891	Bowl		£5-£8	$5-$15	
2906	Bracken Plant Pot	7	£10-£15	$15-$25	
2909	Bracken Bowl	9¾	£8-£12	$10-$20	
2910	Pot		£8-£12	$10-$20	
2919	Bowl		£5-£8	$5-$15	
2921	Oakwood Plant Pot		£12-£18	$15-$30	
2923	Oakwood Bowl	4½	£12-£18	$15-$30	

Bowls, Dishes & Plant Pots

Model No	Model	Size Inches	Market Value		Notes
2948	Bowl		£5-£8	$5-$15	
2953	Bowl		£8-£12	$10-$20	
2965	Pot		£5-£8	$5-$15	
2968	Small Bowl		£8-£12	$10-$20	
2985	Bowl	10½D	£10-£20	$15-$35	
2989	Bowl		£5-£8	$5-$15	
2995	Magnolia Bowl	5	£15-£25	$20-$40	
3000	Wyka Bowl	11D	£12-£18	$15-$30	
3013	Wyka Bowl	32½D	£5-£8	$5-$15	
3022	Magnolia Plant Pot	6¾	£20-£30	$30-$50	
3057	Chesterfield Plant Pot	5	£8-£12	$10-$20	
3058	Chesterfield Plant Pot	6	£12-£18	$15-$30	
3068	Slymcraft Bowl	6½	£5-£8	$5-$15	
3071	Slymcraft Bowl	8¾	£5-£10	$5-$15	
3081	Bowl		£8-£12	$10-$20	
3083	Bowl		£8-£12	$10-$20	
3100	Chesterfield Flower Trough	8½L	£12-£18	$15-$30	
3185	Bowl		£8-£12	$10-$20	
3188	Chesterfield Bowl		£8-£12	$10-$20	
3190	Chesterfield Bowl	9¼L	£8-£12	$10-$20	
3191	Bowl		£8-£12	$10-$20	
3193	Brick Bulb Pot	9L	£8-£12	$10-$20	
3194	Brick Bulb Bowl	6¼L	£8-£12	$10-$20	
3195	Bowl		£8-£12	$10-$20	
3196	Magnolia Bowl	8D	£50-£80	$75-$130	
3212	Bowl		£8-£12	$10-$20	
3213	Magnolia Oval Bowl	14½	£30-£50	$45-$80	
3214	Magnolia Bowl	4¼L	£15-£20	$20-$35	
3215	Magnolia Trough	8½L	£12-£18	$15-$30	
3218	Magnolia Bowl		£12-£18	$15-$30	
3222	Bowl		£8-£12	$10-$20	
3224	Bowl		£8-£12	$10-$20	
3227	Bowl		£8-£12	$10-$20	
3233	Log Shaped Bowl	8L	£12-£18	$15-$30	
3234	Log Shaped Bowl	5½L	£8-£12	$10-$20	
3235	Log Shaped Bowl	4L	£8-£10	$10-$15	
3243	Bowl	9¾L	£12-£18	$15-$30	
3244	Bowl	6L	£12-£18	$15-$30	
3246	Bowl		£10-£15	$15-$25	
3249	Bowl		£8-£12	$10-$20	
3251	Bowl		£8-£12	$10-$20	
3254	Bowl		£8-£12	$10-$20	
3259	Bowl		£8-£12	$10-$20	
3260	Bowl		£8-£12	$10-$20	
3262	Fuchsia Bowl	14L	£30-£50	$45-$80	
3271	Fuchsia Plant Pot		£12-£18	$15-$30	
3280	Log Shaped Bowl	6L	£8-£12	$10-$20	
3287	Lily Oval Bowl	10½L	£30-£50	$45-$80	
3288	Lily Plant Pot	8D	£40-£60	$60-$100	
3291	Lily Plant Pot	7D	£30-£50	$45-$80	
3292	Lily Bowl		£20-£30	$30-$50	
3311	Bird Bowl		£25-£35	$35-$55	
3331	Ribbed Plant Pot		£8-£12	$10-$20	
3332	Square Plant Pot		£8-£12	$10-$20	
3336	Ribbed Square Flower Pot		£8-£12	$10-$20	
3351	Alpine Plant Pot		£10-£15	$15-$25	
3355	Pebbles Bowl	7¾	£12-£18	$15-$30	
3356	Bowl with Figure		£30-£50	$45-$80	
3361	Pebble Plant Pot	5½	£8-£12	$10-$20	
3370	Sea Horse Shell Bowl	10	£30-£50	$45-$80	
3377	Plant Pot	5	£8-£12	$10-$20	
3387	Alpine Bowl		£8-£12	$10-$20	
3388	Alpine Bowl		£10-£15	$15-$25	
3389	Alpine Pot		£10-£15	$15-$25	

Model No	Model	Size Inches	Market Value		Notes
3390	Alpine Pot		£10-£15	$15-$25	
3395	Alpine Pot		£8-£12	$10-$20	
3396	Alpine Pot		£8-£12	$10-$20	
3401	Alpine Bowl		£8-£12	$10-$20	
3415	Pebbles Plant Pot	6	£20-£30	$30-$50	
3419	Pebbles Bowl	7½	£8-£12	$10-$20	
3439	Pebbles Bowl	10¾	£8-£12	$10-$20	
3440	Pebbles Bowl	7½	£8-£12	$10-$20	
3445	Sea Horse Shell Bowl		£20-£30	$30-$50	
3455	Opelle Plant Pot		£12-£18	$15-$30	
3456	Opelle Plant Pot		£10-£15	$15-$25	
3461	Opelle Bowl	5	£8-£12	$10-$20	
3462	Opelle Bowl		£8-£12	$10-$20	
3463	Square Bowl		£8-£12	$10-$20	
3464	Planter	15L	£5-£8	$5-$15	
3465	Opelle Flower Bowl	10½D	£8-£12	$10-$20	
3474	Sea Horse Bowl		£12-£18	$15-$30	
3475	Sea Horse Bowl		£15-£20	$20-$35	
3476	Sea Horse Plant Pot		£12-£18	$15-$30	
3479	Bowl		£5-£8	$5-$15	
3480	Pebbles Plant Pot	5¼	£12-£18	$15-$30	
3482	Pebbles Dish	13½L	£12-£18	$15-$30	
3489	Powder Bowl & Cover		£8-£12	$10-$20	
3495	Tudor Bowl		£8-£12	$10-$20	
3496	Tudor Pot		£8-£12	$10-$20	
3497	Tudor Pot		£8-£12	$10-$20	
3530	New Shell Bowl		£8-£12	$10-$20	
3531	New Shell Bowl		£12-£18	$15-$30	
3533	Bowl		£5-£8	$5-$15	
3534	Bowl		£5-£8	$5-$15	
3537	Fluted Bowl		£8-£12	$10-$20	
3545	Bowl		£5-£8	$5-$15	
3555	Bowl	4D	£8-£12	$10-$20	
3562	New Shell Bowl	12D	£10-£20	$15-$35	
3573	Bowl	5D	£8-£12	$10-$20	
3592	Bowl	11	£8-£12	$10-$20	
3605	Pot		£5-£8	$5-$15	
3608	Fluted Bowl	6D	£10-£15	$15-$25	
3624	Privet Bowl	7D	£8-£12	$10-$20	
3625	Stone Wall Bowl		£8-£12	$10-$20	
3638	Stone Wall Bowl	10½D	£8-£12	$10-$20	
3644	Bowl		£12-£18	$15-$30	
3658	Pot		£5-£8	$5-$15	
3659	Pot		£5-£8	$5-$15	
3663	Bowl		£5-£8	$5-$15	
3665	Bowl		£5-£8	$5-$15	
3666	Bowl		£8-£12	$10-$20	
3681	Fluted Bowl		£8-£12	$10-$20	
3691	Covered Bowl	4	£5-£8	$5-$15	
3696	Chequers Bowl	6¾L	£8-£12	$10-$20	
3697	Bowl	10D	£8-£12	$10-$20	
3698	Chequers Bowl	7¾L	£8-£12	$10-$20	
3699	Chequers Plant Pot		£8-£12	$10-$20	
3700	Chequers Plant Pot		£10-£15	$15-$25	
3701	Chequers Plant Pot		£8-£12	$10-$20	
3710	Palm Leaf Bowl	5½	£8-£12	$10-$20	
3715	Palm Leaf Plant Pot	6	£12-£18	$15-$30	
3716	Palm Leaf Bowl		£12-£18	$15-$30	
3718	Palm Leaf Boat Shaped Bowl		£12-£18	$15-$30	
3719	Palm Leaf Boat Shaped Bowl		£12-£18	$15-$30	
3722	Palm Leaf Plant Pot	5¾	£8-£12	$10-$20	
3726	Palm Leaf Oval Bowl		£8-£12	$10-$20	
3734	Oslo Bowl		£8-£12	$10-$20	
3735	Oslo Bowl		£8-£12	$10-$20	

Bowls, Dishes & Plant Pots

Model No	*Model*	*Size Inches*	*Market Value*		*Notes*
3736	Oslo Bowl		£5-£8	$5-$15	
3737	Oslo Plant Pot	5½	£8-£12	$10-$20	
3738	Oslo Plant Pot	7½	£10-£15	$15-$25	
3743	Oslo Bowl	4¾D	£8-£12	$10-$20	
3806	Bowl	11½L	£10-£15	$15-$25	
3807	Stone Wall Plant Pot	5⅕	£12-£18	$15-$30	
3808	Stone Wall Plant Pot	5¾	£10-£15	$15-$25	
3809	Stone Wall Plant Pot	5½	£8-£12	$10-$20	
3813	Stone Wall Bowl		£5-£8	$5-$15	
3815	Stone Wall Bowl	12L	£12-£18	$15-$30	
3821	Glost Bowl	8½	£8-£12	$10-$20	
3822	Glost Bowl	11L	£10-£15	$15-$25	
3823	Glost Bowl		£10-£15	$15-$25	
3826	Stone Wall Bowl		£8-£12	$10-$20	
3835	Bowl		£8-£12	$10-$20	
3838	Manhattan Bowl		£8-£12	$10-$20	
3843	Fish & Bowl		£8-£12	$10-$20	
3846	Privet Bowl	10L	£8-£12	$10-$20	
3855	Plant Pot	12L	£8-£12	$10-$20	
3860	Linton Bowl		£8-£12	$10-$20	
3861	Linton Bowl		£8-£12	$10-$20	
3868	Begonia Plant Pot		£8-£12	$10-$20	
3871	Begonia Pot		£8-£12	$10-$20	
3872	Begonia Pot		£8-£12	$10-$20	
3873	Begonia Bowl		£8-£12	$10-$20	
3874	Begonia Bowl		£10-£15	$15-$25	
3882	Textured Plant Pot		£10-£15	$15-$25	
3885	Textured Pot		£5-£8	$5-$15	
3886	Textured Pot		£5-£8	$5-$15	
3887	Textured Bowl	7¾L	£8-£12	$10-$20	
3888	Textured Bowl		£8-£12	$10-$20	
3889	Textured Bowl		£5-£8	$5-$15	
3894	Privet Bowl		£5-£8	$5-$15	
3895	Privet Plant Pot		£8-£12	$10-$20	
3896	Privet Plant Pot		£12-£18	$15-$30	
3897	Privet Plant Pot		£15-£20	$20-$35	
3906	Coral Pot		£10-£15	$15-$25	
3910	Coral Pot		£10-£15	$15-$25	
3934	Cactus Pot	3	£8-£12	$10-$20	
3936	Cactus Pot	3	£8-£12	$10-$20	
3940	Manhattan Bowl	6¼	£8-£12	$10-$20	
3941	Manhattan Plant Pot	6¼D	£8-£12	$10-$20	
3942	Manhattan Plant Pot	6¾D	£8-£12	$10-$20	
3943	Manhattan Plant Pot	5D	£8-£12	$10-$20	
3949	Manhattan Bowl		£10-£15	$15-$25	
3989	Pot		£5-£8	$5-$15	
3990	Pot		£8-£12	$10-$20	
3998	Olympus Urn	4	£5-£10	$5-$15	
4002	Maple Plant Pot	5¼D	£12-£18	$15-$30	
4003	Fluted Plant Pot		£10-£15	$15-$25	
4004	Maple Plant Pot	7D	£12-£18	$15-$30	
4005	Stone Wall Pot	4½	£8-£12	$10-$20	
4006	Maple Plant Pot	5¼D	£10-£15	$15-$25	
4007	Bowl		£8-£12	$10-$20	
4013	Maple Bowl	8½D	£8-£12	$10-$20	
4015	Bowl		£5-£8	$5-$15	
4017	Bowl		£5-£8	$5-$15	
4018	Maple Bowl	7¾L	£5-£8	$5-$15	
4019	Manhattan Bowl	4D	£5-£8	$5-$15	
4024	Manhattan Bowl	8⅕D	£8-£12	$10-$20	
4078	Pot		£8-£12	$10-$20	
4080	Olympus Urn	6¼	£8-£12	$10-$20	
4081	Olympus Urn	7	£10-£12	$15-$20	
4083	Pot	11	£12-£18	$15-$30	

Model No	Model	Size Inches	Market Value		Notes
4084	Olympus Urn	10½	£12-£18	$15-$30	
4085	Bowl		£5-£8	$5-$15	
4086	Olympus Bowl	10D	£8-£12	$10-$20	
4104	Bowl	8½	£10-£15	$15-$25	
4107	Bowl	8½	£8-£12	$10-$20	
4109	Embossed Bowl	8½	£8-£12	$10-$20	
4115	Olympus Bowl	7	£8-£12	$10-$20	
4122	Bowl		£8-£12	$10-$20	
4123	Bowl		£8-£12	$10-$20	
4129	Sycamore Bowl	9½D	£8-£12	$10-$20	
4130	Olympus Bowl	4	£8-£12	$10-$20	
4131	Olympus Bowl	5	£8-£12	$10-$20	
4132	Hyacinth Plant Pot	7	£10-£15	$15-$25	
4137	Bowl		£8-£12	$10-$20	
4146	Totem Bowl		£8-£12	$10-$20	
4147	Totem Bowl		£8-£12	$10-$20	
4153	Marina Plant Pot	7D	£12-£18	$15-$30	
4155	Marina Plant Pot	5½	£8-£12	$10-$20	
4156	Marina Plant Pot	6½	£8-£12	$10-$20	
4159	Marina Plant Pot	9½D	£12-£18	$15-$30	
4161	Marina Oval Bowl		£8-£12	$10-$20	
4169	Flora Plant Pot	6½	£10-£15	$15-$25	
4170	Flora Plant Pot	5¾	£10-£15	$15-$25	
4171	Flora Bowl		£5-£8	$5-$15	
4173	Flora Bowl		£8-£12	$10-$20	
4175	Flora Bowl	9D	£8-£12	$10-$20	
4201	Marina Plant Pot	4	£8-£12	$10-$20	
4204	Marina Plant Pot	5	£8-£12	$10-$20	
4205	Sycamore Bowl	7½L	£8-£12	$10-$20	
4210	Sycamore Bowl	5D	£8-£12	$10-$20	
4211	Sycamore Plant Pot	6½D	£8-£12	$10-$20	
4212	Sycamore Plant Pot	6¼D	£10-£15	$15-$25	
4214	Bowl	6D	£5-£8	$5-$15	
4217	Pot Stand		£3-£6	$5-$10	
4218	Agincourt Bowl & Cover	4¼	£8-£12	$10-$20	
4240	Woodland Squirrel Basket		£10-£15	$15-$25	
4265	Autumn Chintz Plant Pot	5	£10-£15	$15-$25	
4278	Bowl		£5-£8	$5-$15	
4279	Pot		£5-£8	$5-$15	
4280	Bowl		£5-£8	$5-$15	
4287	Woodland Plant Pot with Deer		£10-£15	$15-$25	
4289	Woodland Squirrel Bowl	8½D	£8-£12	$10-$20	
4291	Woodland Plant Pot with Squirrel		£10-£15	$15-$25	
4292	Woodland Bowl with Rabbit		£10-£15	$15-$25	
4294	Oval Bowl		£5-£8	$5-$15	
4302	Harmony Plant Pot	7D	£8-£12	$10-$20	
4308	Harmony Bowl		£10-£15	$15-$25	
4309	Harmony Plant Pot	8½D	£8-£12	$10-$20	
4310	Harmony Bowl	6¼L	£8-£12	$10-$20	
4323	Aurora Plant Pot	5	£8-£12	$10-$20	
4324	Aurora Plant Pot	6½	£8-£12	$10-$20	
4325	Aurora Plant Pot	6	£10-£15	$15-$25	
4326	Aurora Plant Pot	8½	£12-£18	$15-$30	
4332	Apollo Bowl		£8-£12	$10-$20	
4334	Manhattan Pot		£5-£8	$5-$15	
4336	Harmony Bowl	4¼D	£5-£8	$5-$15	
4338	Harmony Plant Pot	5D	£8-£12	$10-$20	
4345	Apollo Bowl		£5-£8	$5-$15	
4349	Olympus Pot		£8-£12	$10-$20	
4350	Olympus Pot		£8-£12	$10-$20	
4351	Olympus Pot		£12-£18	$15-$30	
4363	Pot		£5-£8	$5-$15	
4376	Pot		£5-£8	$5-$15	
4380	Pot		£5-£8	$5-$15	

Bowls, Dishes & Plant Pots

Model No	Model	Size Inches	Market Value		Notes
4394	Riverside Bowl		£12-£18	$15-$30	
4521	Plant Pot		£8-£12	$10-$20	
4526	Rhapsody Plant Pot	7½D	£10-£15	$15-$25	
4536	Privet Plant Pot	4	£5-£10	$5-$15	
4539	Privet Plant Pot	4½	£8-£12	$10-$20	
4544	Triangular Bowl		£5-£8	$5-$15	
4547	Riverside Bowl	10D	£25-£35	$35-$55	
4561	Gossamer Plant Pot	6½D	£8-£12	$10-$20	
4562	Tristan Plant Pot		£8-£12	$10-$20	
4575	Autumn Chintz Bowl	5¾D	£8-£12	$10-$20	
4583	Tristan Pot		£5-£8	$5-$15	
4590	Tristan Bowl	5	£8-£12	$10-$20	
4591	Tristan Bowl	6	£10-£15	$15-$25	
4596	Gossamer Plant Pot	6¼D	£12-£18	$15-$30	
4604	Gossamer Bowl	4D	£8-£12	$10-$20	
4611	Bowl	9¼L	£8-£12	$10-$20	
4612	Rhapsody Plant Pot	6¾D	£8-£12	$10-$20	
4613	Rhapsody Plant Pot	9¾D	£12-£18	$15-$30	
4616	Pisces Bowl & Cover		£8-£12	$10-$20	
4620	Rhapsody Bowl	9D	£8-£12	$10-$20	
4635	Spectrum Bowl		£5-£8	$5-$15	
4637	Spectrum Plant Pot	6D	£12-£18	$15-$30	
4640	Spectrum Plant Pot		£10-£15	$15-$25	
4641	Rhapsody Bowl	5¼	£8-£12	$10-$20	
4644	Spectrum Plant Pot	4½D	£8-£12	$10-$20	
4645	Rhapsody Bowl		£5-£8	$5-$15	
4647	Spectrum Bowl	6½D	£8-£12	$10-$20	
4652	Spectrum Bowl	7D	£8-£12	$10-$20	
4653	Spectrum Bowl		£8-£12	$10-$20	
4665	Rhapsody Bowl	5½	£5-£8	$5-$15	
4666	Rhapsody Twin- Handled Bowl		£8-£12	$10-$20	
4670	Bowl	4½	£5-£8	$5-$15	
4678	Assyria Plant Pot	7D	£12-£18	$15-$30	
4692	Iron Bound Barrel Bowl		£8-£12	$10-$20	
4696	Plant Pot		£8-£12	$10-$20	
4697	Plant Pot		£8-£12	$10-$20	
4698	Bowl		£8-£12	$10-$20	
4699	Assyria Plant Pot	6½D	£8-£12	$10-$20	
4731	Bowl		£5-£8	$5-$15	
4757	Iron Bound Basket Plant Pot		£12-£18	$15-$30	
4761	Bowl	5D	£8-£12	$10-$20	
4762	Oval Bowl	7D	£8-£12	$10-$20	
4763	Iron Bound Basket Plant Pot		£8-£12	$10-$20	
4764	Iron Bound Basket Plant Pot		£10-£15	$15-$25	
4774	Etruscan Bowl	4D	£8-£12	$10-$20	
4779	Etruscan Bowl	10D	£10-£20	$15-$35	
4780	Etruscan Bowl	6D	£8-£12	$10-$20	
4781	Etruscan Bowl	8½D	£8-£12	$10-$20	
4782	Etruscan Bowl		£8-£12	$10-$20	
4783	Etruscan Bowl	3½	£5-£8	$5-$15	
4823	Fleur Plant Pot	5¾	£8-£12	$10-$20	
4825	Fleur Plant Pot	4	£8-£12	$10-$20	
4830	Fleur Bowl	5	£8-£12	$10-$20	
4848	Bamboo Bowl		£8-£12	$10-$20	
4886	House in the Glen Bowl	8L	£8-£12	$10-$20	
4887	House in the Glen Basket	6½L	£12-£18	$15-$30	
4907	Sink Tidy Bowl		£20-£30	$30-$50	
4921	Plant Pot		£5-£8	$5-$15	
4922	Plant Pot		£5-£8	$5-$15	
4923	Plant Pot		£5-£8	$5-$15	
4949	Bowl		£5-£8	$5-$15	
5005	Churnet Plant Pot	5	£8-£12	$10-$20	
5006	Churnet Plant Pot	6½	£10-£15	$15-$25	
5008	Churnet Plant Pot	5	£8-£12	$10-$20	

Model No	Model	Size Inches	Market Value		Notes
5009	Churnet Bowl	7	£5-£8	$5-$15	
5010	Churnet Plant Pot	7	£5-£8	$5-$15	
5019	Pot	7D	£8-£12	$10-$20	
5020	Bowl		£5-£8	$5-$15	
5021	Bowl	5	£5-£8	$5-$15	
5022	Rose Bowl & Cover		£8-£12	$10-$20	
5029	Pebble Flower Holder		£8-£12	$10-$20	
5069	Trentham Plant Pot	5	£5-£8	$5-$15	
5070	Trentham Plant Pot	6	£8-£12	$10-$20	
5072	Trentham Bowl	6	£5-£8	$5-$15	
5073	Trentham Bowl		£5-£8	$5-$15	
5074	Trentham Bowl		£5-£8	$5-$15	
5109	Cucumber Bowl		£5-£8	$5-$15	
5110	Grapefruit Bowl		£5-£8	$5-$15	
5128	Strawberry Bowl		£8-£12	$10-$20	
5129	Raspberry Bowl		£8-£12	$10-$20	
5135	Florence Plant Pot	6½	£8-£12	$10-$20	
5137	Florence Plant Pot	5½	£5-£8	$5-$15	
5140	Florence Bowl		£8-£12	$10-$20	
5142	Florence Oval Bowl		£8-£12	$10-$20	
5189	Dolphin Plant Pot		£10-£15	$15-$25	
5193	Bowl	3½	£5-£8	$5-$15	
5240	Plant Pot	6¼	£8-£12	$10-$20	
5245	Harvest Time Plant Pot	5	£15-£20	$20-$35	
5248	Harvest Time Bowl	5L	£8-£12	$10-$20	
5249	Harvest Time Bowl	6D	£18-£25	$25-$40	
5272	Bowl & Cover	4¼	£3-£5	$5-$10	
5273	Rhapsody Bowl		£3-£5	$5-$10	
5274	Vintage Bowl	8¾	£8-£12	$10-$20	
5276	Vintage Plant Pot	7	£8-£12	$10-$20	
5277	Vintage Comport	11½D	£8-£12	$10-$20	
5335	Right Herbert Hanging Bowl		£20-£30	$30-$50	
5336	Right Herbert Hanging Bowl		£20-£30	$30-$50	
5362	Cordon Brun Bowl	7½D	£5-£8	$5-$15	
5369	Bamboo Plant Pot	5¼D	£10-£15	$15-$25	
5371	Bamboo Plant Pot	7½D	£12-£18	$15-$30	
5378	Bamboo Plant Pot	8½D	£12-£18	$15-$30	
5379	Bamboo Plant Pot	9¾D	£12-£18	$15-$30	
5389	Lincoln Plant Pot	6¾	£5-£8	$5-$15	
5390	Lincoln Bowl	13½D	£10-£15	$15-$25	
5398	Canton Bowl & Cover	9	£20-£30	$30-$50	
5399	Canton Bowl & Cover	10½	£22-£28	$30-$45	
5406	Bowl	5	£5-£8	$5-$15	
5457	Anniversary Bowl		£3-£5	$5-$10	
5481	High Tide Bowl		£5-£8	$5-$15	
5482	High Tide Plant Pot	4	£8-£12	$10-$20	
5483	High Tide Plant Pot	5	£10-£15	$15-$25	
5484	High Tide Plant Pot	8¾	£12-£18	$15-$30	
5488	High Tide Flower Holder	9½D	£8-£12	$10-$20	
5489	High Tide Bowl	5¼L	£5-£8	$5-$15	
5500	Autumn Leaves Plant Pot	6	£5-£8	$5-$15	
5503	Autumn Leaves Bowl & Cover		£8-£12	$10-$20	
5505	Autumn Leaves Plant Pot	5	£8-£12	$10-$20	
5506	Autumn Leaves Plant Pot	7	£10-£15	$15-$25	
5533	Pot	4	£5-£8	$5-$15	
5551	Plant Pot Tray		£5-£8	$5-$15	
5552	Plant Pot Tray		£5-£8	$5-$15	
5571	Giant Panda Plant Pot	5½	£20-£30	$30-$50	
5575	Giant Panda Bowl		£20-£30	$30-$50	
5586	Milady Plant Pot	7¾D	£12-£18	$15-$30	
5588	Milady Covered Bowl	5½D	£8-£12	$10-$20	
5590	Milady Plant Pot	6½D	£10-£15	$15-$25	
5591	Milady Plant Pot	5¾D	£10-£15	$15-$25	
5610	Belgravia Bowl		£8-£12	$10-$20	

Bowls, Dishes & Plant Pots

Model No	Model	Size Inches	Market Value		Notes
5611	Belgravia Plant Pot	4¼	£8-£12	$10-$20	
5612	Belgravia Plant Pot	5	£8-£12	$10-$20	
5613	Belgravia Plant Pot	6½	£8-£12	$10-$20	
5614	Belgravia Plant Pot	7½	£10-£15	$15-$25	
5615	Belgravia Plant Pot	8½	£10-£15	$15-$25	

Cats

Model No	Model	Size Inches	Market Value		Notes
42	Cat		£50-£80	$75-$130	
45	Cat/Dog Jug	5	£60-£100	$90-$165	
99	Brown/Black Siamese Cat	5	£50-£80	$75-$130	
100	Siamese Kitten Sitting	4¼	£30-£50	$45-$80	
101	Siamese Kitten Standing		£30-£50	$45-$80	
102	Siamese Kitten Playing		£30-£50	$45-$80	
103	Siamese Kitten in Basket		£30-£50	$45-$80	
104	Cat in Basket		£20-£30	$30-$50	
164	Cat		£20-£30	$30-$50	
184	Cat Boxing	5¾	£100-£200	$150-$330	
843	Laughing Cat with Bow Tie	8	£40-£60	$60-$100	
844	Laughing Cat with Vase	8	£60-£100	$90-$165	
981	Cat Sitting	7¾	£40-£60	$60-$100	
982	Cat Sitting	7¾	£40-£60	$60-$100	
1018	Scared Cat		£20-£30	$30-$50	
1046	Scared Cat	6	£30-£50	$45-$80	
1086	Cat	5	£20-£40	$30-$65	
1087	Cat	7	£30-£50	$45-$80	
1088	Cat	9	£40-£60	$60-$100	
1099	Cat and Basket		£15-£20	$20-$35	
1159	Cat with Corkscrew Tail	6¼	£80-£120	$120-$200	
1162	Cat with Corkscrew Tail	4¾	£50-£80	$75-$130	
1163	Cat with Corkscrew Tail	7¼	£100-£150	$150-$245	
1164	Cat with Corkscrew Tail	11	£200-£300	$295-$495	
1286	Cat with Collar	4	£120-£150	$180-$245	
1287	Cat		£20-£30	$30-$50	
1296	Kittens in a Basket	4	£30-£50	$45-$80	
1313	Scared Cat		£200-£400	$295-$660	
1333	Crouching Cat	4	£80-£120	$120-$200	
1432	Cat	2	£20-£30	$30-$50	
1434	Cat		£20-£30	$30-$50	
1474	Cat Holder		£20-£30	$30-$50	
2066	Cat in Boot		£15-£20	$20-$35	
2120	Cat		£70-£100	$105-$165	
2549	Caricature Cat	5	£40-£60	$60-$100	
2579	Cat		£20-£30	$30-$50	
2722	Cat		£60-£80	$90-$130	
2756	Cat		£20-£30	$30-$50	
2794	Cat		£30-£50	$45-$80	
2795	Cat		£70-£100	$105-$165	
3075	Manx Cat	3⅕	£30-£50	$45-$80	
3102	Kitten		£150-£300	$220-$495	
3121	Scared Cat	3½	£40-£60	$60-$100	
3151	Cat Lying Down	5½L	£30-£50	$45-$80	
3163	Cat		£18-£25	$25-$40	
3167	Sitting Cat	5	£50-£80	$75-$130	
3168	Kitten in Ball of Wool	3¾	£20-£30	$30-$50	
3307	Cat		£20-£30	$30-$50	
3392	Long Necked Cat with Flowers	13¾	£50-£80	$75-$130	
3403	Long Necked Cat	7	£30-£50	$45-$80	
3404	Siamese Caricature Cat	7½	£20-£30	$30-$50	
3406	Caricature Cat	5¾	£50-£80	$75-$130	
3407	Caricature Cat	5½	£40-£60	$60-$100	
3457	Caricature Siamese Cat	13	£50-£80	$75-$130	
3571	Kitten & Basket		£20-£30	$30-$50	
3610	Cat		£25-£50	$35-$80	

Model No	Model	Size Inches	Market Value		Notes
3847	Laughing Cat	6	£30-£50	$45-$80	
3892	Smiling Cat		£40-£60	$60-$100	
3984	Cat		£30-£50	$45-$80	
4077	Manx Cat	3	£50-£80	$75-$130	
4977	Kittens in Boot	5½	£10-£20	$15-$35	
5107	Siamese Cat	9½L	£40-£60	$60-$100	
5111	Siamese Cat	9¾	£40-£60	$60-$100	
5236	Long Haired Cat	8¼L	£40-£60	$60-$100	
5237	Cat	12½L	£40-£60	$60-$100	
5261	Crouching Cat	11½L	£50-£80	$75-$130	
5262	Sitting Cat	7L	£30-£50	$45-$80	
5298	Caricature Cat	7	£30-£50	$45-$80	
5299	Caricature Cat	5¼	£18-£25	$25-$40	
5300	Caricature Cat	4	£15-£20	$20-$35	

Character & Toby Jugs

Model No	Model	Size Inches	Market Value		Notes
306	Cavalier Toby Jug	5¾	£30-£50	$45-$80	
312	Toby Beefeater Jug		£30-£50	$45-$80	
813	Sam Weller Toby Jug	8	£60-£100	$90-$165	
1231	Sam Weller Toby Jug	6	£80-£120	$120-$200	
1288	Character Jug Candle Holder	3	£30-£50	$45-$80	
1289	Character Jug	3¾	£20-£30	$30-$50	
1452	Mr Pickwick Jug	6	£40-£60	$60-$100	
1453	Mr Micawber Jug	6	£40-£60	$60-$100	
1463	Neville Chamberlain Character Jug	6¼	£30-£50	$45-$80	
2815	Robert Burns Character Jug		£30-£50	$45-$80	
2815	William Shakespeare Character Jug		£30-£50	$45-$80	
2888	Uncle Sam Character Jug		£30-£50	$45-$80	
2892	Abraham Lincoln Character Jug		£30-£50	$45-$80	
2899	John F Kennedy Character Jug	6¼	£30-£50	$45-$80	
3106	Robert Burns Character Jug	6¾	£30-£50	$45-$80	
3279	George Bernard Shaw Character Jug	6½	£30-£50	$45-$80	
3799	Lifeboat Man Character Jug		£20-£30	$30-$50	
4400	Mine Host Character Jug		£20-£30	$30-$50	
4401	New Toby Character Jug	7¼	£20-£30	$30-$50	
4402	New Toby Character Jug	5¼	£20-£30	$30-$50	
4403	New Toby Character Jug	4¾	£15-£20	$20-$35	
4404	Old Toby Character Jug	8	£12-£18	$15-$30	
4405	Old Toby Character Jug	4	£12-£18	$15-$30	
4406	Old Toby Character Jug	3	£12-£18	$15-$30	
4407	Coachman Character Jug	6½	£30-£50	$45-$80	
4408	Coachman Character Jug	4	£25-£30	$35-$50	
4409	Auld Mac Character Jug	5½	£25-£30	$35-$50	
4410	Auld Mac Character Jug	3½	£20-£30	$30-$50	
4411	Squire Character Jug	4	£20-£30	$30-$50	
4412	Squire Character Jug	3½	£15-£20	$20-$35	
4413	Jolly Roger Character Jug		£20-£30	$30-$50	
4414	Jolly Roger Character Jug		£15-£20	$20-$35	
4415	Gaffer Character Jug	4¾	£20-£30	$30-$50	
4416	Gaffer Character Jug	2¼	£15-£20	$20-$35	
4417	Fisherman Character Jug	2¼	£15-£20	$20-$35	
4418	Nellie Character Jug		£15-£20	$20-$35	
4419	James Character Jug		£15-£20	$20-$35	
4420	Colonel Character Jug	3¼	£15-£20	$20-$35	
4421	Silas Character Jug	3¼	£15-£20	$20-$35	
4422	King Neptune Character Jug		£15-£20	$20-$35	
4423	King Neptune Character Jug		£15-£20	$20-$35	
4424	King Neptune Character Jug		£12-£18	$15-$30	
4425	Large King Neptune Character Jug		£30-£50	$45-$80	
4426	Santa Claus Character Jug		£30-£50	$45-$80	
4427	Santa Claus Character Jug		£25-£30	$35-$50	
4428	Santa Claus Character Jug		£20-£30	$30-$50	
4429	Santa Claus Character Jug		£15-£20	$20-$35	

Model No	Model	Size Inches	Market Value		Notes
4430	Mr Pickwick Character Jug		£30-£50	$45-$80	
4431	Mr Pickwick Character Jug		£20-£30	$30-$50	
4432	Mr Pickwick Character Jug		£15-£20	$20-$35	
4433	Mr Pickwick Character Jug		£18-£25	$25-$40	
4434	Tony Weller Character Jug		£30-£50	$45-$80	
4435	Tony Weller Character Jug	4¼	£20-£30	$30-$50	
4436	Tony Weller Character Jug		£18-£25	$25-$40	
4437	Tony Weller Character Jug		£15-£20	$20-$35	
4438	Sam Weller Character Jug		£30-£50	$45-$80	
4439	Sam Weller Character Jug		£20-£30	$30-$50	
4440	Sam Weller Character Jug		£18-£25	$25-$40	
4441	Sam Weller Character Jug		£15-£20	$20-$35	
4442	Mrs Bardwell Character Jug		£30-£50	$45-$80	
4443	Mrs Bardwell Character Jug		£25-£30	$35-$50	
4444	Mrs Bardwell Character Jug		£20-£30	$30-$50	
4445	Mrs Bardwell Character Jug		£15-£20	$20-$35	
4446	Mr Winkle Character Jug		£30-£50	$45-$80	
4447	Mr Winkle Character Jug	5½	£25-£30	$35-$50	
4448	Mr Winkle Character Jug	3¼	£18-£25	$25-$40	
4449	Mr Winkle Character Jug	2¼	£15-£20	$20-$35	
4450	Watchman Character Jug	5½	£18-£25	$25-$40	
4451	Watchman Character Jug	4½	£15-£20	$20-$35	
4452	Watchman Character Jug	2	£15-£20	$20-$35	
4453	Cavalier Character Jug		£40-£60	$60-$100	
4454	Cavalier Character Jug		£15-£20	$20-$35	
4455	George Character Jug		£20-£30	$30-$50	
4456	George Character Jug		£15-£20	$20-$35	
4457	Simon Character Jug	4¾	£20-£30	$30-$50	
4458	Simon Character Jug	3½	£15-£20	$20-$35	
4459	Mr Wolfe Character Jug	4½	£20-£30	$30-$50	
4460	Mr Wolfe Character Jug	2¼	£15-£20	$20-$35	
4461	Mandolin Player Character Jug		£20-£30	$30-$50	
4462	Mandolin Player Character Jug		£30-£50	$45-$80	
4463	Mandolin Player Character Jug		£15-£20	$20-$35	
4464	Louis Character Jug		£15-£20	$20-$35	
4465	Marie Character Jug		£15-£20	$20-$35	
4466	Charles Character Jug	3¾	£15-£20	$20-$35	
4467	Cabby Character Jug	3¾	£15-£20	$20-$35	
4468	Milady Character Jug	3¾	£15-£20	$20-$35	
4469	Musketeer Character Jug	6	£20-£30	$30-$50	
4470	Ann Hathaway Character Jug		£20-£30	$30-$50	
4471	Ann Hathaway Character Jug		£15-£20	$20-$35	
4472	Ann Hathaway Character Jug		£12-£18	$15-$30	
4473	William Shakespeare Character Jug		£20-£30	$30-$50	
4474	William Shakespeare Character Jug		£18-£25	$25-$40	
4475	William Shakespeare Character Jug		£15-£20	$20-$35	
4476	Churchill Character Jug	4¼	£20-£30	$30-$50	
4477	Welsh Lady Character Jug		£15-£20	$20-$35	
4478	Shylock Character Jug	7½	£20-£30	$30-$50	
4479	Falstaff Character Jug	6	£20-£30	$30-$50	
4480	Touchstone Character Jug		£20-£30	$30-$50	
4481	Romeo Character Jug		£20-£30	$30-$50	
4482	Juliet Character Jug		£20-£30	$30-$50	
4483	Irish Leprechaun Character Jug		£20-£30	$30-$50	
4484	Duffy Character Jug		£20-£30	$30-$50	
4485	Hamlet Character Jug		£20-£30	$30-$50	
4486	Dick Turpin	5¾	£20-£30	$30-$50	
4487	Cavalier Character Jug	5¾	£20-£30	$30-$50	
4488	Henry VIII Character Jug	4	£20-£30	$30-$50	
4489	Yeoman of The Guard Character Jug		£20-£30	$30-$50	
4490	Life Guard Character Jug	5	£20-£30	$30-$50	
4491	William Shakespeare Character Jug		£20-£30	$30-$50	
4492	George Bernard Shaw Character Jug		£20-£30	$30-$50	
4493	Chelsea Pensioner Character Jug		£20-£30	$30-$50	

Model No	Model	Size Inches	Market Value		Notes
4494	Grenadier Guard Character Jug		£20-£30	$30-$50	
4495	Leprechaun Character Jug		£20-£30	$30-$50	
4496	Fisher Man Character Jug		£20-£30	$30-$50	
4497	Harrods Doorman Character Jug		£20-£30	$30-$50	
5113	Friar Tuck Character Jug	7¾	£30-£50	$45-$80	
5114	Robin Hood Character Jug		£30-£50	$45-$80	
5115	Sheriff of Nottingham Character Jug		£30-£50	$45-$80	
5116	Little John Character Jug		£30-£50	$45-$80	
5117	Maid Marion Character Jug		£30-£50	$45-$80	
5118	Allan A Dale Character Jug		£30-£50	$45-$80	
5198	Fisherman Character Jug	5	£20-£30	$30-$50	
5199	Clerk Character Jug	5	£20-£30	$30-$50	
5200	Horse Dealer Character Jug		£20-£30	$30-$50	
5201	Coal Miner Character Jug		£20-£30	$30-$50	
5202	Bricklayer Character Jug		£20-£30	$30-$50	
5203	Cook Character Jug		£20-£30	$30-$50	
5206	John F Kennedy Character Jug		£20-£30	$30-$50	
5215	George Washington Character Mug		£20-£30	$30-$50	

Comical Animals

25	Fawn/Green Skiing Rabbit	4½	£150-£200	$220-$330	
26	Fawn/Green Injured Skiing Rabbit	3	£150-£200	$220-$330	
27	Fawn/Green Fallen Skiing Rabbit	2¼	£150-£200	$220-$330	
28	Fawn/Green Fallen Skiing Rabbit	3¼	£150-£200	$220-$330	
29	Fawn/Green Fallen Skiing Rabbit	3	£150-£200	$220-$330	
31	Fawn/Green Slipper with Dog	6L	£50-£80	$75-$130	
183	Donkey Laughing	5	£150-£200	$220-$330	
768	Elephant Standing	4	£20-£40	$30-$65	
769	Elephant Standing	6	£20-£40	$30-$65	
770	Elephant Standing	7¼	£30-£60	$45-$100	
771	Elephant Standing	8	£40-£60	$60-$100	
773	Elephant with Howdah	8	£40-£70	$60-$115	
788	Elephant with Howdah	6	£20-£30	$30-$50	
789	Elephant with Howdah	7	£25-£50	$35-$80	
798	Elephant with Howdah		£40-£70	$60-$115	
814	Elephant with Howdah	4	£18-£25	$25-$40	
826	Elephant with Howdah	4	£20-£30	$30-$50	
984	Three Monkeys Hear/Speak/& See No Evil	2¼	£30-£40	$45-$65	
992	Puss in Boots	4	£30-£50	$45-$80	
1157	Mrs Duck in Fancy Dress	8	£150-£200	$220-$330	
1158	Mr Duck (matches 1157)	9	£150-£200	$220-$330	
1172	Mr Pig Dressed	6	£100-£150	$150-$245	
1179	Cockeral in Waistcoat		£100-£200	$150-$330	
1238	Elephant Dressed in Football Kit	8	£400-£600	$595-$990	
1678	Skiing Duck	2	£80-£120	$120-$200	
1679	Skiing Duck	3¾	£100-£150	$150-$245	
1680	Skiing Duck	5¼	£180-£240	$265-$395	
2396	Mother Duck		£180-£240	$265-$395	
2451	Toothache Dog	11	£300-£500	$445-$825	
2455	Toothache Dog	8¼	£150-£250	$220-$415	
2501	Toadstool with Dog Tray		£15-£20	$20-$35	
2807	Two Monkeys on Coconut Posy Vase		£50-£80	$75-$130	
3093	Toothache Dog	4	£30-£50	$45-$80	
3140	Caricature Elephant with Big Ears	5L	£40-£60	$60-$100	
3141	Monkey with Boxing Gloves	5¾	£40-£60	$60-$100	
3183	Toothache Dog	5¼	£40-£60	$60-$100	
3383	Comical Mule Sitting	7½	£30-£50	$45-$80	
3384	Comical Mule Standing	7½	£30-£50	$45-$80	
3422	Funnies Spaniel Dog	4¾	£40-£60	$60-$100	
3423	Funnies English Sheepdog	3	£40-£60	$60-$100	
3424	Funnies Pekinese Dog	3¾	£30-£50	$45-$80	
3425	Funnies Alsatian Dog	3⅓	£30-£50	$45-$80	
3426	Funnies Dachshund Dog	3	£30-£50	$45-$80	

Comical Animals

Model No	Model	Size Inches	Market Value		Notes
3427	Funnies St Bernard Dog	3	£30-£50	$45-$80	
3428	Funnies Poodle Dog	4½	£30-£50	$45-$80	
3429	Funnies Bull Dog	3	£30-£50	$45-$80	
3431	Funnies Scottie Dog	3¼	£30-£50	$45-$80	
3432	Funnies Yorkshire Terrier Dog	3	£30-£50	$45-$80	
3433	Funnies Dog with mouth open	4¼	£30-£50	$45-$80	
3570	Elephant Sitting		£30-£50	$45-$80	
3927	Caricature Fox	7	£50-£80	$75-$130	
5232	Two Monkeys	4	£20-£30	$30-$50	
5555	Stork Carrying Bundle	5½	£12-£18	$15-$30	

Dogs

Model No	Model	Size Inches	Market Value		Notes
16	Bulldog	5¼	£30-£50	$45-$80	
18	Spaniel Dog	5	£60-£100	$90-$165	
19	Saluki Dog		£80-£120	$120-$200	
20	Dog		£40-£60	$60-$100	
34	Dog		£40-£60	$60-$100	
46	Dog Jug	5	£60-£100	$90-$165	
47	Bulldog		£50-£80	$75-$130	
57	Dog		£50-£80	$75-$130	
67	Cairn Terrier Dog	4	£80-£120	$120-$200	
72	Scottie Dog	5¼	£80-£120	$120-$200	
73	Green/Fawn Sitting Dog	4¼	£50-£80	$75-$130	
76	Dog		£20-£30	$30-$50	
89	Scottie Dog Wall Plaque	4	£120-£180	$180-$295	
114	Spaniel Dog Lying Down	7	£200-£300	$295-$495	
115	Spaniel Dog Sitting Down	3	£100-£200	$150-$330	
116	Spaniel Dog Lying Down	3¼L	£100-£200	$150-$330	
145	Scottie Dog	3	£60-£80	$90-$130	
147	Scottie Dog	3¾	£80-£120	$120-$200	
148	Scottie Dog Sitting	3¾	£80-£120	$120-$200	
149	Dog With Chair		£30-£50	$45-$80	
155	Bulldog	3¼	£80-£120	$120-$200	
160	Dog		£20-£30	$30-$50	
161	Dog and Bowl		£20-£30	$30-$50	
162	Terrier Dog with head on paws	2¾	£80-£120	$120-$200	
166	Two Sealyham Dogs	3	£100-£200	$150-$330	
170	Poodle Dog	5¼	£80-£120	$120-$200	
176	Boxer Dog	5¼	£70-£100	$105-$165	
177	Dachshound Dog	5¾	£70-£100	$105-$165	
178	Alsatian Dog Lying	4	£60-£100	$90-$165	
179	Dog		£20-£30	$30-$50	
187	Dog		£15-£20	$20-$35	
188	Dachshund Dog	2¾	£60-£80	$90-$130	
203	Red Setter Dog, Running	4¼	£60-£80	$90-$130	
204	Dog		£20-£30	$30-$50	
209	Boxer Dog	5	£60-£100	$90-$165	
210	Daschund Dog	6	£60-£100	$90-$165	
211	Dog		£20-£30	$30-$50	
212	Dog		£20-£30	$30-$50	
215	Dog		£20-£30	$30-$50	
217	Dog		£20-£30	$30-$50	
743	Airedale Terrier Dog	7	£18-£25	$25-$40	
751	Dog		£30-£50	$45-$80	
752	Pekinese Dog	6	£40-£60	$60-$100	
827	Airedale Dog Vase	4¼	£30-£50	$45-$80	
1038	Bulldog Sitting	3	£20-£30	$30-$50	
1043	Dog	7	£20-£30	$30-$50	
1044	Bulldog with Bow	8	£40-£60	$60-$100	
1045	Bulldog with Bow	10	£60-£100	$90-$165	
1117	Large Head Dog	7	£50-£100	$75-$165	
1118	Monty the Mongrel Dog	6	£30-£50	$45-$80	
1119	Dog with Bow	4	£20-£30	$30-$50	

Model No	Model	Size Inches	Market Value		Notes
1120	Dog	4¾	£20-£30	$30-$50	
1121	Terrier Dog	5¾	£20-£30	$30-$50	
1122	Sealyham Dog	4¾	£20-£30	$30-$50	
1123	Dog	3	£20-£30	$30-$50	
1191	Joey the Dog	5	£30-£50	$45-$80	
1192	Joey the Dog	6	£30-£50	$45-$80	
1193	Joey the Dog	8	£50-£80	$75-$130	
1194	Joey the Dog	9	£60-£100	$90-$165	
1202	Alsation Dog		£60-£100	$90-$165	
1203	Alsation Dog	9	£60-£100	$90-$165	
1205	Scottie Dog	5	£30-£50	$45-$80	
1206	Scottie Dog	6¼	£30-£50	$45-$80	
1207	Scottie Dog	8¾	£40-£60	$60-$100	
1208	Scottie Dog	9	£50-£80	$75-$130	
1209	Scottie Dog	11	£80-£120	$120-$200	
1227	Labrador Dog	5	£30-£50	$45-$80	
1243	Dog with Collar	9	£50-£80	$75-$130	
1244	Dog with Collar	10	£60-£100	$90-$165	
1245	Scottie Dog	6¾	£50-£80	$75-$130	
1246	Sammy Dog	4	£30-£50	$45-$80	
1247	Sammy Dog	5	£40-£60	$60-$100	
1259	Scottie Dog	3¾	£30-£50	$45-$80	
1261	Scottie Dog Standing	8¾	£80-£120	$120-$200	
1262	Scottie Dog Standing	8	£120-£180	$180-$295	
1291	Caricature Dog	3	£120-£180	$180-$295	
1295	Scottie/Griffon Dog	5	£50-£80	$75-$130	
1312	Scottie Dog Posy	8¼D	£40-£60	$60-$100	
1332	Dachshund Caricature	5¼	£40-£60	$60-$100	
1369	Alsation Puppy Dog	5	£25-£50	$35-$80	
1378	Terrier Dog	8	£40-£80	$60-$130	
1379	Terrier Dog	8	£60-£80	$90-$130	
1380	Terrier Dog	11	£100-£150	$150-$245	
1382	Spaniel Dog	8	£50-£80	$75-$130	
1412	Airedale Terrier Dog	9	£250-£350	$370-$580	
1414	Scottie Dog	5	£40-£60	$60-$100	
1415	Cairn Dog	5	£40-£60	$60-$100	
1433	Dog with Paw in Sling	3	£20-£30	$30-$50	
1450	Scottie Dog		£30-£50	$45-$80	
1461	Spaniel Dog	6	£40-£60	$60-$100	
1462	Spaniel Dog	11	£200-£300	$295-$495	
1475	Dog with Paw Raised	8¾	£80-£120	$120-$200	
1476	Dog with Paw Raised	11	£200-£300	$295-$495	
1502	Dog with Paw in Sling	7¼	£150-£250	$220-$415	
1504	Dog Front Paw in Basket	3	£30-£50	$45-$80	
1512	Dog Crouching	3	£60-£80	$90-$130	
1524	Dog with Paw in Sling	6	£100-£200	$150-$330	
1528	Dog Scratching	3	£80-£120	$120-$200	
1533	Dog	14¾	£400-£600	$595-$990	
1546	Dog Bookends		£60-£100	$90-$165	
1548	Collie Dog	5¼	£20-£30	$30-$50	
1594	Dog or Rabbit Ashtray		£20-£30	$30-$50	
1646	Puppy Dog Playing	3	£20-£30	$30-$50	
1647	Puppy Dog Eyes Closed	3	£60-£80	$90-$130	
1715	Dogs Head Cruet on Tray		£60-£80	$90-$130	
1818	Dogs Head Butter Dish		£40-£60	$60-$100	
1849	Dogs Head Preserve Pot	4¼	£30-£50	$45-$80	
1850	Dogs Head Cheese Dish		£50-£80	$75-$130	
1990	Dogs Head Toast Rack & Butter	7¾L	£25-£40	$35-$65	
2025	Spaniel Dog Posy Vase	7L	£20-£30	$30-$50	
2331	Boxer Dog	5¼	£60-£80	$90-$130	
2375	Dog Head Beer Mug	5½	£8-£12	$10-$20	
2421	Dog with Barrel	5¾	£40-£60	$60-$100	
2422	Dog		£40-£60	$60-$100	
2424	Dogs Head Ashtray	6½	£12-£18	$15-$30	

Dogs

Model No	Model	Size Inches	Market Value		Notes
2431	Dogs Head Ashtray	6½L	£15-£20	$20-$35	
2473	Dog with Long Hair	4	£40-£60	$60-$100	
2477	Dog		£20-£30	$30-$50	
2493	St Bernard Dog	5½	£20-£30	$30-$50	
2497	Spaniel Dog	4¼	£30-£50	$45-$80	
2502	Collie Dog	6½	£20-£30	$30-$50	
2503	Terrier Dog	4	£20-£30	$30-$50	
2504	Boston Terrier	5½	£20-£30	$30-$50	
2516	Beagle Ashtray	7½D	£8-£12	$10-$20	
2524	Bloodhound Dog	5	£50-£80	$75-$130	
2528	Setter Dog	5¾	£12-£18	$15-$30	
2536	Dog		£15-£18	$20-$30	
2537	Greyhound Dog	8½	£20-£30	$30-$50	
2538	Airedale Dog	5	£20-£30	$30-$50	
2540	Dog		£20-£30	$30-$50	
2545	Smooth Haired Terrier		£20-£30	$30-$50	
2574	Bulldog		£20-£30	$30-$50	
2580	Dog		£40-£60	$60-$100	
2584	Howling Dog	8½	£40-£60	$60-$100	
2595	Dachshund Dog	4	£40-£60	$60-$100	
2623	Spaniel Dog		£20-£30	$30-$50	
2669	Caricature Dog (not sold separately)		Not known		
2670	Caricature Dog (not sold separately)		Not known		
2671	Caricature Dog (not sold separately)		Not known		
2672	Dog		£20-£30	$30-$50	
2675	Old English Sheepdog	5	£20-£30	$30-$50	
2679	Scottie Dog	4½	£25-£50	$35-$80	
2693	Dog		£20-£30	$30-$50	
2730	Dog		£20-£30	$30-$50	
2731	Dog		£20-£30	$30-$50	
2759	Howling Dog		£50-£80	$75-$130	
2760	Dog		£20-£30	$30-$50	
2761	Dog		£20-£30	$30-$50	
2762	Dachshund Dog		£50-£80	$75-$130	
2764	Dog		£20-£30	$30-$50	
2797	Dog		£20-£30	$30-$50	
2938	Sad Dog	4	£12-£18	$15-$30	
2950	Sad Dog	6¼	£15-£25	$20-$40	
2951	Sad Dog	7¼	£20-£30	$30-$50	
2962	Poodle	5¼	£20-£30	$30-$50	
2971	Poodle	7½	£20-£30	$30-$50	
2973	Dachshund Dog	5L	£20-£30	$30-$50	
2974	Puppy Dog	6½	£18-£25	$25-$40	
3074	Dog		£30-£50	$45-$80	
3077	Dachshund Dog	7½	£40-£60	$60-$100	
3078	Dachshund Dog	5	£30-£50	$45-$80	
3092	Spaniel	4	£20-£30	$30-$50	
3096	Terrier Dog	5½	£20-£30	$30-$50	
3110	Poodle Dog	5¾	£20-£30	$30-$50	
3114	Puppy Dog	3	£12-£18	$15-$30	
3116	Puppy Dog	2¼	£20-£30	$30-$50	
3118	Puppy Dog	4½	£30-£50	$45-$80	
3123	Mongrel Sitting	6½	£30-£50	$45-$80	
3124	Dachshund Dog	4¼	£20-£30	$30-$50	
3125	Alsatian Dog		£30-£50	$45-$80	
3126	Dachshund Dog	4	£20-£30	$30-$50	
3127	St Bernard Dog		£30-£50	$45-$80	
3128	Corgi Dog Sitting	4¼	£20-£30	$30-$50	
3132	Dog And Baskets	2¼	£30-£50	$45-$80	
3133	Corgi Puppy Sitting	3½	£12-£18	$15-$30	
3134	Corgi Puppy	2½	£12-£18	$15-$30	
3135	Corgi Puppy Lying Down	2	£15-£20	$20-$35	
3136	Corgi	4	£20-£30	$30-$50	
3137	Corgi Puppy	3¾	£10-£20	$15-$35	

Model No	Model	Size Inches	Market Value		Notes
3142	Dog		£20-£30	$30-$50	
3143	Dog		£20-£30	$30-$50	
3164	Pekinese Puppy Dog	3½	£10-£20	$15-$35	
3165	Pekinese Dog	3	£10-£20	$15-$35	
3166	Stafford Bull Terrier Dog	5½	£20-£30	$30-$50	
3169	Golden Retriever Dog	5	£18-£25	$25-$40	
3170	Alsatian Dog	6¾	£20-£30	$30-$50	
3171	Alsatian Dog	4	£15-£20	$20-$35	
3173	Chow Dog	5¾	£20-£30	$30-$50	
3174	Poodle Playing	6¾	£20-£30	$30-$50	
3175	Dachshund Dog Begging	6½	£20-£30	$30-$50	
3177	Sealyham Puppy Dog	5	£30-£50	$45-$80	
3178	Dog		£15-£20	$20-$35	
3179	Sealyham Dog	4	£25-£35	$35-$55	
3182	Goofy Dog	6½	£40-£60	$60-$100	
3187	Dog Condiment Set		£50-£80	$75-$130	
3241	Dog		£20-£30	$30-$50	
3275	Spaniel with Pipe	5¼	£40-£60	$60-$100	
3276	Spaniel with Ball	3¼	£30-£50	$45-$80	
3314	Fox Terrier Dog	6¾	£30-£50	$45-$80	
3317	Wire Haired Fox Terrier Dog	6½	£30-£50	$45-$80	
3318	Wire Haired Fox Terrier Sleeping Dog	5L	£30-£50	$45-$80	
3319	Puppy Dog Sitting		£20-£30	$30-$50	
3320	Dachshund Puppy Dog	5½L	£20-£30	$30-$50	
3321	Alsatian Dog	6	£20-£30	$30-$50	
3335	Spaniel Dog Sitting		£12-£18	$15-$30	
3338	Highland Terrier Dog Sitting		£30-£50	$45-$80	
3418	Shetland Sheepdog Puppy		£30-£50	$45-$80	
3447	Cairn Terrier Dog	5	£12-£18	$15-$30	
3500	Labrador Dog	5	£15-£20	$20-$35	
3522	Spaniel Dog		£12-£18	$15-$30	
3552	Pug Dog	5½	£20-£30	$30-$50	
3560	Dog Jumping Wall Vase	3¼	£12-£18	$15-$30	
3561	Basset Hound Dog Sitting	7¾	£30-£50	$45-$80	
3563	Basset Hound Dog Sitting	6¾	£20-£30	$30-$50	
3565	Scottie Dog	3½	£20-£30	$30-$50	
3567	Spaniel Dog	3½	£20-£30	$30-$50	
3586	Dog Lying Down		£20-£30	$30-$50	
3614	Dog Sitting	5	£25-£35	$35-$55	
3615	Dog	5	£25-£35	$35-$55	
3642	Basset Hound Dog		£20-£30	$30-$50	
3675	Dog		£30-£50	$45-$80	
3765	Scottie Dog Sitting		£20-£30	$30-$50	
3766	Poodle Dog Sitting	6	£20-£30	$30-$50	
3767	Corgi Dog Sitting	6	£20-£30	$30-$50	
3798	Spaniel Dog Sitting		£20-£30	$30-$50	
3827	Dog with Slipper in Mouth	5	£25-£30	$35-$50	
3829	Scottie Dog		£30-£50	$45-$80	
3849	Scottie Dog	4	£25-£30	$35-$50	
3913	Jack Russell Dog	4½	£20-£30	$30-$50	
3921	Dog	4	£50-£80	$75-$130	
3923	Dog	2	£40-£60	$60-$100	
3933	Pomeranian Dog	5½	£30-£50	$45-$80	
3968	Dachshund Dog		£20-£30	$30-$50	
3988	Irish Terrier Dog	5	£30-£50	$45-$80	
4097	King Charles Spaniel	5¾	£20-£30	$30-$50	
4113	Great Dane Dog	6	£40-£60	$60-$100	
4227	Scottie Dog & Horseshoe Vase		£8-£12	$10-$20	
4251	Corgi Dog	3	£20-£30	$30-$50	
4252	Spaniel Dog	3	£20-£30	$30-$50	
4528	Dog Vase	9¾	£12-£18	$15-$30	
4709	Hound Lying Down	4L	£12-£18	$15-$30	
4710	Hound Sitting	4½L	£12-£18	$15-$30	
4711	Hound Sniffing	3¼L	£12-£18	$15-$30	

Dogs

Model No	Model	Size Inches	Market Value		Notes
4837	Spaniel Dog		£12-£18	$15-$30	
4846	St Bernard Dog		£20-£30	$30-$50	
4986	Dachshund Dog	8¾L	£20-£30	$30-$50	
4988	West Highland Terrier Dog		£20-£30	$30-$50	
4992	Boxer Dog	5	£20-£30	$30-$50	
4999	Spaniel Dog		£20-£30	$30-$50	
5000	Collie Dog	9L	£20-£30	$30-$50	
5023	Shetland Sheepdog	6¼	£20-£30	$30-$50	
5024	Shetland Sheepdog	7	£25-£50	$35-$80	
5025	Poodle Dog	11¼	£30-£50	$45-$80	
5027	Yorkshire Terrier	6½	£20-£30	$30-$50	
5031	Poodle Dog	9½	£20-£30	$30-$50	
5032	Boxer Dog	8½	£30-£50	$45-$80	
5034	Dalmatian Dog	9L	£20-£30	$30-$50	
5036	Dog Money Box		£20-£30	$30-$50	
5049	Beagle Dog	9½L	£30-£40	$45-$65	
5076	Spaniel Dog	8¾L	£10-£20	$15-$35	
5108	Afghan Hound Dog	9¾	£30-£50	$45-$80	
5112	Alsatian Dog	9½	£20-£30	$30-$50	
5150	Doberman Dog	9½	£30-£50	$45-$80	
5167	Labrador Dog	10½	£20-£30	$30-$50	
5170	Setter Dog	9¼L	£30-£50	$45-$80	
5194	Dogs Eating Bowl	5D	£30-£50	$45-$80	
5205	Welsh Sheepdog	10½L	£20-£30	$30-$50	
5258	Supreme Great Dane Dog	9L	£30-£50	$45-$80	
5259	Supreme Schnauzer Dog	7L	£30-£50	$45-$80	
5260	Supreme Whippet Dog	6L	£30-£50	$45-$80	
5263	Poodle Dog	6½	£20-£30	$30-$50	
5292	Caricature Dog	7	£20-£30	$30-$50	
5293	Caricature Dog	6½	£18-£25	$25-$40	
5294	Caricature Dog	4	£15-£20	$20-$35	
5295	Caricature Dog	7	£30-£50	$45-$80	
5296	Caricature Dog	5¼	£18-£25	$25-$40	
5297	Caricature Dog	4¾	£12-£18	$15-$30	
5301	Caricature Sheep Dog	7	£25-£35	$35-$55	
5302	Caricature Sheep Dog	5¼	£20-£30	$30-$50	
5303	Caricature Sheep Dog	4¾	£18-£25	$25-$40	
5304	Corgi Dog	8½	£25-£35	$35-$55	
5312	Corgi Dog		£25-£35	$35-$55	
5319	Supreme Chihuahua Dog	6¾	£30-£50	$45-$80	
5320	Supreme St Bernard Dog	10½L	£30-£50	$45-$80	
5321	Supreme Corgi Dog	7¾	£30-£50	$45-$80	
5322	Supreme Old English Sheepdog		£30-£50	$45-$80	
5323	Supreme Sealyham Dog	8½L	£30-£50	$45-$80	
5324	Supreme Pyrennean Mountain Dog		£30-£50	$45-$80	
5380	English Sheep Dog		£20-£30	$30-$50	
5381	Skye Terrier Dog	4½	£20-£30	$30-$50	
5434	Springer Spaniel Dog	8L	£30-£50	$45-$80	
5517	Retrievers Dog Head Brooch/Pendant		£20-£30	$30-$50	
5518	Cairns Dog Head Brooch/Pendant		£20-£30	$30-$50	
5519	Poodle Dog Head Brooch/Pendant		£20-£30	$30-$50	
5520	Bulldog Head Brooch/Pendant		£20-£30	$30-$50	
5521	Spaniel Dog Head Brooch/Pendant		£20-£30	$30-$50	
5522	Collie Dog Head Brooch/Pendant		£20-£30	$30-$50	

Egyptian Range

Model No	Model	Size Inches	Market Value		Notes
829	Egyptian Jug	8¾	£50-£80	$75-$130	
831	Egyption Bowl		£15-£20	$20-$35	
832	Egyptian Vase	7¼	£20-£30	$30-$50	
833	Egyptian Vase	9¾	£20-£30	$30-$50	
835	Egyptian Jardiniere	8¾	£20-£30	$30-$50	
837	Egyptian Rose Bowl	4	£15-£20	$20-$35	
838	Egyptian Vase	7	£20-£30	$30-$50	

Model No	Model	Size Inches	Market Value		Notes
839	Egyptian Vase	7	£20-£30	$30-$50	
840	Egyptian Portland Vase	8¼	£30-£40	$45-$65	
841	Egyptian Vase Base (to fit 838)	5	£8-£10	$10-$20	
856	Egyptian Vase	7	£20-£30	$30-$50	
862	Egyptian Clock	9	£40-£60	$60-$100	
863	Egyptian Bowl		£10-£20	$15-$35	
895	Egyptian Vase		£20-£30	$30-$50	
926	Egyptian Plant Pot	4¼	£20-£30	$30-$50	

Farm Animals

Model No	Model	Size Inches	Market Value	
15	Horse	7¾	£30-£50	$45-$80
21	Huntsman & Horse (Renumbered 4707)		£50-£80	$75-$130
55	Pony		£50-£80	$75-$130
60	Horse		£50-£80	$75-$130
95	Horse		£30-£50	$45-$80
107	Foal		£15-£20	$20-$35
109	Foal		£15-£20	$20-$35
124	Horse		£20-£30	$30-$50
125	Horse		£20-£30	$30-$50
135	Horse		£30-£50	$45-$80
140	Horse		£20-£30	$30-$50
141	Foal		£15-£20	$20-$35
167	Horse		£20-£30	$30-$50
205	Foal		£15-£20	$20-$35
206	Foal		£15-£20	$20-$35
207	Horse	6	£30-£50	$45-$80
208	Horse		£20-£30	$30-$50
213	Foal		£15-£20	$20-$35
214	Shetland Pony	5	£50-£80	$75-$130
1100	Pig	10L	£20-£30	$30-$50
1132	Pig		£18-£25	$25-$40
1281	Lamb		£20-£30	$30-$50
1284	Lamb	4	£40-£60	$60-$100
1285	Lamb (similar to 1284)	5	£40-£60	$60-$100
1334	Foal	4	£20-£30	$30-$50
1373	Goat	4L	£50-£80	$75-$130
1374	Donkey	4L	£50-£80	$75-$130
1422	Horse	5¾	£60-£100	$90-$165
1427	Lamb	5¾	£80-£120	$120-$200
1428	Donkey	4¼	£30-£50	$45-$80
1431	Calf	3	£30-£50	$45-$80
1447	Foal Lying Down	3	£30-£50	$45-$80
1486	Pig		£30-£50	$45-$80
1505	Set of Six Lambs	1	£280-£340	$415-$560
1508	Foal	5	£40-£60	$60-$100
1659	Lamb	4¾	£30-£50	$45-$80
1660	Lamb	6	£80-£120	$120-$200
1661	Lamb	8	£250-£350	$370-$580
2668	Lamb (not sold separately)		Not known	
3119	Horse	6½	£20-£30	$30-$50
3129	Horse And Tack	6½	£20-£30	$30-$50
3130	Horse	6½	£20-£30	$30-$50
3131	Donkey		£20-£30	$30-$50
3138	Donkey with Cart	4	£30-£50	$45-$80
3139	Donkey	4	£25-£35	$35-$55
3144	Horse	5	£20-£30	$30-$50
3145	Foal	4¼	£20-£30	$30-$50
3149	Cart Horse		£30-£50	$45-$80
3150	Foal	4	£18-£25	$25-$40
3155	Cart Horse	7½	£18-£25	$25-$40
3172	Goat	5	£35-£55	$50-$90
3176	Horse	7¼	£20-£30	$30-$50
3180	Horse	9	£25-£50	$35-$80

Farm Animals

Model No	Model	Size Inches	Market Value		Notes
3240	Pig		£20-£30	$30-$50	
3337	Pig	3½	£12-£18	$15-$30	
3762	Horse		£20-£30	$30-$50	
3930	Prestige Bull	142½	£100-£150	$150-$245	
4707	Horse & Rider	9L	£80-£120	$120-$200	
4708	Pony & Rider	6L	£70-£100	$105-$165	
4839	Galloway Bull	2¼	£12-£18	$15-$30	
4872	Shire Horse with Harness		£30-£50	$45-$80	
4873	Shire Horse		£25-£30	$35-$50	
4963	Shire Horse	7	£20-£30	$30-$50	
4978	Shire Horse	7	£20-£30	$30-$50	
5035	Hunter Horse	12½	£50-£80	$75-$130	
5125	Shire Horse	9¾L	£20-£30	$30-$50	
5131	Donkey		£40-£60	$60-$100	
5197	Galloway Bull	5	£50-£100	$75-$165	
5207	Galloway Bull	5¾	£40-£60	$60-$100	
5213	Modus Horse	9½L	£30-£60	$45-$100	

Figures

Model No	Model	Size Inches	Market Value		Notes
39	Red Riding Hood Figure 1950s		£150-£200	$220-$330	
111	Girl		£60-£100	$90-$165	
112/3	Boys		£60-£100	$90-$165	
327	Boys Head Plaque		£40-£60	$60-$100	
329	Girls Head Plaque		£40-£60	$60-$100	
847	Covent Garden Flower Girl Figure	10	£60-£100	$90-$165	
865	Covent Garden Flower Seller Figure	10	£70-£100	$105-$165	
880	30s Style Figurine	8	£40-£60	$60-$100	
881	Spanish Lady Figurine	9	£50-£80	$75-$130	
887	Curtsying Lady Figurine	5	£50-£80	$75-$130	
888	Lady Dressed in Hat & Muff Figurine	6	£50-£100	$75-$165	
889	Lady in Bonnet & Shawl Figurine	7¼	£50-£80	$75-$130	
890	Lady Holding Flowers Figurine		£50-£80	$75-$130	
919	Figurine of Lady holding Skirt	8	£50-£80	$75-$130	
920	Figurine of Lady with Skirts held out	8	£50-£80	$75-$130	
930	Pierrette Figurine (matches 931)	9¾	£120-£180	$180-$295	
931	Pierrot Figurine (matches 930)	9¾	£120-£180	$180-$295	
989	Footballer		£150-£200	$220-$330	
1022	Black Boy & Banjo Figurine	5	£150-£180	$220-$295	
1023	Boy Soldier Figurine		£50-£80	$75-$130	
1033	Indian Chief on Rock	7¼	£70-£100	$105-$165	
1035	Figurine of Lady Seated		£60-£80	$90-$130	
1036	Red Riding Hood		£80-£120	$120-$200	
1037	Girl snd Donkey on Base	7	£40-£60	$60-$100	
1042	Boy and Donkey on Base	7	£40-£60	$60-$100	
1080	Figurine of a Lady	5	£60-£100	$90-$165	
1081	Red Riding Hood Figure	5	£60-£100	$90-$165	
1154	Figurine of Boy Whistling		£100-£150	$150-$245	
1161	Shy Girl		£80-£120	$120-$200	
1170	Girl with Banjo (matches 1022)	5	£100-£150	$150-$245	
1237	Figurines Bride & Groom		£40-£60	$60-$100	
1258	Sailor and Rum Keg	9	£70-£100	$105-$165	
1319	Sailor Figurine		£70-£100	$105-$165	
1326	Figurine Posy Holder	3	£60-£80	$90-$130	
1336	Figurine Posy Holder	7¼	£50-£100	$75-$165	
1663	Airman	6	£150-£200	$220-$330	
1664	Soldier		£150-£200	$220-$330	
2736	Figure of Boy		£60-£80	$90-$130	
2822	Figure possibly a Saint		£220-£280	$325-$460	
2824	Prototype Figure of St Francis of Assisi	9½	£250-£350	$370-$580	
2829	Boy /Girl/Other Posy Holder	4¾	£40-£60	$60-$100	
2842	Figure		£60-£80	$90-$130	
2845	Girl		£60-£80	$90-$130	
2887	Figure		£60-£80	$90-$130	

Model No	Model	Size Inches	Market Value		Notes
2895	St Joan of Arc Figure		£200-£300	$295-$495	
2903	Prototype St Nicholas & Child Figure		£200-£300	$295-$495	
3111	Girl "Pam"	3	£60-£100	$90-$165	
3112	Boy "Paul"	3¾	£60-£100	$90-$165	
3113	Boy "Pete"	3¼	£60-£100	$90-$165	
4249	Tray with Figure		£8-£12	$10-$20	
4836	Stand with Figure		£10-£15	$15-$25	
4836	Stand with Figure		£10-£15	$15-$25	
4973	Boy and Dog		£10-£15	$15-$25	
5313	Staffordshire Rustic Emily with Dog		£50-£80	$75-$130	
5314	Staffordshire Rustic Alice with Goat		£50-£80	$75-$130	
5315	Staffordshire Rustic Adam the Gamekeeper	10	£50-£80	$75-$130	
5316	Staffordshire Rustic Katie the Goose Girl		£50-£80	$75-$130	

Gnomes, Pixies & Goblins

Model No	Model	Size Inches	Market Value		Notes
74	Garden Gnome Sitting	7¾	£200-£300	$295-$495	
75	Garden Gnome Sitting	6	£200-£300	$295-$495	
81	Garden Gnome Relaxing	8L	£200-£300	$295-$495	
82	Garden Gnome Relaxing	8L	£200-£300	$295-$495	
83	Garden Gnome Playing Banjo	8	£200-£300	$295-$495	
87	Garden Gnome Standing	7¼	£200-£300	$295-$495	
108	Garden Gnome Relaxing	10	£300-£400	$445-$660	
110	Garden Gnome Sitting	11	£300-£400	$445-$660	
113	Garden Gnome Relaxing	11	£300-£400	$445-$660	
320	Gnome Wall Vase	7	£80-£120	$120-$200	
353	Log & Gnome Bulb Bowl	8	£40-£60	$60-$100	
355	Tree House & Gnome Jug	7¾	£60-£100	$90-$165	
707	Mushroom with Pixie/Gnome/ Rabbit Flower Holder	3	£40-£60	$60-$100	
708	Wheelbarrow with Flowers/Gnome/ Pixie Flower Holder	5L	£40-£60	$60-$100	
747	Barrow and Pixie Flower Holder		£20-£30	$30-$50	
842	Goblin on Mound	6¾	£40-£60	$60-$100	
845	Goblin Vase "Billikens"	7¼	£30-£50	$45-$80	
962	Garden Gnome Standing	5	£60-£100	$90-$165	
1021	Pixie sitting beneath Mushroom	3	£120-£180	$180-$295	
1024	Garden Gnome Knees Clasped	4	£50-£90	$75-$150	
1092	Garden Gnome Standing	8¼	£60-£100	$90-$165	
1093	Garden Gnome Standing	9	£80-£120	$120-$200	
1094	Garden Gnome	14	£150-£200	$220-$330	
1095	Garden Gnome with Flower Pot	8¼	£50-£100	$75-$165	
1097	Garden Gnome with Flower Pot	9	£60-£100	$90-$165	
1169	Lucky Pixie	6¾	£20-£30	$30-$50	
1196	Gnome & Mushroom Jug	8	£30-£50	$45-$80	
1221	Garden Gnome with Wheelbarrow	8	£80-£120	$120-$200	
1222	Goblin	6¾	£50-£100	$75-$165	
1420	Lucky Pixie, Toadstool & Squirrel	3	£30-£50	$45-$80	
1421	Lucky Pixie Sitting	3	£30-£50	$45-$80	
1480	Posy with Gnome in centre	6¾D	£20-£30	$30-$50	
1481	Posy with Gnome in centre	9¾D	£10-£20	$15-$35	
1513	Rabbit & Gnome Plant Pot Holder	7D	£30-£50	$45-$80	
1969	Mushroom Jug with Gnome as Handle	8	£40-£60	$60-$100	
2158	Pixie on Mushroom	3¼	£50-£80	$75-$130	
2275	Pixie & Log Posy Vase	5L	£10-£20	$15-$35	
2276	Pixie Posy Basket	5L	£10-£20	$15-$35	
2277	Watering Can Posy Vase with Pixie	3	£20-£30	$30-$50	
2289	Pixie Bowl	6½L	£40-£60	$60-$100	
2295	Acorn & Pixie Plant Holder	7	£20-£30	$30-$50	
2339	Mushroom & Pixie Bowl	9D	£40-£60	$60-$100	
2346	Mushroom & Pixie Bowl	8½	£30-£50	$45-$80	
2799	Gnome on Bamboo Posy Vase	3	£25-£50	$35-$80	
4766	Large Gnome		£30-£50	$45-$80	
4769	Gnome	3½	£20-£30	$30-$50	

Gnomes, Pixies & Goblins

Model No	Model	Size Inches	Market Value		Notes
4847	Gnome		£20-£30	$30-$50	
4929	Pixie		£20-£30	$30-$50	

Jugs

Model No	Model	Size Inches	Market Value		Notes
36	Jug	16	£30-£50	$45-$80	
43	Duck Jug		£50-£80	$75-$130	
216	Jug		£5-£8	$5-$15	
218	Sanora Jug		£8-£12	$10-$20	
219	Jug		£5-£8	$5-$15	
222	Sanora Jug	7¼	£10-£20	$15-$35	
245	Sanora Jug	3	£10-£20	$15-$35	
260	Misty Morn/Rosslyn Jug	8	£10-£20	$15-$35	
272	Rosslyn/Misty Morn Jug	12	£10-£20	$15-$35	
304	Cavalier/Country Jug	3	£20-£30	$30-$50	
305	Cavalier/Country Jug	2¼	£10-£20	$15-$35	
307	Cavalier/Country Jug	4¼	£15-£20	$20-$35	
309	Cavalier/Country Jug	6	£15-£20	$20-$35	
330	Acorn Jug With Squirrel Handle		£100-£200	$150-$330	
334	Hydrangea Jug		£10-£20	$15-$35	
336	Swallow Jug		£8-£12	$10-$20	
344	Hydrangea Jug		£10-£20	$15-$35	
350	Hydrangea Jug		£10-£20	$15-$35	
351	Hydrangea Jug		£10-£20	$15-$35	
360	Jug	6¾	£5-£10	$5-$15	
363	Jug/Vase	7¼	£15-£20	$20-$35	
364	Jug/Vase	9	£15-£20	$20-$35	
386	Jug	8	£10-£20	$15-$35	
393	Jug		£8-£12	$10-$20	
394	Jug		£8-£12	$10-$20	
395	Jug		£8-£12	$10-$20	
397	Jug		£8-£12	$10-$20	
398	Pink/Green Jug	3	£10-£20	$15-$35	
400	Miniature Jug	3	£10-£20	$15-$35	
401	Miniature Jug	3	£10-£20	$15-$35	
402	Jug		£5-£8	$5-$15	
406	Dorethy Bag Jug	7	£20-£30	$30-$50	
407	Jug		£5-£8	$5-$15	
423	Jug		£5-£8	$5-$15	
427	Jug	9	£10-£20	$15-$35	
441	Jug		£5-£8	$5-$15	
453	Jug	3	£10-£15	$15-$25	
456	Jug		£5-£8	$5-$15	
457	Jug		£5-£8	$5-$15	
461	Sanora Jug	7	£15-£20	$20-$35	
463	Jug	6¾	£10-£20	$15-$35	
464	Sanora Jug	5	£12-£18	$15-$30	
465	Vine Patterned Jug	8	£12-£18	$15-$30	
478	Vine Patterned Jug		£10-£20	$15-$35	
480	Diamond Jug		£8-£12	$10-$20	
486	Jug	10	£12-£18	$15-$30	
487	Jug	8¾	£10-£15	$15-$25	
490	Australian Flowers Sydney Jug	5	£10-£15	$15-$25	
499	Jug		£8-£12	$10-$20	
501	Australian Flowers Sydney Jug		£10-£20	$15-$35	
518	Sanora Jug		£10-£20	$15-$35	
544	Green/Blue Budgie Jug	9	£40-£60	$60-$100	
551	Jug		£8-£12	$10-$20	
557	Slymcraft/Steppes Jug	7	£10-£15	$15-$25	
560	Green Duck Jug	6	£20-£30	$30-$50	
561	Jug	4¼	£8-£12	$10-$20	
563	Jug	7¾	£12-£18	$15-$30	
571	Steppes/Rouge Jug	9	£15-£20	$20-$35	
572	Iceberg/Penquin Jug	8	£20-£30	$30-$50	

Model No	Model	Size Inches	Market Value		Notes
573	Jugs 1-5	8¾H	£15-£30	$20-$50	
596	Jug		£5-£8	$5-$15	
606	Jug		£5-£8	$5-$15	
666	Octagonal Jug 3 Sizes	8H	£15-£35	$20-$55	
716	Jug		£8-£12	$10-$20	
754	Jug		£8-£12	$10-$20	
886	Jug	8	£20-£30	$30-$50	
917	Harvest Poppy Jug	8	£15-£20	$20-$35	
935	Jug		£8-£12	$10-$20	
954	Jug		£10-£20	$15-$35	
956	Jug		£10-£20	$15-$35	
964	Cornflower Jug	7	£20-£30	$30-$50	
1000	Jug		£20-£30	$30-$50	
1001	Ribbed Jug	7	£20-£30	$30-$50	
1070	Flower Jug	10	£30-£50	$45-$80	
1071	Flower Jug	7	£15-£20	$20-$35	
1078	Jug with Flowers	7	£20-£30	$30-$50	
1091	Cider Jug		£20-£30	$30-$50	
1108	Jug	8	£20-£30	$30-$50	
1112	Bacchanti Flower Jug	8	£30-£50	$45-$80	
1114	Hollyhocks Jug	8¾	£50-£80	$75-$130	
1115	Acorn & Squirrel Jug	9	£40-£60	$60-$100	
1116	Dragon Handle Jug	9¾	£30-£50	$45-$80	
1125	Bacchanti Flower Jug	7	£30-£50	$45-$80	
1138	Stork Handled Jug	10	£60-£100	$90-$165	
1139	Diamond Shaped Jug	8	£20-£40	$30-$65	
1147	Jug	6	£40-£50	$60-$80	
1150	Flower Jug	5¼	£20-£30	$30-$50	
1167	Stag Handled Jug	8	£80-£120	$120-$200	
1189	Flower Jug	11	£30-£50	$45-$80	
1195	Acorn & Squirrel Jug	7	£40-£60	$60-$100	
1252	Flower Jug	6	£15-£20	$20-$35	
1253	Flower Jug	6¼	£10-£15	$15-$25	
1254	Flower Jug	6	£10-£15	$15-$25	
1273	Rope Flower Jug	6	£20-£30	$30-$50	
1274	Hollyhock Flower Jug	8	£30-£50	$45-$80	
1276	Shell Flower Jug	6	£20-£30	$30-$50	
1277	Shell Flower Jug	7	£22-£28	$30-$45	
1281	Shell Flower Jug	10¾	£30-£50	$45-$80	
1301	Jug		£8-£12	$10-$20	
1305	Birds Nest Flower Jug	8	£100-£150	$150-$245	
1310	Rope Jug	6	£20-£30	$30-$50	
1318	Bunny Handled Jug	9¾	£60-£100	$90-$165	
1342	Jug	7¾	£20-£30	$30-$50	
1344	Jug	9	£15-£30	$20-$50	
1348	Deco Jug	12	£30-£40	$45-$65	
1356	Autumn Jug	6	£20-£30	$30-$50	
1359	Autumn Jug	12	£30-£50	$45-$80	
1363	Jug	7¼	£20-£30	$30-$50	
1367	Jug	6	£10-£15	$15-$25	
1370	Budgerigar Jug	7	£80-£120	$120-$200	
1404	Jug	6	£15-£20	$20-$35	
1405	Jug		£20-£30	$30-$50	
1406	Jug	11	£20-£30	$30-$50	
1409	Jug	5¼	£20-£30	$30-$50	
1410	Jug	8	£20-£30	$30-$50	
1411	Jug		£20-£30	$30-$50	
1417	Jug	6	£15-£20	$20-$35	
1418	Jug	8¼	£15-£20	$20-$35	
1419	Jug	11¼	£30-£50	$45-$80	
1435	Barrel Cider Jug	8	£25-£50	$35-$80	
1551	Small Jug	3	£8-£12	$10-$20	
1553	Jug	3	£8-£12	$10-$20	
1580	Dahlia Graduated Set of 3 Jugs	6¼H	£10-£20	$15-$35	

Jugs

Model No	Model	Size Inches	Market Value		Notes
1584	Dahlia Jug	4	£10-£15	$15-$25	
1605	Dahlia Jug	6	£15-£20	$20-$35	
1612	Jug	7	£8-£12	$10-$20	
1618	Jug		£8-£12	$10-$20	
1623	Jug		£8-£12	$10-$20	
1624	Jug	6	£12-£18	$15-$30	
1625	Jug	6	£10-£20	$15-$35	
1640	Jug	7	£10-£20	$15-$35	
1641	Jug	6	£10-£20	$15-$35	
1643	Dahlia Flower Jug	11¾	£15-£20	$20-$35	
1655	Flower Jug	8	£12-£18	$15-$30	
1685	Jug	7	£10-£15	$15-$25	
1697	Jug		£5-£8	$5-$15	
1698	Green Leaf Jug	3	£8-£12	$10-$20	
1705	Jug		£8-£12	$10-$20	
1710	Jug		£15-£20	$20-$35	
1716	Jug		£10-£15	$15-$25	
1728	Barrel Jug	3¼	£10-£15	$15-$25	
1729	Jug		£10-£15	$15-$25	
1737	Jug		£8-£12	$10-$20	
1744	Jug	5	£10-£15	$15-$25	
1745	Bumpy Jug	6	£10-£15	$15-$25	
1746	Flower Jug	6	£12-£18	$15-$30	
1751	Flower Jug		£10-£15	$15-$25	
1756	Jug		£10-£20	$15-$35	
1778	Jug		£10-£20	$15-$35	
1779	Dragon Jug	9	£60-£100	$90-$165	
1782	Jug	6	£10-£20	$15-$35	
1790	Jug		£8-£12	$10-$20	
1794	Jug	4	£12-£18	$15-$30	
1795	Jug	6	£10-£15	$15-$25	
1814	Neptune Jug	2	£5-£10	$5-$15	
1815	Neptune Graduated Set of 3 Jugs		£10-£15	$15-$25	
1824	Jug	9¾	£15-£20	$20-$35	
1854	Wild Duck Jug	8	£20-£30	$30-$50	
1866	Blackberry Jug		£12-£18	$15-$30	
1875	Leaf Graduated Set of 3 Jugs		£12-£18	$15-$30	
1876	Blackberry Set of 3 Jugs		£15-£20	$20-$35	
1886	Blackberry Jug		£10-£15	$15-$25	
1890	Leaf Jug	2	£12-£18	$15-$30	
1904	Jug		£8-£12	$10-$20	
1926	Jug		£10-£15	$15-$25	
1938	Hobnail Jug		£10-£15	$15-$25	
1943	Hobnail Set of 3 Jugs		£20-£30	$30-$50	
1945	Cider Jug		£15-£20	$20-$35	
1958	Squirrel Jug	7¼	£20-£30	$30-$50	
1959	Squirrel Jug	8	£30-£50	$45-$80	
1960	Stork Jug	10	£60-£100	$90-$165	
1962	Hollyhock Jug	8	£30-£50	$45-$80	
1970	Jug	5¼	£10-£15	$15-$25	
1971	Jug	5¼	£10-£15	$15-$25	
1985	Jug		£10-£15	$15-$25	
1986	Jug		£10-£15	$15-$25	
1987	Jug		£10-£15	$15-$25	
1988	Jug		£10-£15	$15-$25	
1989	Jug		£10-£15	$15-$25	
1993	Mini Squirrel Jug	3	£20-£30	$30-$50	
1995	Jug		£15-£20	$20-$35	
2007	Jug		£8-£12	$10-$20	
2036	Ivyleaf Jug	8¼	£20-£25	$30-$40	
2037	Ivyleaf Jug	6	£18-£25	$25-$40	
2045	Ivyleaf Jug	3	£12-£18	$15-$30	
2071	Ivyleaf Jug	6	£20-£30	$30-$50	
2072	Ivyleaf Jug	6	£20-£30	$30-$50	

Model No	Model	Size Inches	Market Value		Notes
2073	Ivyleaf Jug	6	£20-£30	$30-$50	
2077	Ivyleaf Jug	8	£20-£30	$30-$50	
2078	Ivyleaf Jug	7¼	£20-£30	$30-$50	
2086	Seagull Jug	6¼	£50-£80	$75-$130	
2087	Chrys Jug		£12-£18	$15-$30	
2093	Chrys Jug	3	£12-£18	$15-$30	
2094	Chrys Jug	6	£18-£25	$25-$40	
2095	Chrys Jug	7¼	£20-£30	$30-$50	
2096	Chrys Jug	9	£25-£50	$35-$80	
2103	Chrys Jug	6¾	£15-£20	$20-$35	
2104	Chrys Jug	5¾	£20-£30	$30-$50	
2165	Thistle Jug	3½	£8-£12	$10-$20	
2185	Raphique Jug		£5-£10	$5-$15	
2201	Small Jug		£5-£10	$5-$15	
2210	Jug		£8-£12	$10-$20	
2341	Nuleef Jug		£20-£30	$30-$50	
2363	Nuleef Jug		£8-£10	$10-$15	
2373	Floral Jug		£12-£18	$15-$30	
2554	Jug		£8-£12	$10-$20	
2557	Small Jug		£5-£8	$5-$15	
2577	Kitchen Jug	7¼	£12-£18	$15-$30	
2581	Jug		£8-£12	$10-$20	
2582	Jug		£5-£8	$5-$15	
2583	Jug		£5-£8	$5-$15	
2590	Jug		£5-£8	$5-$15	
2738	Monkey Jug		£20-£30	$30-$50	
2809	Jug		£5-£8	$5-$15	
2813	Monkey Jug		£12-£18	$15-$30	
2941	Jug	7½	£8-£12	$10-$20	
2944	Jug		£5-£8	$5-$15	
2978	Avon Shaped Jug	3	£8-£12	$10-$20	
2996	Wyka Jug	3¾	£12-£18	$15-$30	
3009	Wyka Jug	8	£18-£25	$25-$40	
3203	Jug	6¾	£8-£12	$10-$20	
3204	Avon Jug	4½	£8-£12	$10-$20	
3258	Jug		£5-£8	$5-$15	
3282	Flower Jug	15	£30-£50	$45-$80	
3397	Alpine Flower Jug	10	£20-£30	$30-$50	
3569	Avon Jug	6½	£10-£15	$15-$25	
3584	Flower Jug	11	£20-£30	$30-$50	
3604	Jug with Butterfly Handle		£8-£12	$10-$20	
3606	Cream Jug with Butterfly Handle		£8-£12	$10-$20	
3727	Jug		£8-£12	$10-$20	
3832	Jug		£10-£15	$15-$25	
3834	Wisdom & Providence Jug	9½	£10-£15	$15-$25	
4043	Nouveau Jug		£10-£15	$15-$25	
4044	Nouveau Jug		£10-£15	$15-$25	
4045	Nouveau Jug		£10-£15	$15-$25	
4124	Jug		£8-£12	$10-$20	
4268	Pewter Coloured Jug	5	£5-£8	$5-$15	
4271	Agincourt Jug	4¼	£8-£12	$10-$20	
4272	Agincourt Jug	6	£8-£12	$10-$20	
4368	Agincourt Jug	6	£8-£12	$10-$20	
4744	Leaves Jug	4	£8-£12	$10-$20	
4745	Beech Leaf Jug	4	£8-£12	$10-$20	
4746	Leaves Jug	4	£8-£12	$10-$20	
4747	Ash Leaf Jug	4	£8-£12	$10-$20	
4785	Jug	3	£5-£8	$5-$15	
4788	Jug	3	£5-£8	$5-$15	
5148	Leaf Jug And Stand		£8-£12	$10-$20	
5172	Alton Cream Jug	4	£3-£5	$5-$10	
5243	Harvest Time Flower Jug	8¾	£20-£30	$30-$50	
5246	Harvest Time Jug	5½	£12-£18	$15-$30	
5325	New Cavalier Jug	8	£20-£30	$30-$50	

Jugs

Model No	Model	Size Inches	Market Value		Notes
5329	New Cavalier Jug	6	£10-£15	$15-$25	
5388	Lincoln Jug	8	£5-£8	$5-$15	
5420	Severn Jug No 4	4	£5-£8	$5-$15	
5429	Severn Jug No 3	5½	£5-£8	$5-$15	
5430	Severn Jug No 2	5¾	£5-£8	$5-$15	
5435	Limited Edition Pipers Whiskey Jug		£20-£30	$30-$50	
5441	Hollington Miniature Teapot & Jug		£12-£18	$15-$30	
5442	Miniature Jug	3	£10-£15	$15-$25	
5443	Miniature Jug	3	£10-£15	$15-$25	
5444	Hollington Miniature Jug		£10-£15	$15-$25	
5445	Hollington Miniature Jug		£10-£15	$15-$25	
5446	Hollington Miniature Jug		£10-£15	$15-$25	
5452	Anniversary Cream Jug		£3-£5	$5-$10	
5469	Hollington Jug	9	£12-£18	$15-$30	
5470	Hollington Jug	9	£12-£18	$15-$30	
5471	Hollington Jug	9	£12-£18	$15-$30	
5472	Hollington Jug	9	£12-£18	$15-$30	
5473	Hollington Jug	7½	£8-£12	$10-$20	
5474	Hollington Jug	7½	£8-£12	$10-$20	
5475	Hollington Jug	7½	£8-£12	$10-$20	
5476	Hollington Jug	7½	£8-£12	$10-$20	
5501	Autumn Leaves Jug	8	£8-£12	$10-$20	
5509	Autumn Leaves Jug	7	£8-£12	$10-$20	
5573	Giant Panda Jug	9	£25-£35	$35-$55	
5574	Giant Panda Jug	8½	£20-£30	$30-$50	
5597	1904 Jug	9	£8-£12	$10-$20	

Miscellaneous

No	Model	Size Inches	Market Value		
58	Lamp		£40-£60	$60-$100	
71	Eagle Lamp Base		£80-£120	$120-$200	
119	Cottage		£15-£20	$20-$35	
121	Candlestick		£8-£12	$10-$20	
143	Flower Holder		£8-£12	$10-$20	
144	Flower Holder		£8-£12	$10-$20	
154	Ashtray		£3-£5	$5-$10	
176	Clock	16	£50-£70	$75-$115	
182	Boat		£10-£15	$15-$25	
185	Jardiniere	5	£20-£30	$30-$50	
196	Misty Morn Ginger Jar	9	£15-£20	$20-$35	
197	Misty Morn Ginger Jar	11¾	£15-£20	$20-$35	
202	Candlestick		£10-£15	$15-$25	
230	Clock	11	£30-£50	$45-$80	
302	Jardiniere	8	£30-£50	$45-$80	
322	Jardiniere		£12-£18	$15-$30	
341	Jardiniere	6	£15-£20	$20-$35	
342	3 Piece Garniture	7	£15-£20	$20-$35	
350	Jardiniere	5	£10-£20	$15-$35	
369	Fern Pot	7	£10-£20	$15-$35	
372	Tankard		£5-£8	$5-$15	
373	Tankard		£5-£8	$5-$15	
376	Jardiniere	7	£20-£30	$30-$50	
390	Dish & Cover		£10-£20	$15-$35	
391	Cigarette Box		£10-£20	$15-$35	
399	Shell Jardiniere	4	£20-£40	$30-$65	
408	Basket		£8-£12	$10-$20	
409	Jardiniere	10L	£20-£30	$30-$50	
414	Vine Patterned Basket	10L	£10-£20	$15-$35	
428	Jardiniere		£10-£20	$15-$35	
433	Clock (with Budgie)	9¾	£30-£50	$45-$80	
445	Twin-Handled Jardiniere	8	£15-£20	$20-$35	
449	Fern Pot	14	£20-£30	$30-$50	
466	Jardiniere		£10-£15	$15-$25	
467	Jardiniere		£10-£15	$15-$25	

Model No	Model	Size Inches	Market Value		Notes
474	Twin Handled Jardiniere		£12-£18	$15-$30	
482	Clock	12	£30-£50	$45-$80	
494	Flower Holder	3¼	£10-£20	$15-$35	
503	Jardiniere		£10-£15	$15-$25	
507	Lamp		£12-£18	$15-$30	
510	Clock		£30-£50	$45-$80	
512	Shell Jardiniere	7¾	£15-£20	$20-$35	
513	Shell Jardiniere	7¾	£15-£20	$20-$35	
514	Shell Jardiniere	7¾	£15-£20	$20-$35	
520	Clock	14	£30-£50	$45-$80	
522	Round Plinth	14¾D	£10-£15	$15-$25	
545	Budgie Basket	8	£40-£60	$60-$100	
545	Budgie Basket	8	£40-£60	$60-$100	
546	Green/Blue Budgie Jardiniere	6	£50-£70	$75-$115	
552	Urn		£8-£12	$10-$20	
553	Urn		£8-£12	$10-$20	
602	Jardiniere	5	£15-£20	$20-$35	
604	Clock	12	£30-£50	$45-$80	
605	Heart Shaped Clock	10¾	£35-£60	$50-$100	
608	Heart Shaped Clock	12¾	£50-£80	$75-$130	
615	Sea Shell Jardiniere	6¾	£20-£30	$30-$50	
616	Sea Shell Jardiniere	9	£25-£40	$35-$65	
618	Jardiniere	8¾	£15-£20	$20-$35	
645	Clock	11	£30-£50	$45-$80	
649	Wild Duck Clock	10	£30-£50	$45-$80	
649	Clock	10	£30-£50	$45-$80	
651	Clock	9¾	£40-£60	$60-$100	
667	Candlestick		£8-£12	$10-$20	
670	Candlestick		£8-£12	$10-$20	
689	Treetrunk & Blue Tit Jardiniere	11	£60-£80	$90-$130	
694	Clock Set, with Couple in Garden		£50-£80	$75-$130	
695	Clock Set 3 piece		£50-£100	$75-$165	
696	Clock Set with Couple in Garden		£80-£120	$120-$200	
696	Clock	10¾	£30-£50	$45-$80	
716	Jardiniere with Couple in Garden	11D	£20-£40	$30-$65	
744	Clock	10	£30-£50	$45-$80	
756	Nautilus Range Jardiniere	9	£30-£50	$45-$80	
757	Wild Duck Jardiniere		£20-£30	$30-$50	
783	Clock	10	£40-£60	$60-$100	
803	Wild Duck Candlestick	6	£10-£20	$15-$35	
804	Wild Duck Box	3	£12-£18	$15-$30	
805	Wild Duck Box	2	£12-£18	$15-$30	
809	Wild Duck Jardiniere	5	£15-£30	$20-$50	
831	Clock		£30-£50	$45-$80	
864	Sphinx on Base	6	£30-£50	$45-$80	
891	Dutch Clog		£10-£15	$15-$25	
893	Jardiniere	7¾	£20-£30	$30-$50	
902	Ginger Jar	8¾	£20-£30	$30-$50	
945	Palestine Pot & Cover	5¼	£30-£50	$45-$80	
948	Palestine Pastille Burner	9	£40-£60	$60-$100	
983	Basket		£20-£30	$30-$50	
1135	Cauldron	4¾	£8-£12	$10-$20	
1212	Candle Holder	4	£10-£20	$15-$35	
1218	Dutch Clog		£10-£15	$15-$25	
1266	Ashtray		£10-£20	$15-$35	
1292	Chick Ashtray	4¼	£50-£80	$75-$130	
1293	Duck Ashtray	3	£40-£60	$60-$100	
1335	Hip Flask	4	£10-£20	$15-$35	
1338	Yacht		£20-£40	$30-$65	
1339	Yacht	9¾	£30-£50	$45-$80	
1366	Ashtray various animal designs	6¾	£20-£30	$30-$50	
1400	Selection of Miniatures	1	£20-£40	$30-$65	
1441	Cigarette Barrel		£5-£10	$5-$15	
1442	Barrel Match Holder		£8-£12	$10-$20	

Miscellaneous

Model No	Model	Size Inches	Market Value		Notes
1449	Flower Stand (matches 1448)		£10-£15	$15-$25	
1454	Ashtray various animal designs	5¼	£15-£20	$20-$35	
1455	Pond Ashtray with animals	5¾D	£15-£30	$20-$50	
1473	Basket		£30-£50	$45-$80	
1482	Candlestick		£15-£20	$20-$35	
1482	Ashtray		£5-£10	$5-$15	
1485	Candlestick with Animal or Flower	4	£15-£20	$20-$35	
1496	Basket	7	£15-£20	$20-$35	
1531	Banjo Ashtray	6¾	£15-£20	$20-$35	
1547	Muscial Instrument Ashtray	6¾L	£15-£20	$20-$35	
1573	Armchair Ashtray	4¾	£10-£15	$15-$25	
1610	Basket		£8-£12	$10-$20	
1622	Fireplace with Animal Ashtray		£30-£50	$45-$80	
1622	Fireplace Ashtray		£20-£30	$30-$50	
1630	Wishing Well		£5-£10	$5-$15	
1657	Basket		£10-£15	$15-$25	
1667	Ashtray with Figures	5D	£30-£50	$45-$80	
1672	Candle Holder		£8-£12	$10-$20	
1676	Lamp Base		£10-£20	$15-$35	
1723	Lamp		£15-£20	$20-$35	
1727	Lamp Base	6¾	£30-£50	$45-$80	
1752	Basket		£15-£20	$20-$35	
1755	Basket		£10-£15	$15-$25	
1773	Basket		£8-£12	$10-$20	
1777	Basket	3	£10-£15	$15-$25	
1780	Basket	5	£10-£15	$15-$25	
1796	Basket	4¼	£8-£12	$10-$20	
1819	Basket	4	£8-£12	$10-$20	
1820	Trinket Box	3¼	£20-£30	$30-$50	
1825	Ashtray		£10-£20	$15-$35	
1829	Basket	9L	£10-£15	$15-$25	
1857	Wild Duck Lamp Base	8	£50-£80	$75-$130	
1882	Candle Holder	1	£12-£18	$15-$30	
1897	Ashtray	5D	£5-£10	$5-$15	
1903	Diamond Shape Box	2¼	£15-£20	$20-$35	
1905	Lamp Base		£8-£12	$10-$20	
1931	Box		£8-£10	$10-$15	
1975	Box		£8-£12	$10-$20	
1976	Commemorative Ashtray Elizabeth II		£20-£30	$30-$50	
1982	Fern Pot		£10-£15	$15-$25	
1983	Fern Pot		£10-£15	$15-$25	
1984	Fern Pot		£10-£15	$15-$25	
1991	Basket		£8-£12	$10-$20	
1996	Basket with Dog or various others	2	£20-£30	$30-$50	
1997	Heart Shaped Box & Cover	4D	£20-£30	$30-$50	
1998	Open Barrel		£5-£10	$5-$15	
2022	Heart Shaped Box & Cover	3D	£20-£30	$30-$50	
2030	Basket		£10-£15	$15-$25	
2039	Ivyleaf Dish	3	£8-£10	$10-$15	
2042	Basket		£8-£12	$10-$20	
2054	Dish with Animal	5	£15-£20	$20-$35	
2064	Ivyleaf Dish	13L	£12-£18	$15-$30	
2070	Ivyleaf Lamp Base	6	£25-£35	$35-$55	
2074	Ivyleaf Dish	10¾L	£15-£25	$20-$40	
2085	Basket		£8-£12	$10-$20	
2088	Ivyleaf Cheese Dish		£25-£35	$35-$55	
2089	Ivyleaf Candy Box	2	£15-£20	$20-$35	
2111	Seagull Candy Box	5D	£25-£30	$35-$50	
2168	Thistle Candlestick	2¾	£10-£15	$15-$25	
2174	Candlestick		£5-£8	$5-$15	
2206	Candlestick		£8-£12	$10-$20	
2221	Lamp		£12-£18	$15-$30	
2313	Holder		£5-£8	$5-$15	
2323	Lace Candleholder	3½	£5-£8	$5-$15	

Model No	Model	Size Inches	Market Value		Notes
2343	Horses Head Mug	5½	£8-£12	$10-$20	
2376	Fox Head Beer Mug	5½	£8-£12	$10-$20	
2432	Horse Beer Mug		£8-£12	$10-$20	
2433	Hounds Head Beer Mug		£8-£12	$10-$20	
2435	Horse Beer Mug		£8-£12	$10-$20	
2437	Fox Beer Mug		£8-£12	$10-$20	
2466	Water Wheel		£8-£12	$10-$20	
2509	Barrel with Animals		£10-£20	$15-$35	
2517	Fox Ashtray	7½D	£8-£12	$10-$20	
2518	Horse Ashtray	7½D	£8-£12	$10-$20	
2519	Leaf		£8-£12	$10-$20	
2520	Leaf		£8-£12	$8-$12	
2521	Horse Head Bookends	4¼	£50-£80	$75-$130	
2522	Fish Bookends	4¾	£80-£120	$120-$200	
2533	Round Ashtray		£8-£12	$10-$20	
2552	Bookends		£20-£30	$30-$50	
2573	Match Holder		£8-£12	$10-$20	
2603	Moulin De Lecq Inn Beer Mug		£8-£12	$10-$20	
2627	Bottle Holder		£5-£8	$5-$15	
2642	Horse Beer Mug		£8-£12	$10-$20	
2681	Blacksmiths Anvil		£8-£12	$10-$20	
2685	Luggage Trunk		£12-£18	$15-$30	
2686	Ashtray		£8-£12	$10-$20	
2703	Lemon Juicer		£8-£12	$10-$20	
2723	Bottle Holder		£8-£12	$10-$20	
2788	Bamboo Basket	8¼	£8-£12	$10-$20	
2789	Cot		£8-£12	$10-$20	
2826	Wagner Bookend	4¼	£40-£60	$60-$100	
2863	Dutch Clog	5½	£8-£12	$10-$20	
2865	Chalice		£8-£12	$10-$20	
2866	Book Support		£8-£12	$10-$20	
2881	Wine Cup		£8-£12	$10-$20	
2984	Basket		£5-£8	$5-$15	
2987	Basket		£5-£8	$5-$15	
3076	Flower Holder		£8-£12	$10-$20	
3080	Basket		£8-£12	$10-$20	
3086	Round Ashtray (used for adverts)	6¼	£10-£15	$15-$25	
3099	Candle Holder		£8-£12	$10-$20	
3105	Ashtray		£3-£8	$5-$15	
3122	Ashtray		£18-£25	$25-$40	
3197	Basket		£8-£12	$10-$20	
3219	Tankard	5	£10-£15	$15-$25	
3220	Tankard	5	£10-£15	$15-$25	
3226	Tankard	5	£10-£15	$15-$25	
3231	Triple Candle Holder	13L	£20-£30	$30-$50	
3273	Fox Mask Tankard	4¾	£8-£12	$10-$20	
3274	Hounds Head Tankard	4¾	£8-£12	$10-$20	
3274	Stoke City Tankard	4¾	£8-£12	$10-$20	
3278	Horse Head Tankard	4¾	£12-£18	$15-$30	
3306	Tankard		£8-£12	$10-$20	
3333	Cupid Flower Holder	5½	£8-£12	$10-$20	
3340	Ginger Jar & Cover	6	£8-£12	$10-$20	
3352	Ginger Jar		£8-£12	$10-$20	
3372	Elephant Tea Caddy "Ringtons"	8½	£12-£18	$15-$30	
3394	Ashtray	5¾L	£5-£8	$5-$15	
3409	Ashtray	5¾	£2-£5	$5-$10	
3410	Ashtray		£3-£5	$5-$10	
3435	Horses Ashbox		£12-£18	$15-$30	
3436	Fish Ashbox		£12-£18	$15-$30	
3437	Duck Ashbox		£12-£18	$15-$30	
3438	Plinth		£3-£5	$5-$10	
3446	Basket		£5-£8	$5-$15	
3467	Ashtray		£3-£5	$5-$10	
3481	Pebbles Ashtray	6½	£5-£8	$5-$15	

Miscellaneous

Model No	Model	Size Inches	Market Value		Notes
3488	Tankard	4¾	£5-£8	$5-$15	
3488	Nottingham Forest FC Tankard	4¾	£8-£12	$10-$20	
3550	Lamp Base	16½	£25-£30	$35-$50	
3553	Vintage Urn	7	£15-£20	$20-$35	
3559	Vintage Urn	5	£10-£15	$15-$25	
3566	Barrel Box		£8-£12	$10-$20	
3578	Vintage Urn	10½	£12-£18	$15-$30	
3579	Vintage Urn	11	£15-£20	$20-$35	
3617	Twin Handled Baby Feeder		£8-£12	$10-$20	
3621	Ashtray	6L	£3-£5	$5-$10	
3641	Ashtray		£3-£8	$5-$15	
3660	Ashtray on Feet		£5-£8	$5-$15	
3674	Tyre Ashtray	6½D	£8-£12	$10-$20	
3675	Grandfather Clock		£20-£30	$30-$50	
3682	Ashtray	4L	£3-£5	$5-$10	
3683	Pebble Lamp Base	12	£30-£50	$45-$80	
3706	Menu Holder	6	£12-£15	$15-$25	
3709	Card Holder	3L	£8-£12	$10-$20	
3712	Square Ashtray		£3-£5	$5-$10	
3730	Ashtray		£3-£5	$5-$10	
3742	Baby Mug	3¼	£5-£8	$5-$15	
3756	Birds Head Pie Funnel		£10-£20	$15-$35	
3760	Ashtray		£3-£6	$5-$10	
3788	Nursery Ware Egg Cup		£10-£15	$15-$25	
3791	Nursery Ware Baby Plate	6D	£12-£18	$15-$30	
3802	Seaman Jones Money Box		£20-£30	$30-$50	
3803	Tudor Lamp Base	10	£25-£30	$35-$50	
3804	Lamp Base	10¾	£20-£30	$30-$50	
3805	Lamp		£20-£30	$30-$50	
3849	Fish on Base		£12-£18	$15-$30	
3928	Lamp Base		£15-£20	$20-$35	
3937	Wisdon & Providence Tankard		£8-£12	$10-$20	
3953	Maple Leaf Ashtray	6½D	£8-£12	$10-$20	
3954	Maple Leaf Tankard		£5-£8	$5-$15	
3958	Hyacinth Lamp Base		£18-£25	$25-$40	
3959	Textured Lamp Base	10	£18-£25	$25-$40	
3961	Macklestone Lamp Base		£20-£30	$30-$50	
3962	Lamp Base	12	£18-£25	$25-$40	
3963	Extension To Lamp	8	£3-£5	$5-$10	
3975	Wisdom & Providence Tankard		£8-£12	$10-$20	
3976	Macklestone Lamp Base	10	£12-£18	$15-$30	
3978	Wisdon & Providence Tankard		£8-£12	$10-$20	
3979	Macklestone Lamp Base		£20-£30	$30-$50	
3996	Suede Ashtray	5¼D	£8-£12	$10-$20	
4009	Suede Ashtray		£5-£8	$5-$15	
4027	Ashtray	6¼D	£5-£8	$5-$15	
4034	Totem Beaker		£5-£8	$5-$15	
4052	Nouveau Beaker		£5-£8	$5-$15	
4066	Ashtray		£3-£5	$5-$10	
4090	Fish Tankard		£5-£8	$5-$15	
4094	Manhattan Lamp Base	10	£20-£30	$30-$50	
4111	Shamrock Posy/Ashtray	6L	£5-£8	$5-$15	
4112	Candleholder	8	£5-£8	$5-$15	
4118	Ashtray	4D	£3-£5	$5-$10	
4120	Ashtray	6½D	£3-£5	$5-$10	
4136	Ashtray		£3-£5	$5-$10	
4145	Totem Ashtray	4L	£3-£5	$5-$10	
4183	Tankard		£8-£12	$10-$20	
4184	Hounds Head Jar		£8-£12	$10-$20	
4192	Leather Covered Tankard		£5-£8	$5-$15	
4200	Pewter Effect Tankard		£5-£8	$5-$15	
4245	Tankard	5½	£3-£6	$5-$10	
4245	Hereford Cider Tankard	5½	£8-£12	$10-$20	
4246	Horseshoe Ashtray		£3-£5	$5-$10	

Model No	Model	Size Inches	Market Value		Notes
4247	Lining	7	£1-£2	$1-$5	
4248	Lining		£1-£2	$1-$5	
4261	Lining	5	£1-£2	$1-$5	
4288	Woodland Ashtray with Deer		£8-£12	$10-$20	
4293	Woodland Ashtray with Deer		£8-£12	$10-$20	
4352	Tankard		£5-£8	$5-$15	
4355	Horses Head & Horseshoe Ashtray		£8-£12	$10-$20	
4369	Lining		£1-£2	$1-$5	
4381	Ashtray	6D	£3-£5	$5-$10	
4383	Cigarette Box		£5-£8	$5-$15	
4387	Fish Head Tankard	6	£12-£18	$15-$30	
4388	Evening Fantasy Ashtray	5½	£3-£5	$5-$10	
4389	Tobacco Jar		£8-£12	$10-$20	
4395	Riverside Candle Holder	3¾	£12-£18	$15-$30	
4396	Hollyberry Candle Holder		£12-£18	$15-$30	
4397	Square Ashtray	4D	£5-£8	$5-$15	
4500	Christmas Pudding Teapot		£30-£50	$45-$80	
4524	Riverside Ashtray	5½D	£5-£8	$5-$15	
4527	Ashtray		£3-£5	$5-$10	
4566	Fish Head Tankard	5	£12-£18	$15-$30	
4567	Fish Head Tankard	5½	£10-£15	$15-$25	
4569	Evening Fantasy Urn	6¼	£8-£12	$10-$20	
4574	Drinking Horn Tankard	6¾	£8-£12	$10-$20	
4601	Iron Bound Basket on six feet		£5-£8	$5-$15	
4621	Tankard		£5-£8	$5-$15	
4622	Hound Head Tankard		£5-£8	$5-$15	
4623	Fox Head Tankard		£5-£8	$5-$15	
4624	Horse Head Tankard		£5-£8	$5-$15	
4628	Drinking Horn Tankard	8	£12-£18	$15-$30	
4632	Riding Boot Tankard		£8-£12	$10-$20	
4664	Iron Bound Basket on six feet		£10-£15	$15-$25	
4667	Flower Holder	6	£5-£8	$5-$15	
4724	Hockey Ball Tankard	4¾	£20-£30	$30-$50	
4727	Fishing Tankard	4¾	£20-£30	$30-$50	
4735	Tankard		£8-£12	$10-$20	
4736	Thistle Tankard	4¾	£8-£12	$10-$20	
4758	Bottle	10	£8-£12	$10-$20	
4767	Leather Spirit Measure		£8-£12	$10-$20	
4768	Scotland Thistle Dish	6D	£5-£8	$5-$15	
4770	Chrys Candle Holder		£8-£12	$10-$20	
4776	Etruscan Plant Pot	6½D	£10-£15	$15-$25	
4777	Etruscan Plant Pot	4¼D	£8-£12	$10-$20	
4778	Etruscan Plant Pot	7½D	£12-£18	$15-$30	
4810	Embossed Village Tankard		£5-£8	$5-$15	
4831	Croft Thimble		£20-£30	$30-$50	
4849	Flower Holder Picture Frame		£12-£18	$15-$30	
4868	Plum Preserve Lid (4865/4871)		£20-£30	$30-$50	
4914	Fish Mug		£5-£8	$5-$15	
4945	Coffin Ashtray		£8-£12	$10-$20	
4959	Tankard		£5-£8	$5-$15	
4960	Tankard		£5-£8	$5-$15	
4961	Tankard		£5-£8	$5-$15	
4962	Tankard		£5-£8	$5-$15	
4967	Mosaic Mug	4¾	£8-£12	$10-$20	
4972	Stand For Galloway Bull		£10-£20	$15-$35	
4974	Chicken Pomander		£8-£12	$10-$20	
4975	Floral Pomander		£8-£12	$10-$20	
4976	Ships Lanterns Bookends	6¾	£50-£80	$75-$130	
4987	Basket	4	£8-£12	$10-$20	
4989	Frog Pomander		£8-£12	$10-$20	
5011	Churnet Plinth For 5010		£3-£5	$5-$10	
5030	Coco De Mer Tankard		£8-£12	$10-$20	
5052	Pigs Head Thimble		£20-£30	$30-$50	
5053	Castle Thimble		£20-£30	$30-$50	

Miscellaneous

Model No	Model	Size Inches	Market Value		Notes
5054	Rose Thimble		£20-£30	$30-$50	
5056	Heart Thimble		£20-£30	$30-$50	
5057	Leaning Tower of Pisa Thimble		£20-£30	$30-$50	
5058	Windmill Thimble		£20-£30	$30-$50	
5059	Circus Clown Thimble		£20-£30	$30-$50	
5060	Wishing Well Thimble		£20-£30	$30-$50	
5061	Unicorn Thimble		£20-£30	$30-$50	
5062	Lion Thimble		£20-£30	$30-$50	
5063	Cigarette Box	4¼	£8-£12	$10-$20	
5064	Ashtray		£8-£12	$10-$20	
5065	Ships Wheel Ashtray		£8-£12	$10-$20	
5090	Tankard	4¼	£5-£8	$5-$15	
5098	Tankard		£8-£12	$10-$20	
5100	Pen Tray		£8-£12	$10-$20	
5130	Ashtray & Cover		£3-£5	$5-$10	
5136	Florence Candle Holder		£5-£8	$5-$15	
5138	Florence Twin Candle Holder		£8-£12	$10-$20	
5144	Rodek Ashtray		£3-£5	$5-$10	
5145	Lesney Sand Buggy Ashtray		£20-£30	$30-$50	
5146	Lesney Aeroplane Ashtray		£20-£30	$30-$50	
5153	Series Mug		£3-£5	$5-$10	
5154	Series Mug		£3-£5	$5-$10	
5155	Series Mug		£3-£5	$5-$10	
5156	Series Mug		£3-£5	$5-$10	
5157	Series Mug		£3-£5	$5-$10	
5158	Series Mug		£3-£5	$5-$10	
5159	Series Mug		£3-£5	$5-$10	
5160	Series Mug		£3-£5	$5-$10	
5161	Series Mug		£3-£5	$5-$10	
5162	Series Mug		£3-£5	$5-$10	
5163	Series Mug		£3-£5	$5-$10	
5165	Winston Churchill Bust	8	£50-£80	$75-$130	
5195	Cats Eating Bowl	5D	£30-£50	$45-$80	
5214	Loving Cup		£5-£9	$5-$15	
5217	Tankard	4	£3-£5	$5-$10	
5218	Tankard	4	£3-£5	$5-$10	
5219	Tankard	4	£3-£5	$5-$10	
5221	Volvo Tankard		£8-£12	$10-$20	
5222	Benskins Indian Tankard (Ltd Edition)		£50-£100	$75-$165	
5235	Cushion (for cat)		£5-£8	$5-$15	
5270	Tankard	4¼	£5-£8	$5-$15	
5271	Tankard	3¼	£3-£5	$5-$10	
5275	Vintage Urn	9	£20-£30	$30-$50	
5280	Vintage Urn	9	£8-£12	$10-$20	
5281	Tankard	6¾	£5-£8	$5-$15	
5282	Tankard	8	£8-£12	$10-$20	
5283	Tankard		£5-£8	$5-$15	
5284	Tankard		£5-£8	$5-$15	
5285	Leaf		£5-£8	$5-$15	
5286	Dish Cloth Bowl		£20-£30	$30-$50	
5288	Geest Ashtray		£3-£5	$5-$10	
5309	Ashtray	6¾L	£3-£5	$5-$10	
5310	Ashtray		£3-£5	$5-$10	
5311	Ashtray		£3-£5	$5-$10	
5317	Candlestick	6	£5-£8	$5-$15	
5318	Embossed Candlestick	6	£5-£8	$5-$15	
5326	New Cavalier Punch Bowl		£20-£30	$30-$50	
5328	New Cavalier Tankard	6¾	£10-£15	$15-$25	
5330	New Cavalier Wine Goblet		£8-£12	$10-$20	
5331	New Cavalier Ashtray		£3-£5	$5-$10	
5332	New Cavalier Loving Cup		£8-£12	$10-$20	
5333	New Cavalier Tankard	4	£10-£15	$15-$25	
5334	New Cavalier Decanter		£8-£12	$10-$20	
5367	Ashtray		£3-£5	$5-$10	

Model No	Model	Size Inches	Market Value		Notes
5368	Ashtray		£3-£5	$5-$10	
5382	Horseshoe Ashtray		£3-£5	$5-$10	
5384	Ashtray		£3-£5	$5-$10	
5385	Pomander		£5-£8	$5-$15	
5393	Canton Ginger Jar	12½	£25-£35	$35-$55	
5394	Canton Ginger Jar	10½	£25-£35	$35-$55	
5395	Canton Ginger Jar	7	£20-£30	$30-$50	
5403	Ashtray		£2-£3	$2-$5	
5404	Limited Edition Leyland Lorry		£150-£250	$220-$415	
5405	Ashtray		£2-£3	$2-$5	
5407	Ashtray		£2-£3	$2-$5	
5433	Hound Lamp Base	5	£20-£30	$30-$50	
5436	Limited Edition Pipers Whiskey Ashtray		£12-£18	$15-$30	
5437	Limited Edition Guinness Ashtray		£12-£18	$15-$30	
5438	Bell with Dove		£5-£8	$5-$15	
5440	Tyre Ashtray		£3-£5	$5-$10	
5448	Anniversary Goblet	5	£5-£8	$5-$15	
5451	Anniversary Trinket Box	5½L	£5-£8	$5-$15	
5456	Anniversary Loving Cup		£8-£12	$10-$20	
5458	Anniversary Ashtray		£3-£5	$5-$10	
5459	Anniversary Candlestick		£5-£8	$5-$15	
5460	Anniversary Bell		£5-£8	$5-$15	
5478	Nursery Ware Egg Cup Truck		£60-£100	$90-$165	
5479	Nursery Ware Egg Cup Steam Engine		£60-£100	$90-$165	
5487	High Tide Basket		£8-£12	$10-$20	
5507	Autumn Leaves Trinket Box		£8-£12	$10-$20	
5508	Autumn Leaves Candle Stick		£5-£8	$5-$15	
5523	Horses Head Brooch/Pendant		£20-£30	$30-$50	
5524	Horses Head Brooch/Pendant		£20-£30	$30-$50	
5525	Horses Head Brooch/Pendant		£20-£30	$30-$50	
5535	Croft Bell	5¾	£8-£12	$10-$20	
5538	Croft Clock	8D	£20-£30	$30-$50	
5553	Cradle	4½	£10-£15	$15-$25	
5581	Large Plaque		£8-£12	$10-$20	
5589	Milady Candle Stick	4	£8-£12	$10-$20	
5594	Milady Hand Mirror		£8-£12	$10-$20	
5644	Wedding Cake Thimble with Box		£20-£30	$30-$50	
5996	Desk Top Newspaper Holder		£12-£18	$15-$30	
5997	Desk Top Match Box Tray		£12-£18	$15-$30	
5998	Desk Top Match Box Pen Holder		£12-£18	$15-$30	
5999	Desk Top Sack Pen Holder		£12-£18	$15-$30	
6000	Desk Top Scrap Paper Tray		£12-£18	$15-$30	
6001	Desk Top Gift Wrapped Box		£8-£12	$10-$20	
6002	Desk Top Carrier Bag Pen Holder		£12-£18	$15-$30	
6002	Carrier Bag Pen Holder made for Harrods		£15-£20	$20-$35	
6003	Desk Top Money Box Parcel		£12-£18	$15-$30	
6004	Desk Top Paper Weight		£12-£18	$15-$30	
6005	Desk Top String Dispenser		£12-£18	$15-$30	

Novelties

136	Tortoise Bowl & Cover	2¼	£60-£100	$90-$165	
165	Top Hat With Kitten	3	£150-£200	$220-$330	
181	Top Hat		£10-£15	$15-$25	
185	Mermaid		£30-£50	$45-$80	
196	Shoe		£15-£20	$20-$35	
280	Hat Flower Holder	6D	£15-£20	$20-$35	
299	Nut Basket Hat	7D	£10-£20	$15-$35	
354	Tree & Bunny Wall Vase	6	£40-£60	$60-$100	
429	Log		£5-£8	$5-$15	
720	Hat		£15-£20	$20-$35	
723	Hat		£15-£20	$20-$35	
762	Owl Clock	10	£60-£100	$90-$165	
961	Shoe		£10-£15	$15-$25	

Novelties

Model No	Model	Size Inches	Market Value		Notes
1145	Squirrel Wool Holder	8	£80-£120	$120-$200	
1171	Windmill	5	£60-£80	$90-$130	
1230	Shoe Ashtray		£10-£20	$15-$35	
1270	Hare Match Holder	3	£25-£30	$35-$50	
1320	Shoe Ashtray	2	£10-£20	$15-$35	
1459	Hare Serviette Ring		£30-£50	$45-$80	
1472	Car	1	£120-£180	$180-$295	
1484	Top Hat with Kitten	4	£20-£30	$30-$50	
1590	Pair of Rabbit Match Holders	2	£40-£60	$60-$100	
2051	Old Slipper with Dog	3	£20-£30	$30-$50	
2060	Old Boot	4¼	£12-£18	$15-$30	
2332	Sock	3¼	£8-£12	$10-$20	
2425	Chimney with Cat/Owl or Stork	4	£30-£50	$45-$80	
2438	Pekinese Ashtray	5¼L	£12-£18	$15-$30	
2560	Shoe		£8-£12	$10-$20	
2597	Bootee	2¼	£10-£15	$15-$25	
2897	Stocking		£8-£12	$10-$20	
2939	Wheelbarrow		£8-£12	$10-$20	
3019	Pig Money Box	5½	£12-£18	$15-$30	
3239	Elephant Money Box	4¼	£30-£50	$45-$80	
3346	Pigs Head Money Box		£12-£18	$15-$30	
3542	Mr Sylvac Advertising Figure		£150-£200	$220-$330	
3626	Top Hat	4	£10-£15	$15-$25	
3711	Irish Harp	5½	£8-£12	$10-$20	
3750	Pineapple Mug		£8-£12	$10-$20	
3754	Cats Head Money Box		£20-£30	$30-$50	
3763	Lifeboat Mans Head Money Box		£20-£30	$30-$50	
3770	Cats Head Money Box		£20-£30	$30-$50	
3830	Stone Wall Slipper		£8-£12	$10-$20	
3837	Teddy Bear Policeman Money Box		£20-£30	$30-$50	
3839	Bunnies Bank Money Box		£30-£50	$45-$80	
3840	Cowboy Money Box		£25-£30	$35-$50	
3841	Indian Money Box		£25-£30	$35-$50	
3875	Begonia Slipper		£5-£8	$5-$15	
3935	Squirrel Money Box	6¾	£30-£50	$45-$80	
4125	Golf Ashtray		£5-£10	$5-$15	
4188	Irish Pig Money Box		£20-£30	$30-$50	
4360	Pig Money Box		£20-£30	$30-$50	
4361	Owl Money Box	5½	£20-£30	$30-$50	
4546	Fox Egg Cup Stand & Cups		£100-£150	$150-$245	
4549	Apple Sauce Face Pot	5¾	£25-£35	$35-$55	
4551	Bread Sauce Face Pot	4	£25-£35	$35-$55	
4553	Beetroot Face Pot	5	£25-£35	$35-$55	
4557	Bread Sauce Face Pot		£25-£35	$35-$55	
4565	Cucumber Face Pot	6	£25-£35	$35-$55	
4570	Skull Tankard	4	£15-£20	$20-$35	
4582	Boot Shaped Tankard	6¾	£12-£18	$15-$30	
4584	Boot Shaped Tankard	6¾	£12-£18	$15-$30	
4627	Lochness Monster Souvenir		£8-£12	$10-$20	
4712	Golf Ball Preserve Pot		£20-£30	$30-$50	
4713	Football Preserve Pot		£20-£30	$30-$50	
4715	Rugby Ball Preserve Pot		£20-£30	$30-$50	
4716	Tennis Ball Preserve Pot		£20-£30	$30-$50	
4717	Hockey Ball Preserve Pot		£20-£30	$30-$50	
4719	Golf Ball Tankard	4¾	£20-£30	$30-$50	
4721	Football Tankard	4¾	£20-£30	$30-$50	
4722	Rugby Ball Tankard	5½	£20-£30	$30-$50	
4723	Tennis Ball Tankard	4¾	£20-£30	$30-$50	
4728	Soccer Tankard	4¾	£20-£30	$30-$50	
4750	Coleslaw Face Pot	5¾	£50-£80	$75-$130	
4751	Tomato Face Pot	5¾	£30-£50	$45-$80	
4752	Piccalilli Face Pot	5¾	£50-£80	$75-$130	
4753	Chutney Face Pot	5	£20-£30	$30-$50	
4754	Parsley Face Pot	5¾	£50-£80	$75-$130	

Model No	Model	Size Inches	Market Value		Notes
4755	Pickled Cabbage Face Pot	5¼	£40-£60	$60-$100	
4756	Onion Face Pot	5¾	£15-£20	$20-$35	
4760	Humpty Dumpty Egg Separator		£40-£60	$60-$100	
4841	Top Hat with Cat & Dog		£20-£30	$30-$50	
4874	Boot Tankard		£8-£12	$10-$20	
4895	Lemon Face Pot	5½	£30-£50	$45-$80	
4896	Orange Face Pot	4½	£30-£50	$45-$80	
4897	Plum Face Pot		£30-£50	$45-$80	
4898	Blackberry Face Pot		£30-£50	$45-$80	
4899	Raspberry Face Pot		£30-£50	$45-$80	
4906	Pan Scourer Face Pot	3¼	£20-£30	$30-$50	
4906	Beef Stock Cubes Face Pot	3¼	£20-£30	$30-$50	
4906	Chicken Stock Face Pot	3¼	£20-£30	$30-$50	
4915	Tartare Sauce Face Pot	4¾	£40-£60	$60-$100	
4990	Mouse Pomander		£8-£12	$10-$20	
4991	Squirrel Pomander		£8-£12	$10-$20	
5037	Frog Money Box		£20-£30	$30-$50	
5039	Owl Money Box	8	£20-£30	$30-$50	
5048	Horseradish Face Pot	4¼	£50-£80	$75-$130	
5091	Tortoise Money Box	6¾	£12-£18	$15-$30	
5092	Owl Money Box	5¾	£12-£18	$15-$30	
5093	Squirrel Money Box	6¾	£12-£18	$15-$30	
5096	Bulldog Money Box	6¾	£12-£18	$15-$30	
5097	Frog Money Box	5¼	£12-£18	$15-$30	
5101	Caricature Tortoise Money Box		£12-£18	$15-$30	
5102	Caricature Elephant Money Box		£12-£18	$15-$30	
5103	Caricature Bloodhound Money Box		£12-£18	$15-$30	
5104	Teddy Bear Money Box (with and without eyes)		£12-£18	$15-$30	
5105	Caricature Chipmunk Money Box		£12-£18	$15-$30	
5106	Caricature Owl Money Box		£12-£18	$15-$30	
5126	Onion Face Pot	4	£20-£30	$30-$50	
5127	Beetroot Face Pot	4	£20-£30	$30-$50	
5149	Mr Pickwick Pomander		£20-£30	$30-$50	
5208	Face Mug		£8-£12	$10-$20	
5431	Owl Lamp Base	4¼	£20-£30	$30-$50	
5432	Tortoise Lamp Base	4½	£20-£30	$30-$50	
5466	Four Chicken Eggcups & Stand		£12-£18	$15-$30	
5468	Nessie Cruet Set		£30-£50	$45-$80	
5480	Teddy Bear Jam Pot		£12-£18	$15-$30	
5530	Beer Mug Money Box		£10-£15	$15-$25	
5532	Beer Mug Money Box		£10-£15	$15-$25	
5548	Nosey Parker Vinegar Bottle		£50-£100	$75-$165	
5549	Nosey Parker Pepper	5	£50-£80	$75-$130	
5550	Nosey Parker Salt	5¾	£50-£80	$75-$130	
5554	Pair of Baby Boots	4½	£12-£18	$15-$30	
5576	Giant Panda Money Box	4¼	£30-£40	$45-$65	
5655	Pig Mug		£8-£12	$10-$20	
5656	Bear Money Box	5¼	£20-£30	$30-$50	
5657	Pig Money Box	6½	£20-£30	$30-$50	
5659	Elephant Money Box	6¾	£20-£30	$30-$50	
5660	Cheshire Cat Money Box	6¼	£20-£30	$30-$50	
5661	Basset Hound Money Box		£20-£30	$30-$50	
5662	Fish Money Box	7½L	£20-£30	$30-$50	
6006	Beer Can		£12-£18	$15-$30	
6128	Letter P Money Box		£12-£18	$15-$30	

Posy Vases

Model No	Model	Size Inches	Market Value		Notes
123	Anemome Posy Dish	9¾D	£20-£40	$30-$65	
126	Anemome Posy Dish	7D	£20-£40	$30-$65	
127	Anemome Posy Dish	9D	£20-£40	$30-$65	
127	Anemome Posy Dish	9	£20-£40	$30-$65	
129	Hat Shaped Posy	4D	£20-£40	$30-$65	
278	Posy/Vase		£5-£8	$5-$15	

Posy Vases

Model No	Model	Size Inches	Market Value		Notes
279	Posy/Vase		£5-£8	$5-$15	
452	Posy		£5-£8	$5-$15	
454	Posy		£5-£8	$5-$15	
724	Nautilus Range Posie	9D	£30-£50	$45-$80	
1003	Posy Holder		£5-£10	$5-$15	
1064	Bunny Posy Holder	4¼	£50-£80	$75-$130	
1127	Swan Posy Holder	5	£15-£25	$20-$40	
1186	Posy Bowl	8D	£10-£15	$15-$25	
1235	Diamond Shaped Posy	2	£5-£10	$5-$15	
1248	Posy Ring	8D	£5-£10	$5-$15	
1249	Posy Bowl	6D	£5-£10	$5-$15	
1250	Posy Bowl	6D	£5-£10	$5-$15	
1251	Diamond Shaped Posy Bowl	7L	£8-£12	$10-$20	
1314	Posy Trough	1	£5-£10	$5-$15	
1315	Posy	6L	£5-£8	$5-$15	
1316	Posy	8L	£5-£8	$5-$15	
1317	Posy	12L	£8-£12	$10-$20	
1324	Posy Trough	11L	£10-£15	$15-$25	
1325	Posy Trough	10L	£10-£15	$15-$25	
1337	Flower Seller Posy Holder	6¼	£40-£60	$60-$100	
1340	Yacht Posy Holder	12	£70-£100	$105-$165	
1352	Posy Holder	6	£30-£50	$45-$80	
1353	Posy Holder	6	£15-£20	$20-$35	
1393	Yacht Posy Holder	6¾	£30-£50	$45-$80	
1394	Yacht Posy Holder	8	£40-£60	$60-$100	
1397	Horse Shoe Posy		£8-£12	$10-$20	
1416	Koala Bear Vase	5	£60-£100	$90-$165	
1479	Posy with various animals	8L	£25-£50	$35-$80	
1479	Posy with Lady	8L	£20-£30	$30-$50	
1487	Koala Bear Posy Log	4	£30-£50	$45-$80	
1488	Posy	3L	£10-£20	$15-$35	
1892	Posy Ring		£5-£10	$5-$15	
1893	Posy Ring		£5-£10	$5-$15	
1899	Posy		£8-£12	$10-$20	
1909	Floral Posy	2	£8-£12	$10-$20	
1930	Floral Posy Bowl		£12-£18	$15-$30	
1954	Floral Posy Bowl		£10-£20	$15-$35	
1957	Floral Posy Bowl		£10-£15	$15-$25	
1965	Posy Vase	6L	£8-£12	$10-$20	
1966	Posy Vase	4L	£5-£8	$5-$15	
1967	Posy Vase	8L	£10-£15	$15-$25	
1992	Round Posy	6D	£8-£12	$10-$20	
1999	Posy Vase		£8-£12	$10-$20	
2006	Floral Posy	1	£10-£15	$15-$25	
2023	Posy Vase	7L	£5-£8	$5-$15	
2033	Ivyleaf Posy	7L	£10-£15	$15-$25	
2101	Chrys Posy	6¾D	£8-£12	$10-$20	
2102	Chrys Posy	8	£8-£12	$10-$20	
2122	Floral Posy Bowl	2	£10-£15	$15-$25	
2131	Rope Oval Posy	8L	£8-£12	$10-$20	
2133	Floral Posy		£15-£20	$20-$35	
2178	Raphique Posy	8¼L	£8-£10	$10-$15	
2215	Posy Trough		£5-£12	$5-$20	
2278	Flower Pot Posy with Pixie	3	£20-£30	$30-$50	
2311	Floral Posy		£10-£15	$15-$25	
2510	Floral Posy Bowl		£10-£20	$15-$35	
2525	Floral Posy Bowl		£15-£25	$20-$40	
2547	Bamboo Posy	4¾	£5-£8	$5-$15	
2745	Bamboo Posy Holder		£5-£8	$5-$15	
2767	Bamboo Posy		£5-£8	$5-$15	
2783	Moselle Cherub Posy Vase		£10-£20	$15-$35	
2793	Posy Vase		£8-£12	$10-$20	
2798	Owl on Tree Posy Vase	3¾	£25-£50	$35-$80	
2800	Fox on Pine Cone Posy Vase	3	£25-£50	$35-$80	

Model No	Model	Size Inches	Market Value		Notes
2886	Posy		£8-£12	$10-$20	
2970	Factory Gift Posy	5½L	£20-£30	$30-$50	
3014	Oak Leaf Posy	10½L	£10-£15	$15-$25	
3017	Posy		£5-£8	$5-$15	
3018	Bracken Posy		£5-£8	$5-$15	
3101	Lily Posy Vase	10L	£50-£80	$75-$130	
3239	Elephant Posy	5½	£20-£30	$30-$50	
3289	Lily Posy Vase	7¼L	£20-£30	$30-$50	
3313	Cupid Flower Posy	4¾	£12-£18	$15-$30	
3325	Cupid Flower Posy	5½	£8-£12	$10-$20	
3360	Pebble Posy Vase	12½L	£12-£18	$15-$30	
3363	Posy Vase	9½L	£5-£8	$5-$15	
3365	Posy Vase	7½L	£5-£8	$5-$15	
3366	Posy Vase	4	£5-£8	$5-$15	
3391	Alpine Posy Bar		£5-£8	$5-$15	
3420	Pebbles Posy Vase	8½L	£8-£12	$10-$20	
3521	Posy Vase		£5-£8	$5-$15	
3532	New Shell Posy	8½L	£10-£15	$15-$25	
3536	Posy Vase		£5-£8	$5-$15	
3556	Log Posy Vase		£5-£8	$5-$15	
3556	Log Posy Vase with Animal		£20-£30	$30-$50	
3702	Posy Bar		£5-£8	$5-$15	
3703	Posy		£5-£8	$5-$15	
3707	Posy		£5-£8	$5-$15	
3854	Linton Posy		£5-£8	$5-$15	
3862	Linton Slipper Posy		£5-£8	$5-$15	
3867	Begonia Posy	7L	£8-£12	$10-$20	
3881	Textured Posy		£8-£12	$10-$20	
3899	Privet Posy Ring		£5-£8	$5-$15	
3902	Coral Posy		£8-£12	$10-$20	
3945	Manhattan Posy		£3-£6	$5-$10	
3951	Manhattan Posy	5L	£5-£8	$5-$15	
3952	Manhattan Posy		£5-£10	$5-$15	
3987	Totem Posy		£3-£6	$5-$10	
4016	Posy Vase		£5-£8	$5-$15	
4158	Marina Posy	8L	£8-£12	$10-$20	
4167	Flora Posy Ring	6D	£8-£12	$10-$20	
4172	Flora Posy		£5-£8	$5-$15	
4178	Marina Posy		£5-£8	$5-$15	
4213	Sycamore Posy		£5-£8	$5-$15	
4231	Woodland Posy with Deer		£8-£12	$10-$20	
4239	Wooodland Posy with Deer		£8-£12	$10-$20	
4276	Posy		£5-£8	$5-$15	
4281	Posy Vase	7L	£5-£8	$5-$15	
4282	Posy		£5-£8	$5-$15	
4298	Harmony Pot		£5-£8	$5-$15	
4300	Harmony Posy		£5-£8	$5-$15	
4538	Privet Posy		£3-£5	$5-$10	
4560	Autumn Chintz Posy		£5-£8	$5-$15	
4579	Hollyberry Posy		£8-£12	$10-$20	
4580	Hollyberry Posy Ring		£8-£12	$10-$20	
4598	Tristan Posy		£5-£8	$5-$15	
4605	Gossamer Posy		£5-£8	$5-$15	
4642	Spectrum Posy		£5-£8	$5-$15	
4671	Posy Ring	7½D	£5-£8	$5-$15	
4672	Horseshoe Posy		£5-£8	$5-$15	
4673	Posy Bar	5½L	£3-£5	$5-$10	
4674	Posy Bar	7¾L	£5-£8	$5-$15	
4675	Posy Bar	9¾L	£8-£12	$10-$20	
4676	Posy Bar	13¼L	£10-£15	$15-$25	
4677	Posy Tray		£5-£8	$5-$15	
4889	House in the Glen Posy	9½D	£12-£18	$15-$30	
4890	House in the Glen Posy		£10-£15	$15-$25	
5028	Kingfisher Posy Log		£8-£12	$10-$20	

Posy Vases

Model No	Model	Size Inches	Market Value		Notes
5375	Bamboo Posy	8L	£5-£8	$5-$15	
5376	Bamboo Posy Vase	11L	£5-£8	$5-$15	
5377	Bamboo Posy Vase	6¾L	£5-£8	$5-$15	

Rabbits

Model No	Model	Size Inches	Market Value		Notes
44	Rabbit Jug	5	£60-£100	$90-$165	
150	Rabbit Holder		£30-£50	$45-$80	
151	Rabbit Posy Vase		£100-£200	$150-$330	
323	Lop Ear Bunny & Mushroom Wall Vase	7¼	£80-£120	$120-$200	
901	Match Striker Rabbit		£20-£30	$30-$50	
973	Rabbit Posy Vase		£15-£20	$20-$35	
990	Snub Nose Bunny	5	£30-£50	$45-$80	
1026	Bunny	7¾	£50-£80	$75-$130	
1027	Bunny	8¼	£70-£100	$105-$165	
1028	Bunny	10¾	£80-£120	$120-$200	
1057	Rabbit		£15-£20	$20-$35	
1065	Bunny	6	£50-£80	$75-$130	
1066	Rabbit		£50-£80	$75-$130	
1067	Bunny	4	£30-£50	$45-$80	
1181	Rabbit Ashtray		£40-£60	$60-$100	
1182	Rabbit	2	£30-£40	$45-$65	
1200	Rabbit		£20-£30	$30-$50	
1255	Rabbit Coaster Holder & Mats	5	£100-£150	$150-$245	
1294	Rabbit Ashtray	5L	£50-£80	$75-$130	
1302	Lop-Eared Rabbit	5	£50-£80	$75-$130	
1303	Lop-Eared Rabbit	7	£80-£120	$120-$200	
1304	Lop-Eared Rabbit	8	£100-£150	$150-$245	
1311	Rabbit Bookends (& other designs)	4	£80-£120	$120-$200	
1311	Rabbit Bookends (& other designs)	5	£60-£100	$90-$165	
1312	Rabbit Posy	8¼D	£40-£60	$60-$100	
1371	Crouching Hare	3	£80-£120	$120-$200	
1386	Rabbit	3¼	£20-£30	$30-$50	
1388	Crouching Hare	5	£100-£150	$150-$245	
1389	Crouching Hare	7	£200-£300	$295-$495	
1398	Rabbit Wall Plaque		£100-£150	$150-$245	
1457	Bunnie and Tree Stump Holder	3	£30-£50	$45-$80	
1497	Rabbit Crouching	3L	£80-£120	$120-$200	
1509	Lop Eared Rabbit	4¾	£30-£50	$45-$80	
1510	Lop Eared Rabbit on Mushroom Vase	5	£40-£60	$60-$100	
1511	Rabbit with Ears Back	13	£300-£500	$445-$825	
1523	Rabbit	4	£200-£300	$295-$495	
1525	Rabbit with Ears Back	8	£180-£240	$265-$395	
1526	Rabbit	10	£200-£300	$295-$495	
1529	Rabbit	3	£100-£150	$150-$245	
1530	Rabbit	5	£300-£500	$445-$825	
1532	Bunnies Nose to Nose Ashtray	3¼	£30-£40	$45-$65	
1534	Bunnies Nose to Nose	2	£30-£50	$45-$80	
1546	Lop Eared Rabbit Bookends	4	£60-£100	$90-$165	
1724	Rabbit & Tree Lamp		£80-£120	$120-$200	
1948	Rabbit Honey Pot with Bee on Cover	3¼	£40-£60	$60-$100	
1978	Rabbit Jug	8	£50-£80	$75-$130	
2427	Rabbit		£40-£60	$60-$100	
2687	Rabbit with Skies		£30-£50	$45-$80	
2688	Rabbit with Skies		£30-£50	$45-$80	
2689	Rabbit with Skies		£25-£30	$35-$50	
2955	Crouching Rabbit		£300-£500	$445-$825	
2980	Rabbit with Bow Tie	6	£30-£50	$45-$80	
3097	Rabbit	6½	£30-£50	$45-$80	
3322	Lop Eared Rabbit		£30-£50	$45-$80	
3326	Lop Eared Rabbit		£40-£60	$60-$100	
3327	Rabbit		£30-£50	$45-$80	
3328	Rabbit		£30-£50	$45-$80	
4070	Rabbit Flower Jug	9½	£40-£60	$60-$100	

Model No	Model	Size Inches	Market Value		Notes
4234	Rabbit		£20-£30	$30-$50	
4838	Two Rabbits		£18-£25	$25-$40	
4928	Rabbit	2	£20-£30	$30-$50	
5257	Rabbit (used for ornaments)		Not known		
5289	Thumper Lop Eared Rabbit		£30-£50	$45-$80	
5290	Thumper Lop Eared Rabbit		£18-£25	$25-$40	
5291	Thumper Lop Eared Rabbit	4	£15-£20	$20-$35	
5305	Rabbit (Large) Ltd Information		Not known		
5306	Rabbit(Medium) Ltd Information		Not known		
5307	Rabbit (Small) Ltd Information		Not known		
5658	Rabbit Money Box	6¾	£20-£30	$30-$50	

Tablewares & Kitchenwares

Model No	Model	Size Inches	Market Value		Notes
171	Container		£3-£5	$5-$10	
180	Container		£5-£8	$5-$15	
201	Tray		£8-£12	$10-$20	
253	Dovedale Bowl		£10-£20	$15-$35	
266	Springbok Honeypot		£15-£20	$20-$35	
267	Springbok Cream Jug		£10-£15	$15-$25	
268	Springbok Sugar Bowl		£10-£15	$15-$25	
292	Dovedale Jug	8	£15-£20	$20-$35	
293	Dovedale Jug	10	£20-£40	$30-$65	
294	Cavalier/Country Sweet Box	5L	£10-£20	$15-$35	
296	Mug		£3-£5	$5-$10	
297	Tray		£5-£8	$5-$15	
300	Cavalier Jug	5	£10-£20	$15-$35	
301	Cavalier Jug	4	£10-£20	$15-$35	
308	Beaker		£4-£6	$5-$10	
313	Cavalier Jar		£10-£20	$15-$35	
314	Cake Basket		£10-£20	$15-$35	
325	Country Scene Teapot		£12-£18	$15-$30	
326	Country Scene Sugar Bowl		£5-£8	$5-$15	
328	Country Scene Honey Pot		£12-£18	$15-$30	
331	Hydrangea Teapot		£10-£20	$15-$35	
332	Hydrangea Honeypot		£10-£20	$15-$35	
339	Hydrangea Sugarbowl		£5-£10	$5-$15	
340	Country Scene Tray		£8-£12	$10-$20	
341	Country Scene Tray		£8-£12	$10-$20	
342	Hydrangea Cheese Dish		£15-£20	$20-$35	
345	Hydrangea Coffee Pot		£10-£20	$15-$35	
352	Hydrangea Mug		£5-£10	$5-$15	
366	Hydrangea Fruit Saucer		£10-£20	$15-$35	
403	Coffee Pot		£12-£18	$15-$30	
404	Teapot		£12-£18	$15-$30	
405	Tray		£5-£8	$5-$15	
424	Toast Rack		£5-£8	$5-$15	
431	Tray		£5-£8	$5-$15	
440	Centre Piece	7	£30-£50	$45-$80	
455	Dovecote Jug		£8-£12	$10-$20	
458	Honey Pot		£10-£15	$15-$25	
460	Tray		£5-£8	$5-$15	
482	Tray		£5-£8	$5-$15	
491	Sauce Jug	5	£8-£12	$10-$20	
497	Dovecote Fruit Dish	13	£10-£20	$15-$35	
506	Butter Dish		£8-£12	$10-$20	
516	Onion Sauce Bowl	5D	£20-£30	$30-$50	
525	Tray		£5-£8	$5-$15	
526	Leaf Tray	8	£5-£10	$5-$15	
527	Cone Tray	8	£5-£10	$5-$15	
528	Tray		£5-£10	$5-$15	
529	Dovecote Butter Dish	5D	£8-£12	$10-$20	
530	Dovecote Cheese Dish	4	£10-£15	$15-$25	
531	Dovecote Fruit Basket	11¼	£10-£20	$15-$35	

Tablewares & Kitchenwares

Model No	Model	Size Inches	Market Value		Notes
532	Dovecote Teapot		£10-£20	$15-$35	
533	Dovecote Sugar Bowl	3	£5-£10	$5-$15	
534	Dovecote Cream Jug	3¼	£5-£10	$5-$15	
534	Dovecote Cream Jug	3¼	£5-£10	$5-$15	
535	Dovecote Honey Pot	4	£10-20	$15-$35	
536	Dovecote Cucumber Dish	12	£10-£20	$15-$35	
542	Dovecote Cup and Plate		£10-£15	$15-$25	
542	Tray		£12-£18	$15-$30	
577	Dovecote Teapot		£12-£18	$15-$30	
584	Honey Pot	3	£15-£20	$20-$35	
594	Tray	13L	£15-£25	$20-$40	
619	Butter Dish Cow Finial	5L	£10-£20	$15-$35	
620	Butter Pot		£5-£8	$5-$15	
620	Butter Pot		£5-£8	$5-$15	
621	Cheese Dish Mouse on Cover	7¾	£15-£25	$20-$40	
640	Tray		£15-£20	$20-$35	
643	Cheese Dish	7L	£25-£40	$35-$65	
654	Sandwich Set	12L	£15-£20	$20-$35	
672	Sweet Box		£10-£15	$15-$25	
674	Oval Plate		£15-£30	$20-$50	
674	Oval Plate		£15-£30	$20-$50	
683	Butter/Cheese Dish	3	£15-£20	$20-$35	
717	Tray		£5-£8	$5-$15	
719	Tray		£5-£8	$5-$15	
849	Cheese Dish from Southsea	5¼L	£15-£20	$20-$35	
903	Harvest Poppy Pot & Cover	8¾	£20-£30	$30-$50	
1090	Mug	3	£5-£10	$5-$15	
1134	Cauldron Jug	2	£10-£15	$15-$25	
1183	Cruet	2	£20-£30	$30-$50	
1184	Honey Pot		£10-£15	$15-$25	
1185	Butter Dish		£10-£15	$15-$25	
1197	Cake Stand		£15-£20	$20-$35	
1198	Cress Dish	11¼L	£15-£20	$20-$35	
1213	Butter Dish		£10-£20	$15-$35	
1216	Biscuit Barrel	7	£20-£30	$30-$50	
1322	Toast Rack	6L	£15-£30	$20-$50	
1362	Sugar Shaker	5	£15-£20	$20-$35	
1364	Mug (Matches 1363)	3¼	£8-£12	$10-$20	
1365	Jam Pot	4¼	£10-£15	$15-$25	
1392	Toast Rack	2	£30-£50	$45-$80	
1436	Barrel Mug		£8-£10	$10-$15	
1437	Barrel Jam Pot		£8-£12	$10-$20	
1438	Barrel Butter Dish		£10-£15	$15-$25	
1439	Barrel Cruet	2¾	£30-£50	$45-$80	
1440	Barrel Butter Dish/Sweet Tray	4L	£5-£10	$5-$15	
1443	Barrel Sauce Bottle Holder		£8-£12	$10-$20	
1445	Barrel Sauce Boat	5¼L	£10-£15	$15-$25	
1446	Barrel Biscuit Jar		£10-£15	$15-$25	
1456	Barrel Mug		£5-£10	$5-$15	
1470	Cruet		£15-£20	$20-$35	
1537	Strawberry Pot & Cover	3L	£15-£20	$20-$35	
1552	Mug	3	£8-£12	$10-$20	
1572	Dahlia Cruet		£20-£30	$30-$50	
1579	Dahlia Mug	3	£8-£12	$10-$20	
1581	Dahlia Honey Pot	4	£10-£20	$15-$35	
1582	Dahlia Butter Dish	4	£8-£12	$10-$20	
1583	Dahlia Sugar Pot	3¼D	£8-£12	$10-$20	
1585	Dahlia Teapot	6	£20-£30	$30-$50	
1586	Dahlia Cheesedish & Cover	7¼L	£10-£20	$15-$35	
1587	Dahlia Biscuit Barrel	6	£15-£20	$20-$35	
1588	Dahlia Pot		£8-£12	$10-$20	
1589	Stackable Bowls with Cover	4D	£10-£15	$15-$25	
1591	Rectangular Dish		£10-£20	$15-$35	
1595	Dahlia Milk Jug	8	£12-£20	$15-$35	

Model No	Model	Size Inches	Market Value		Notes
1600	Dahlia Mug	4	£10-£15	$15-$25	
1614	Mug	4	£5-£12	$5-$20	
1660	Toast Rack		£8-£12	$10-$20	
1691	Lemonade Set		£15-£20	$20-$35	
1693	Leaf Teapot		£15-£20	$20-$35	
1695	Sugar Bowl/Honey Pot	3	£8-£10	$10-$15	
1696	Butter Dish/Bowl	4	£10-£15	$15-$25	
1699	Sugar Bowl	4D	£8-£12	$10-$20	
1700	Sugar Bowl	3D	£8-£12	$10-$20	
1703	Teapot		£15-£20	$20-$35	
1711	Mug		£5-£10	$5-$15	
1713	Plate		£5-£10	$5-$15	
1717	Mug		£5-£10	$5-$15	
1720	Cruet		£10-£15	$15-$25	
1725	Salt & Pepper		£15-£20	$20-$35	
1727	Teapot		£20-£30	$30-$50	
1733	Tray		£5-£10	$5-$15	
1747	Neptune Cheese Dish		£15-£20	$20-$35	
1748	Neptune Tray		£12-£18	$15-$30	
1749	Teapot		£12-£18	$15-$30	
1765	Sugar Bowl		£5-£10	$5-$15	
1768	Sweet Dish		£8-£12	$10-$20	
1769	Butter Dish		£10-£15	$15-$25	
1770	Sugar Bowl		£5-£8	$5-$15	
1771	Mug		£5-£8	$5-$15	
1775	Cavalier Beer Mug	5	£15-£20	$20-$35	
1776	Primrose Cheese Dish		£15-£20	$20-$35	
1791	Embossed Dish	4¼L	£8-£12	$10-$20	
1797	Neptune Dish		£10-£15	$15-$25	
1798	Neptune Double Tray		£12-£18	$15-$30	
1801	Cavalier Jug	8	£18-£25	$25-$40	
1812	Neptune Teapot	5	£20-£30	$30-$50	
1861	Blackberry Dimond Shape Tray	12L	£15-£20	$20-$35	
1862	Blackberry Dish	11¾	£18-£25	$25-$40	
1864	Blackberry Square Dish	8D	£12-£18	$15-$30	
1867	Blackberry Preserve Pot	4	£15-£20	$20-$35	
1868	Blackberry Butter Dish & Cover	3	£10-£15	$15-$25	
1869	Blackberry Cream Jug	3¾	£10-£15	$15-$25	
1870	Blackberry Preserve Pot	3	£10-£15	$15-$25	
1871	Blackberry Sugar Bowl	2	£10-£15	$15-$25	
1872	Blackberry Cheese Dish	6L	£15-£20	$20-$35	
1873	Blackberry Toast Rack	5¼L	£15-£20	$20-$35	
1874	Blackberry Double Dish	10L	£15-£20	$20-$35	
1878	Blackberry Mug		£8-£12	$10-$20	
1884	Teapot		£20-£25	$30-$40	
1887	Butter & Toast Rack		£12-£18	$15-$30	
1888	Honey Pot		£8-£12	$10-$20	
1889	Leaf Teapot		£25-£30	$35-$50	
1891	Sugar Bowl		£8-£12	$10-$20	
1907	Tray		£8-£12	$10-$20	
1908	Blackberry Coffee Cup	2	£10-£15	$15-$25	
1915	Biscuit Barrel		£15-£20	$20-$35	
1916	Biscuit Barrel		£15-£20	$20-$35	
1918	Biscuit Barrel	8	£15-£20	$20-$35	
1929	Teapot		£15-£20	$20-$35	
1936	Mug		£5-£10	$5-$15	
1937	Hobnail Honey Pot	4	£8-£12	$10-$20	
1942	Teapot		£15-£20	$20-$35	
1946	Hobnail Cheese Dish		£10-£15	$15-$25	
1947	Double Tray		£8-£12	$10-$20	
1953	Teapot		£15-£20	$20-$35	
1974	Honey Pot		£10-£15	$15-$25	
1994	Tray		£5-£8	$5-$15	
2003	Tray		£5-£10	$5-$15	

Tablewares & Kitchenwares

Model No	Model	Size Inches	Market Value		Notes
2005	Tray		£5-£10	$5-$15	
2019	Chrys Tray		£10-£15	$15-$25	
2021	Tray		£5-£10	$5-$15	
2032	Ivyleaf Tray & Holder	8L	£15-£25	$20-$40	
2038	Tray		£5-£10	$5-$15	
2040	Tray		£5-£10	$5-$15	
2046	Ivyleaf Honey Pot	4	£12-£18	$15-$30	
2068	Ivyleaf Watercress Dish	9L	£15-£20	$20-$35	
2080	Tray		£5-£8	$5-$15	
2105	Chrys Jam Pot & Cover	4	£12-£18	$15-$30	
2106	Jam Pot & Cover		£8-£12	$10-$20	
2107	Tray		£8-£12	$10-$20	
2138	Shallow Dish		£8-£12	$10-$20	
2142	Shallow Dish	8½L	£5-£8	$5-$15	
2169	Tray		£5-£8	$5-$15	
2170	Tray		£5-£8	$5-$15	
2172	Raphique Jam Pot	5½	£8-£12	$10-$20	
2177	Raphique Honey Pot	5½	£8-£12	$10-$20	
2179	Raphique Butter Dish	6¾L	£8-£12	$10-$20	
2184	Raphique Cruet Set		£15-£25	$20-$40	
2186	Salt & Pepper		£10-£15	$15-$25	
2188	Raphique Teapot		£20-£30	$30-$50	
2196	Cheese Dish		£12-£18	$15-$30	
2197	Butter Dish		£8-£12	$10-$20	
2202	Tray		£5-£8	$5-$15	
2203	Teapot		£15-£20	$20-$35	
2211	Toast Rack		£5-£8	$5-$15	
2214	Tray		£8-£12	$10-$20	
2223	Lace Dish	5¼	£8-£12	$10-$20	
2226	Cactus Honey Pot		£8-£12	$10-$20	
2244	Lace Jam/Honey Pot		£5-£8	$5-$15	
2245	Cactus Dish	4¼L	£12-£18	$15-$30	
2271	Lace Jam/Honey Pot	4¾	£8-£12	$10-$20	
2285	Tray		£5-£8	$5-$15	
2298	Lace Cruet		£5-£8	$5-$15	
2299	Lace Dish	11D	£8-£12	$10-$20	
2319	Nuleef Tray	11¼	£12-£18	$15-$30	
2337	Lace Cheese Dish		£12-£18	$15-$30	
2335	Nuleef Jam/Honey Pot		£10-£20	$15-$35	
2336	Nuleef Bonbon Dish		£10-£15	$15-$25	
2342	Nuleef Mug		£5-£8	$5-$15	
2344	Beer Mug		£8-£12	$10-$20	
2347	Lace Sweet Dish	5¼	£12-£18	$15-$30	
2348	Nuleef Toast Rack		£10-£20	$15-$35	
2349	Nuleef Condiment Set		£12-£18	$15-$30	
2351	Nuleef Graduated Jugs	5½	£10-£15	$15-$25	
2353	Nuleef Watercress Dish & Stand	12½L	£10-£15	$15-$25	
2354	Nuleef Double Dish		£8-£12	$10-$20	
2355	Nuleef Dish	8¼	£5-£8	$5-$15	
2356	Nuleef Butter Dish		£20-£30	$30-$50	
2357	Nuleef Cheese Dish		£30-£50	$45-$80	
2358	Nuleef Triple Dish		£20-£30	$30-$50	
2359	Nuleef Dish		£12-£18	$15-$30	
2369	Butter Dish		£8-£12	$10-$20	
2370	Tray		£5-£8	$5-$15	
2394	Beer Mug		£5-£8	$5-$15	
2395	Beer Mug		£5-£8	$5-$15	
2400	Plume Dish		£8-£12	$10-$20	
2402	Plume Plant Pot Holder		£10-£20	$15-$35	
2403	Plume Cheese Dish		£12-£18	$15-$30	
2409	Plume Cruet		£12-£18	$15-$30	
2410	Plume Jam/Honey Pot		£8-£12	$10-$20	
2411	Plume Butter Dish		£12-£18	$15-$30	
2436	Beer Mug		£8-£12	$10-$20	

Model No	Model	Size Inches	Market Value		Notes
2511	Tray		£5-£8	$5-$15	
2555	Kitchen Jam/Honey Pot		£8-£12	$10-$20	
2562	Moselle Cherub Comport	8¾	£50-£80	$75-$130	
2563	Tray		£5-£8	$5-$15	
2566	Moselle Cake Plate	12D	£30-£50	$45-$80	
2570	Mug		£5-£8	$5-$15	
2571	Teapot		£15-£25	$20-$40	
2575	Cheese Dish		£15-£20	$20-$35	
2576	Kitchen Cruet	3½	£10-£15	$15-$25	
2585	Butter Dish		£10-£15	$15-$25	
2586	Kitchen Jar		£10-£15	$15-$25	
2587	Kitchen Jar		£10-£15	$15-$25	
2588	Kitchen Jar		£10-£15	$15-$25	
2589	Sugar Sifter		£10-£15	$15-$25	
2591	Watercress Dish & Stand		£12-£18	$15-$30	
2592	Large Bowl		£8-£12	$10-$20	
2602	Laronde Dish		£8-£12	$10-$20	
2604	Teapot		£30-£50	$45-$80	
2605	Kitchen Teapot		£18-£25	$25-$40	
2611	Laronde Basket	8½	£10-£15	$15-$25	
2612	Laronde Cruet		£10-£15	$15-$25	
2615	Laronde Jam/Honey Pot	5	£5-£8	$5-$15	
2619	Laronde Cheese Dish		£8-£12	$10-$20	
2620	Laronde Dish	13½	£8-£12	$10-$20	
2621	Laronde Dish		£8-£12	$10-$20	
2633	Sugar Shaker		£8-£12	$10-$20	
2634	Laronde Triple Dish		£10-£15	$15-$25	
2663	Plate		£5-£8	$5-$15	
2684	Tray	8½	£8-£12	$10-$20	
2721	Egg Separator		£5-£8	$5-$15	
2725	Tray		£5-£8	$5-$15	
2726	Watercress Dish & Stand		£12-£18	$15-$30	
2763	Egg Cup		£5-£8	$5-$15	
2880	Tray		£8-£12	$10-$20	
2885	Apple Blossom Plate	9¼D	£20-£30	$30-$50	
2913	Tray		£5-£8	$5-$15	
2916	Biscuit Barrel		£12-£18	$15-$30	
2940	Serviette Ring		£10-£15	$15-$25	
2945	Mug		£5-£8	$5-$15	
2947	Mug		£5-£8	$5-$15	
2956	Wyka Jam Pot	5½	£8-£12	$10-$20	
2957	Cheese Dish		£10-£15	$15-$25	
2958	Jam Pot		£8-£12	$10-$20	
2959	Butter Dish		£8-£12	$10-$20	
2960	Tray		£5-£8	$5-$15	
2961	Large Bowl		£8-£12	$10-$20	
2966	Teapot		£25-£50	$35-$80	
2967	Teapot		£25-£50	$35-$80	
2969	Teapot		£20-£30	$30-$50	
2976	Avon Shaped Teapot	6¾	£20-£30	$30-$50	
2977	Avon Shaped Sugar Bowl		£5-£8	$5-$15	
2982	Avon Shaped Teapot	5	£20-£30	$30-$50	
2986	Watercress Dish & Stand	10½D	£12-£18	$15-$30	
2988	Tray		£5-£8	$5-$15	
2990	Watercress Dish & Stand		£8-£12	$10-$20	
2998	Wyka Butter Dish	7L	£8-£12	$10-$20	
2999	Cheese Dish		£8-£12	$10-$20	
3001	Wyka Cruet	4¾	£18-£25	$25-$40	
3002	Wyka Sandwich Tray	12½	£8-£12	$10-$20	
3003	Wyka Double Tray	12½L	£8-£12	$10-$20	
3004	Wyka Triple Tray	15L	£12-£18	$15-$30	
3005	Wyka Toast Rack	10½L	£12-£18	$15-$30	
3007	Wyka Watercress Dish & Stand		£8-£12	$10-$20	
3010	Wyka Butter Dish	7¼	£12-£18	$15-$30	

Tablewares & Kitchenwares

Model No	Model	Size Inches	Market Value		Notes
3012	Wyka Mug	5½	£8-£12	$10-$20	
3020	Jar		£5-£8	$5-$15	
3186	Tray		£5-£8	$5-$15	
3206	Avon Butter Dish	7L	£12-£18	$15-$30	
3207	Avon Cheese Dish		£12-£18	$15-$30	
3208	Avon Sandwich Tray	13½L	£8-£12	$10-$20	
3209	Avon Honey Jar	4	£5-£8	$5-$15	
3237	Tray		£8-£12	$10-$20	
3238	Avon Cup	3	£5-£8	$5-$15	
3245	Jar		£8-£12	$10-$20	
3253	Cup		£5-£8	$5-$15	
3257	Plate	9D	£8-£12	$10-$20	
3261	Plate	10D	£8-£12	$10-$20	
3262	Avon Plate	8D	£5-£8	$5-$15	
3263	Avon Plate		£5-£8	$5-$15	
3264	Avon Cereal Bowl	6¼D	£5-£8	$5-$15	
3265	Avon Fruit Bowl		£8-£12	$10-$20	
3267	Avon Cake Plate	11½D	£8-£12	$10-$20	
3268	Avon Cake Stand	8D	£12-£15	$15-$25	
3269	Avon Fruit Bowl	9½D	£10-£15	$15-$25	
3270	Avon Soup Bowl		£5-£8	$5-$15	
3281	Cup		£3-£5	$5-$10	
3296	Avon 4 Piece Condiment Set		£12-£18	$15-$30	
3297	Avon Cheese Board & Knife	10¾L	£12-£18	$15-$30	
3299	Avon Toast Rack	8½L	£10-£15	$15-$25	
3304	Beaker		£8-£12	$10-$20	
3315	Avon Coffee Pot	9	£8-£12	$10-$20	
3353	Avon Coffee Pot		£12-£18	$15-$30	
3354	Square Jar & Cover		£8-£12	$10-$20	
3357	Blossom Jar		£8-£12	$10-$20	
3359	Square Jar		£8-£12	$10-$20	
3367	Square Etched Jar		£8-£12	$10-$20	
3378	Feather Tray	8½L	£10-£15	$15-$25	
3405	Jar	6	£5-£8	$5-$15	
3408	Beaker		£5-£8	$5-$15	
3411	Mug		£5-£8	$5-$15	
3413	Ears of Wheat Beaker		£5-£8	$5-$15	
3417	Jar & Cover		£5-£8	$5-$15	
3421	Honey Pot		£8-£12	$10-$20	
3442	Beaker		£5-£8	$5-$15	
3452	Tea Cup Embossed		£3-£5	$5-$10	
3454	Hors d'oeuvre Dish		£12-£18	$15-$30	
3468	Fluted Cup		£3-£5	$5-$10	
3484	Feather Celery Tray	14½L	£15-£20	$20-$35	
3485	Feather Salad Bowl	12D	£18-£25	$25-$40	
3486	Desert Bowl	4½	£5-£8	$5-$15	
3502	Feather Twin Tray	10L	£12-£18	$15-$30	
3503	Feather Triple Tray	12L	£12-£18	$15-$30	
3504	Feather Dish	12L	£12-£18	$15-$30	
3505	Feather Condiment Set & Tray	9¾	£12-£18	$15-$30	
3506	Feather Twin Tray	11L	£12-£18	$15-$30	
3507	Feather Cress Dish	10D	£12-£18	$15-$30	
3508	Feather Cheese Dish		£12-£18	$15-$30	
3509	Feather Biscuit Jar		£12-£18	$15-$30	
3510	Feather Sectioned Dish		£12-£18	$15-$30	
3511	Feather Butter Dish & Cover		£12-£18	$15-$30	
3512	Feather Twin Dish	11L	£12-£18	$15-$30	
3513	Feather Beaker		£12-£18	$15-$30	
3514	Feather Honey/Preserve Pot		£15-£20	$20-$35	
3515	Feather Dish	6½	£8-£12	$10-$20	
3516	Tea Cup		£3-£5	$5-$10	
3519	Cup		£3-£5	$5-$10	
3520	Butter Dish		£8-£12	$10-$20	
3543	Cup		£3-£5	$5-$10	

Model No	Model	Size Inches	Market Value		Notes
3544	Cup		£3-£5	$5-$10	
3546	Beer Mug	4½	£3-£5	$5-$10	
3547	Magnolia Cup & Saucer		£5-£8	$5-$15	
3554	Butter Dish with Butterfly Finial		£20-£30	$30-$50	
3564	Tea Cup Butterfly Handle		£5-£8	$5-$15	
3576	Honey Pot with Butterfly		£15-£20	$20-$35	
3581	Vegetable Dish		£12-£18	$15-$30	
3582	Soup Bowl		£5-£8	$5-$15	
3589	Cheese Dish Board & Dish		£12-£18	$15-$30	
3590	Woven Pattern Pot	4	£8-£12	$10-$20	
3594	Oval Meat Dish	16½L	£10-£20	$15-$35	
3596	Feather Jug		£12-£18	$15-$30	
3597	Woven Pattern Pot		£8-£12	$10-$20	
3599	Feather Sugar Bowl		£8-£12	$10-$20	
3600	Feather Jug		£8-£12	$10-$20	
3601	Feather Jug		£12-£18	$15-$30	
3607	Sugar Bowl with Butterfly Handle		£8-£12	$10-$20	
3609	Coffee Can		£5-£8	$5-$15	
3611	Gravy Boat & Stand		£10-£15	$15-$25	
3613	Beehive Honey Pot	5½	£12-£18	$15-$30	
3616	Embossed Pot		£8-£12	$10-$20	
3619	Condiment Set with Butterfly		£20-£30	$30-$50	
3620	Teapot with Butterfly Handle		£20-£30	$30-$50	
3622	Jar		£5-£8	$5-$15	
3623	Embossed Pot		£5-£8	$5-$15	
3627	Jar		£5-£8	$5-$15	
3628	Coffee Pot		£10-£15	$15-$25	
3629	Jar		£5-£8	$5-$15	
3630	Coffee Pot		£10-£15	$15-$25	
3632	Beer Tankard	5	£8-£12	$10-$20	
3633	Meat Dish	12L	£8-£12	$10-$20	
3634	Mug		£5-£8	$5-$15	
3635	Sugar Bowl		£5-£8	$5-$15	
3636	Tray	15½L	£5-£8	$5-$15	
3637	Embossed Jar	6	£5-£8	$5-$15	
3640	Embossed Coffee Pot		£12-£18	$15-$30	
3645	Tray		£5-£8	$5-$15	
3646	Embossed Mug		£5-£8	$5-$15	
3647	Web Coffee Pot		£12-£18	$15-$30	
3648	Sugar Bowl		£5-£8	$5-$15	
3649	Sugar Bowl		£5-£8	$5-$15	
3650	Web Mug		£5-£8	$5-$15	
3661	Beer Mug	6½	£5-£8	$5-$15	
3664	Mug		£5-£8	$5-$15	
3667	Sugar Bowl	3½	£5-£8	$5-$15	
3668	Teapot		£12-£18	$15-$30	
3669	Cream Jug	4½	£5-£8	$5-$15	
3670	Coffee Pot		£12-£18	$15-$30	
3671	Teacup		£3-£5	$5-$10	
3672	Embossed Teacup		£3-£5	$5-$10	
3673	Butter Dish		£8-£12	$10-$20	
3676	Jar	6	£5-£8	$5-$15	
3677	Cheese Dish		£12-£18	$15-$30	
3679	Butter Dish Butterfly Handle		£12-£18	$15-$30	
3685	Honey Pot	5½	£8-£12	$10-$20	
3686	Butter Dish		£8-£12	$10-$20	
3687	Coffee Pot		£12-£18	$15-$30	
3688	Beaker		£5-£8	$5-$15	
3708	Butter Dish		£10-£15	$15-$25	
3713	Condiment Set	9½L	£12-£18	$15-$30	
3728	Cream Jug		£8-£12	$10-$20	
3729	Web Cream Jug		£8-£12	$10-$20	
3744	Butterfly Bread & Butter Plate		£8-£12	$10-$20	
3745	Butterfly Sandwich Plate		£8-£12	$10-$20	

Model No	Model	Size Inches	Market Value		Notes
3746	Teapot with Butterfly		£8-£12	$10-$20	
3747	Tudor Mug		£8-£12	$10-$20	
3748	Mug		£5-£8	$5-$15	
3749	Embossed Mug		£8-£12	$10-$20	
3751	Mug		£8-£12	$10-$20	
3753	Jar		£5-£8	$5-$15	
3757	Teacup		£3-£5	$5-$10	
3758	Jar		£5-£8	$5-$15	
3759	Fluted Plate	10D	£5-£8	$5-$15	
3761	Tray	15L	£5-£8	$5-$15	
3764	Square Jar		£5-£8	$5-$15	
3768	Triple Tray		£8-£12	$10-$20	
3771	Wishing Well Cheese Dish		£12-£18	$15-$30	
3772	Wishing Well Honey Pot		£12-£18	$15-$30	
3773	Wishing Well Butter Dish		£12-£18	$15-$30	
3818	Stone Wall Tray	7L	£5-£8	$5-$15	
3828	Avon Coffee Pot	8¼	£12-£18	$15-$30	
3831	Stone Wall Tray	13L	£5-£8	$5-$15	
3833	Jar		£5-£8	$5-$15	
3836	Coffee Pot		£8-£12	$10-$20	
3858	Linton Pot		£10-£15	$15-$25	
3859	Linton Pot		£8-£12	$10-$20	
3876	Begonia Tray		£5-£8	$5-$15	
3890	Textured Tray		£5-£8	$5-$15	
3893	Coral Tray		£5-£8	$5-$15	
3908	Avon Sugar Bowl		£5-£8	$5-$15	
3909	Avon Sugar Bowl		£5-£8	$5-$15	
3914	Avon Egg Cup	2½	£3-£6	$5-$10	
3915	Lisbon Bread Plate		£5-£8	$5-$15	
3919	Mug		£5-£8	$5-$15	
3920	Mug		£5-£8	$5-$15	
3922	Mug		£5-£8	$5-$15	
3926	Mug		£5-£8	$5-$15	
3931	Jar		£3-£8	$5-$15	
3948	Manhattan Tray	13½L	£8-£12	$10-$20	
3950	Manhattan Tray	7½	£5-£8	$5-$15	
3955	Maple Leaf Tray		£5-£8	$5-$15	
3973	Mug		£5-£8	$5-$15	
3977	Totem Cheese Dish		£8-£12	$10-$20	
3981	Coffee Mug		£5-£8	$5-$15	
3982	Totem Honey Pot	5½	£5-£8	$5-$15	
3985	Coffee Pot		£12-£18	$15-$30	
3986	Totem Butter Dish	6L	£8-£12	$10-$20	
3991	Tulip Tray		£5-£8	$5-$15	
4014	Totem Condiment Set & Tray		£12-£18	$15-$30	
4020	Totem Dish		£8-£12	$10-$20	
4021	Coffee Filter		£3-£8	$5-$15	
4022	Totem Oil & Vinegar Set on Tray		£8-£12	$10-$20	
4025	Coffee Filter		£8-£12	$10-$20	
4026	Sugar Bowl		£5-£8	$5-$15	
4028	Cream Jug		£5-£8	$5-$15	
4029	Totem Toast Rack		£5-£8	$5-$15	
4030	Totem Cheese Board & Knife		£8-£12	$10-$20	
4031	Totem 4x Egg Cups on Stand		£8-£12	$10-$20	
4032	Totem Triple Tray	13L	£8-£12	$10-$20	
4033	Totem Sugar Bowl	4D	£5-£8	$5-$15	
4035	Totem Double Tray		£5-£8	$5-$15	
4036	Totem Sandwich Tray	13L	£5-£8	$5-$15	
4037	Totem Coffee Jug	8¼	£8-£12	$10-$20	
4038	Totem Mug	4	£8-£12	$10-$20	
4039	Totem Cream Jug	3	£3-£5	$5-$10	
4040	Totem Jug		£3-£5	$5-$10	
4041	Nouveau Storage Jar		£5-£10	$5-$15	
4042	Nouveau Storage Jar		£5-£10	$5-$15	

Model No	Model	Size Inches	Market Value		Notes
4046	Nouveau Teapot		£10-£15	$15-$25	
4047	Nouveau Teapot		£10-£15	$15-$25	
4048	Nouveau Coffee Jug		£10-£15	$15-$25	
4049	Nouveau Cheese Dish		£10-£15	$15-$25	
4050	Nouveau Butter Dish		£10-£15	$15-$25	
4051	Nouveau Sugar Bowl		£3-£5	$5-$10	
4053	Nouveau Sugar Shaker		£5-£8	$5-$15	
4054	Nouveau Honey Pot		£10-£15	$15-$25	
4055	Nouveau Mixing Bowl		£10-£15	$15-$25	
4056	Nouveau Mixing Bowl		£8-£12	$10-$20	
4057	Nouveau Egg Separator		£5-£8	$5-$15	
4058	Nouveau Lemon Squeezer		£5-£8	$5-$15	
4059	Nouveau Condiment Set		£8-£12	$10-$20	
4060	Nouveau Vinegar Bottle		£5-£8	$5-$15	
4061	Nouveau Spice Jar		£5-£8	$5-$15	
4065	Mug		£5-£8	$5-$15	
4067	Coffee Pot		£8-£12	$10-$20	
4071	Double Egg Cup		£5-£8	$5-$15	
4072	Coffee Filter		£5-£8	$5-$15	
4073	Beaker		£5-£8	$5-$15	
4074	Jam Pot		£5-£8	$5-$15	
4075	Totem Honey Pot		£8-£12	$10-$20	
4076	Coffee Pot		£8-£12	$10-$20	
4082	Coffee Percolator		£10-£15	$15-$25	
4087	Cream Jug		£5-£8	$5-$15	
4088	Sugar Bowl		£5-£8	$5-$15	
4089	Cream Jug	4½	£5-£8	$5-$15	
4095	Totem Tea Cup		£3-£5	$5-$10	
4099	Coffee Strainer		£8-£12	$10-$20	
4101	Coffee Filter		£5-£8	$5-$15	
4102	Totem Coffee Filter		£5-£8	$5-$15	
4106	Totem Coffee Pot	6¼	£18-£25	$25-$40	
4108	Mug		£5-£8	$5-$15	
4133	Storage Jar		£5-£8	$5-$15	
4134	Totem Teapot		£8-£12	$10-$20	
4135	Teapot		£8-£12	$10-$20	
4137	Teacup		£3-£5	$5-$10	
4139	Spice Jar		£5-£8	$5-$15	
4140	Totem Teapot		£12-£18	$15-$30	
4141	Totem Saucer		£1-£2	$2-$5	
4142	Totem Breakfast Cup		£2-£5	$2-$10	
4143	Totem Storage Jar	7	£8-£12	$10-$20	
4144	Totem Teapot		£12-£18	$15-$30	
4148	Totem Spice Jar	4½	£5-£8	$5-$15	
4149	Totem Cheese Dish	8¼L	£8-£12	$10-$20	
4150	Totem Jar	8	£8-£12	$10-$20	
4151	Totem Egg Separator		£3-£5	$5-$10	
4154	Marina Tray	7½L	£5-£8	$5-$15	
4176	Totem Sugar Shaker		£8-£12	$10-$20	
4177	Totem Sauce Bat And Stand		£8-£12	$10-$20	
4179	Totem Jug	6¼	£12-£18	$15-$30	
4180	Coffee Percolator		£12-£18	$15-$30	
4182	Totem Egg Cups & Stand		£8-£12	$10-$20	
4185	Irish Sugar Bowl		£8-£12	$10-$20	
4186	Irish Cream Jug		£5-£8	$5-$15	
4187	Irish Sugar Bowl		£8-£12	$10-$20	
4189	Mug		£5-£8	$5-$15	
4190	Basket Coffee Percolator		£8-£12	$10-$20	
4191	Beaker		£5-£8	$5-$15	
4193	Totem Sauce Boat & Stand		£5-£8	$5-$15	
4194	Basket Coffee Percolator		£8-£12	$10-$20	
4195	Tray	7½D	£5-£8	$5-$15	
4196	Triangular Tray		£5-£8	$5-$15	
4197	Square Tray		£5-£8	$5-$15	

Model No	Model	Size Inches	Market Value		Notes
4198	Oblong Tray		£5-£8	$5-$15	
4202	Totem Coffee Pot	11½	£8-£12	$10-$20	
4216	Sugar Bowl		£5-£8	$5-$15	
4220	Totem Storage Jar	7½	£8-£12	$10-$20	
4221	Totem Plate	10D	£5-£8	$5-$15	
4222	Totem Plate	8D	£3-£6	$5-$10	
4223	Totem Plate	7½D	£2-£5	$2-$10	
4224	Totem Teapot	6¾	£8-£12	$10-$20	
4225	Totem Lemon Squeezer		£5-£8	$5-$15	
4235	Totem Coffee Pot		£8-£12	$10-$20	
4237	Totem Coffee Percolator	9¾	£12-£18	$15-$30	
4244	Tray	7L	£5-£8	$5-$15	
4253	Agincourt Tankard	4¾	£8-£12	$10-$20	
4254	Agincourt Tankard	5½	£8-£12	$10-$20	
4255	Agincourt Tankard	6½	£8-£12	$10-$20	
4256	Beaker		£5-£8	$5-$15	
4257	Beaker		£5-£8	$5-$15	
4259	Agincourt Coffee Jug	14½	£12-£15	$15-$25	
4260	Embossed Mug		£5-£8	$5-$15	
4262	Cauldron Jam Pot with Pixie Finial		£10-£15	$15-$25	
4267	Agincourt Tankard	6¼	£8-£12	$10-$20	
4269	Embossed Honey Jar		£5-£8	$5-$15	
4270	Agincourt Tankard	4¼	£8-£12	$10-$20	
4273	Agincourt Tankard	4¼	£8-£12	$10-$20	
4274	Agincourt Tankard	4½	£8-£12	$10-$20	
4275	Agincourt Tankard	3	£8-£12	$10-$20	
4283	Mug		£5-£8	$5-$15	
4295	Agincourt Tankard	5	£5-£8	$5-$15	
4296	Agincourt Tankard	3½	£5-£8	$5-$15	
4311	Agincourt Tankard	6½	£5-£8	$5-$15	
4312	Honey Pot		£8-£12	$10-$20	
4313	Totem Mug		£5-£8	$5-$15	
4314	Embossed Jam Pot		£8-£12	$10-$20	
4315	Agincourt Cruet		£8-£12	$10-$20	
4316	Agincourt Mustard Pot		£5-£8	$5-$15	
4317	Agincourt Tankard	4¼	£5-£8	$5-$15	
4318	Agincourt Tankard	5¼	£5-£8	$5-$15	
4333	Coffee Percolator		£8-£12	$10-$20	
4335	Shell Tray	6L	£5-£8	$5-$15	
4337	Oval Tray		£4-£8	$5-$15	
4339	Coffee Mug	4	£10-£15	$15-$25	
4342	Embossed Coffee Mug	4¾	£5-£8	$5-$15	
4343	Oslo Coffee Mug	4½	£5-£8	$5-$15	
4344	Coffee Mug		£5-£8	$5-$15	
4346	Cordon Brun Coffee Pot		£18-£25	$25-$40	
4348	Embossed Coffee Mug	4¾	£5-£8	$5-$15	
4354	Shell Tray		£10-£15	$15-$25	
4356	Totem Plate		£3-£6	$5-$10	
4357	Totem Plate		£3-£6	$5-$10	
4358	Jam Pot		£3-£6	$5-$10	
4359	Shell Tray	6L	£5-£8	$5-$15	
4362	Starway Mug		£5-£8	$5-$15	
4370	Coffee Pot		£8-£12	$10-$20	
4372	Cup		£3-£5	$5-$10	
4378	Starway Coffee Pot	11½	£12-£18	$15-$30	
4382	Sugar Bowl		£3-£5	$5-$10	
4384	Starway Cream Jug	4	£5-£8	$5-$15	
4386	Beaker		£5-£8	$5-$15	
4390	Starway Sugar Bowl	4	£5-£8	$5-$15	
4398	Hollyberry Tray	8L	£10-£15	$15-$25	
4399	Hollyberry Tray	6L	£10-£15	$15-$25	
4501	Concord Mug		£5-£8	$5-$15	
4502	Three Piece Condiment		£5-£8	$5-$15	
4503	Sugar Bowl		£5-£8	$5-$15	

Model No	Model	Size Inches	Market Value		Notes
4504	Cream Jug		£5-£8	$5-$15	
4505	Butter Dish		£3-£5	$5-$10	
4506	Cheese Dish		£8-£12	$10-$20	
4507	Sandwich Tray		£5-£8	$5-$15	
4508	Cup		£3-£6	$5-$10	
4509	Tray	9L	£5-£8	$5-$15	
4510	Coffee Pot		£8-£12	$10-$20	
4512	Coffee Pot		£8-£12	$10-$20	
4513	Preserve Pot		£5-£8	$5-$15	
4514	Plate	8D	£5-£8	$5-$15	
4522	Teapot		£8-£12	$10-$20	
4525	Cheese Dish with Cat & Mouse		£8-£12	$10-$20	
4530	Hollyberry Honeypot	4	£12-£18	$15-$30	
4541	Cow Cream Jug		£20-£30	$30-$50	
4543	Cow Butter Dish	7	£12-£18	$15-$30	
4571	Coffee Percolator		£8-£12	$10-$20	
4572	Pisces Sauce Boat & Stand		£12-£18	$15-$30	
4576	Hollyberry Cheese Dish		£15-£20	$20-$35	
4577	Hollyberry Condiment & Stand		£18-£25	$25-$40	
4585	Salt & Pepper		£5-£8	$5-$15	
4587	Starway Jug & Cover	6¾	£8-£12	$10-$20	
4600	Butter Dish Barrel with Cow Finial		£18-£25	$25-$40	
4633	Hollyberry Mug	4½	£8-£12	$10-$20	
4634	Hollyberry Tray	9L	£15-£20	$20-$35	
4639	Rhapsody Comport	9D	£10-£15	$15-$25	
4649	Spectrum Comport	9¾D	£10-£20	$15-$35	
4668	Starway Cup		£2-£4	$2-$5	
4669	Pisces Salt & Pepper		£18-£25	$25-$40	
4682	Embossed Owl Mug		£8-£12	$10-$20	
4683	Leaf Pattern Mint Sauce Boat & Stand		£8-£12	$10-$20	
4684	Pisces Plate	10½D	£8-£12	$10-$20	
4685	Pisces Plate	13½D	£10-£15	$15-$25	
4686	Starway Saucer		£1-£2	$1-$5	
4690	Assyria Plate	13½D	£8-£12	$10-$20	
4700	Preserve Jar		£8-£12	$10-$20	
4703	Leaf Tray		£5-£8	$5-$15	
4705	Pisces Plate	5	£8-£12	$10-$20	
4706	Pisces Plate	7¾D	£8-£12	$10-$20	
4714	Cricket Ball Preserve Pot		£20-£30	$30-$50	
4718	Bowls Preserve Pot		£20-£30	$30-$50	
4720	Cricket Ball Tankard	4¾	£20-£30	$30-$50	
4725	Bowls Tankard	4¾	£20-£30	$30-$50	
4726	Capstan Tankard	4	£20-£30	$30-$50	
4734	Iron Bound Basket Honey Pot		£8-£12	$10-$20	
4759	Mint Sauce Boat		£8-£12	$10-$20	
4765	Stand	4¾	£1-£2	$1-$5	
4771	Ice Jug		£5-£8	$5-$15	
4793	Starway Coffee Pot		£8-£12	$10-$20	
4795	Ice Jug		£5-£8	$5-$15	
4797	Medway Coffee Pot	9½	£12-£18	$15-$30	
4801	Medway Mug	4¾	£8-£12	$10-$20	
4802	Medway Sugar Bowl	4½	£5-£8	$5-$15	
4806	Medway Cream Jug	4	£5-£8	$5-$15	
4807	Brazil Coffee Pot	9½	£20-£30	$30-$50	
4809	Croft Teapot	6½	£20-£30	$30-$50	
4811	Croft Plate	8D	£8-£12	$10-$20	
4812	Croft Honey Pot	5½	£12-£18	$15-$30	
4813	Croft Cream Jug	3	£12-£18	$15-$30	
4814	Croft Sugar Bowl	4½D	£12-£18	$15-$30	
4815	Croft Cheese Dish		£20-£30	$30-$50	
4816	Croft Butter Dish		£20-£30	$30-$50	
4817	Croft Mug	5½	£5-£8	$5-$15	
4818	Croft Tea Cup		£2-£4	$2-$5	
4819	Croft Saucer		£1-£2	$1-$5	

Tablewares & Kitchenwares

Model No	Model	Size Inches	Market Value		Notes
4820	Croft Plate	7½D	£8-£12	$10-$20	
4821	Croft Plate	8D	£8-£12	$10-$20	
4822	Croft Cottage Plate	7¾D	£8-£12	$10-$20	
4832	Croft Condiment Set		£20-£30	$30-$50	
4833	Croft Storage Jar	8½	£20-£30	$30-$50	
4834	Croft Teapot	5¾	£20-£30	$30-$50	
4843	Medway Tea Cup		£3-£5	$5-$10	
4844	Medway Tea Cup		£3-£5	$5-$10	
4850	Brazil Leaf Saucer	6½D	£3-£5	$5-$10	
4851	Brazil Leaf Tea Cup		£3-£5	$5-$10	
4852	Brazil Leaf Sugar Bowl	4½D	£8-£12	$10-$20	
4853	Brazil Leaf Cream Jug	4	£8-£12	$10-$20	
4865	Preserve Pot	3	£5-£8	$5-$15	
4866	Strawberry Preserve Lid (4865/4871)		£20-£30	$30-$50	
4867	Blackberry Preserve Lid (4865/4871)		£20-£30	$30-$50	
4867	Raspberry Preserve Lid (4865/4871)		£20-£30	$30-$50	
4871	Preserve Pot	3	£5-£8	$5-$15	
4875	Medway Plate	7¾D	£3-£5	$5-$10	
4876	Medway Preserve Pot	5½	£5-£8	$5-$15	
4877	Medway Cheese Dish		£8-£12	$10-$20	
4878	Medway Dinner Plate		£3-£5	$5-$10	
4879	Medway Soup Bowl	6½D	£2-£5	$2-$10	
4880	Medway Teapot		£12-£18	$15-$30	
4881	Medway Sandwich Tray		£3-£6	$5-$10	
4882	Medway Butter Dish		£8-£12	$10-$20	
4888	House in the Glen Tray		£5-£8	$5-$15	
4901	Cereal Bowl		£3-£5	$5-$10	
4902	Beef Dripping Holder	4½	£8-£12	$10-$20	
4903	Pork Dripping Holder	4½	£8-£12	$10-$20	
4904	Lard Holder	4½	£8-£12	$10-$20	
4905	Soup Bowl		£8-£12	$10-$20	
4908	Embossed Vegetable Soup Bowl & Cover		£10-£20	$15-$30	
4931	Teapot Strainer & Stand		£8-£12	$10-$20	
5001	Embossed Rose Saucer		£1-£2	$1-$5	
5002	Embossed Rose Cup		£3-£5	$5-$10	
5033	Embossed Celery Jug	8½	£20-£30	$30-$50	
5038	Tea Bag Holder	6L	£12-£18	$15-$30	
5041	Coffee Bag Holder	6L	£8-£12	$10-$20	
5042	Embossed Spring onion Vase		£8-£12	$10-$20	
5043	Embossed Corn on The Cob Dish		£8-£12	$10-$20	
5047	Tea Bag Dispenser		£8-£12	$10-$20	
5050	Swan Pie Funnel		£8-£12	$10-$20	
5077	Coffee Bag Holder		£8-£12	$10-$20	
5078	Tea Cup		£1-£2	$1-$5	
5079	Tea Saucer		£1-£3	$1-$5	
5080	Plate	7½	£3-£5	$5-$10	
5081	Sugar Bowl	3¼	£2-£5	$2-$10	
5082	Cream Jug	4¾	£2-£5	$2-$10	
5083	Coffee Pot	9	£12-£18	$15-$30	
5084	Plate	11D	£8-£12	$10-$20	
5085	Sandwich Tray	13½L	£5-£8	$5-$15	
5086	Salt & Pepper		£5-£8	$5-$15	
5087	Tea Pot	5	£8-£12	$10-$20	
5088	Tea Pot	6¾	£8-£12	$10-$20	
5089	Cream Jug		£2-£4	$2-$5	
5124	Mug		£5-£8	$5-$15	
5143	Rodek Ham Stand		£5-£8	$5-$15	
5147	Muffin Dish, Cover & Stand		£10-£15	$15-$25	
5151	Banana Split Dish		£8-£12	$10-$20	
5168	Sunflower Butter Dish	5D	£8-£12	$10-$20	
5169	Sunflower Butter Dish	6L	£12-£18	$15-$30	
5171	Alton Coffee Pot		£12-£18	$15-$30	
5173	Alton Tea Cup		£3-£5	$5-$10	
5174	Alton Salt & Pepper		£5-£8	$5-$15	

Model No	Model	Size Inches	Market Value		Notes
5175	Alton Sugar Bowl	4½D	£3-£5	$5-$10	
5176	Alton Tea Saucer		£1-£2	$1-$5	
5177	Alton Plate	7¾	£3-£5	$5-$10	
5179	Bread & Butter Plate	11½D	£8-£12	$10-$20	
5180	Alton Butter Dish	5¼L	£8-£12	$10-$20	
5181	Alton Cheese Dish		£8-£12	$10-$20	
5182	Alton Preserve Pot	5¾	£5-£8	$5-$15	
5183	Alton Cereal Bowl	7½D	£3-£5	$5-$10	
5185	Dolphin Cereal Bowl	8½L	£15-£20	$20-$35	
5187	Dolphin Tray		£8-£12	$10-$20	
5191	Dolphin Basket		£8-£12	$10-$20	
5204	Coffee Mug	4	£4-£8	$5-$15	
5241	Cup		£3-£5	$5-$10	
5242	Washing Up Brush Holder	6	£20-£30	$30-$50	
5244	Harvest Time Basket		£12-£18	$15-$30	
5308	Teabag Pot	5½	£12-£18	$15-$30	
5337	Cordon Brun Jug	6¼	£5-£8	$5-$15	
5338	Cordon Brun Jug	6½	£5-£8	$5-$15	
5339	Cordon Brun Jug	5¾	£5-£8	$5-$15	
5340	Cordon Brun Jug	4¾	£3-£5	$5-$10	
5341	Cordon Brun Storage Jar	7¾	£5-£8	$5-$15	
5342	Cordon Brun Storage Jar	5	£5-£8	$5-$15	
5343	Cordon Brun Salt & Pepper		£5-£8	$5-$15	
5344	Cordon Brun Salt Jar	8½	£8-£12	$10-$20	
5345	Cordon Brun Preserve Pot		£8-£12	$10-$20	
5347	Cordon Brun Teapot		£12-£18	$15-$30	
5348	Cordon Brun Mug		£3-£5	$5-$10	
5349	Cordon Brun Butter Dish		£5-£8	$5-$15	
5350	Cordon Brun Cheese Dish	7¼L	£8-£12	$10-$20	
5351	Cordon Brun Preserve Pot Holder		£3-£5	$5-$10	
5352	Cordon Brun Tea Cup		£2-£4	$2-$5	
5353	Cordon Brun Saucer		£1-£2	$1-$5	
5354	Cordon Brun Plate	7½D	£3-£5	$5-$10	
5355	Cordon Brun Plate	8D	£4-£6	$5-$10	
5356	Cordon Brun Egg Cup & Stand		£3-£5	$5-$10	
5357	Cordon Brun Sugar Sifter		£5-£8	$5-$15	
5358	Cordon Brun Spoon Rest		£3-£5	$5-$10	
5359	Cordon Brun Egg Separator		£3-£5	$5-$10	
5360	Cordon Brun Lemon Squeezer		£3-£5	$5-$10	
5361	Cordon Brun Spice Jar	4¾	£8-£12	$10-$20	
5363	Cordon Brun Comport	6	£12-£18	$15-$30	
5364	Cordon Brun Double Egg Cup		£5-£8	$5-$15	
5365	Cordon Brun Teapot Stand		£1-£3	$1-$5	
5366	Cordon Brun Toast Rack		£4-£6	$5-$10	
5383	Honey Bee Pot	5	£30-£50	$45-$80	
5386	Lincoln Tray	8½L	£5-£8	$5-$15	
5396	Canton Jar	13	£30-£50	$45-$80	
5397	Canton Jar	9	£30-£50	$45-$80	
5400	Severn Salt & Pepper		£5-£8	$5-$15	
5402	Severn Cheese Dish	9¾L	£8-£12	$10-$20	
5408	Tray		£4-£6	$5-$10	
5409	English Rose Teapot	5	£12-£18	$15-$30	
5410	English Rose Sugar Bowl		£3-£5	$5-$10	
5411	English Rose Cream Jug		£3-£5	$5-$10	
5412	English Rose Tea Saucer		£1-£2	$1-$5	
5413	English Rose Plate	7¾	£3-£5	$5-$10	
5414	English Rose Tea Cup		£3-£5	$5-$10	
5415	English Rose Salt & Pepper		£5-£8	$5-$15	
5416	English Rose Preserve Pot		£5-£8	$5-$15	
5417	English Rose Cheese Dish		£8-£12	$10-$20	
5418	English Rose Butter Dish		£8-£12	$10-$20	
5419	Severn Tea Pot	6½	£12-£18	$15-$30	
5421	Mug		£3-£5	$5-$10	
5422	Honey Pot	5	£5-£8	$5-$15	

Tablewares & Kitchenwares

Model No	Model	Size Inches	Market Value		Notes
5423	Tea Time Clock Face Teapot & Mug		£30-£40	$45-$65	
5424	Butter Dish	6¾	£8-£12	$10-$20	
5425	Three Teabag Teapot	6½	£20-£30	$30-$50	
5426	Two Teabag Teapot	5¾	£18-£25	$25-$40	
5427	One Teabag Teapot	4	£15-£20	$20-$35	
5428	Teapot Stand	6D	£5-£8	$5-$15	
5447	Anniversary Honey Pot	5	£5-£8	$5-$15	
5449	Anniversary Teapot		£12-£18	$15-$30	
5450	Anniversary Plate	10D	£8-£12	$10-$20	
5453	Anniversary Teacup		£3-£5	$5-$10	
5454	Anniversary Saucer		£1-£2	$1-$5	
5455	Anniversary Tea Plate	6¼D	£5-£8	$5-$15	
5465	Chicken Shaped Egg Cup		£3-£5	$5-$10	
5529	Beer Mugs Salt & Pepper		£8-£12	$10-$20	
5531	Beer Mug Salt		£8-£12	$10-$20	
5536	Croft Jug	7	£10-£15	$15-$25	
5537	Croft Coffee Pot	9	£18-£25	$25-$40	
5547	Clown Honey Pot		£18-£25	$25-$40	
5563	Tray		£8-£12	$10-$20	
5620	Tapestry Tea Cup		£3-£5	$5-$10	
5621	Tapestry Saucer		£1-£2	$1-$5	
5622	Tapestry Tea Plate	6¼D	£5-£8	$5-$15	
5623	Tapestry Mug	5½	£5-£8	$5-$15	
5624	Tapestry Sugar Bowl		£3-£5	$5-$10	
5625	Tapestry Cream Jug		£4-£8	$5-$15	
5626	Tapestry Tea Pot	5	£8-£12	$10-$20	
5627	Tapestry Sandwich Tray	12¾L	£5-£10	$5-$15	
5628	Tapestry Salt & Pepper		£5-£8	$5-$15	
5629	Tapestry Butter Dish		£8-£12	$10-$20	
5630	Tapestry Cheese Dish		£8-£12	$10-$20	
5631	Tapestry Preserve Pot	4½	£12-£18	$15-$30	
5634	Teapot		£12-£18	$15-$30	
5635	Teapot		£12-£18	$15-$30	
5636	Teapot		£10-£15	$15-$25	
5637	Teapot		£10-£15	$15-$25	
5670	Tudor Cottage Tea Pot		£20-£30	$30-$50	
5671	Tudor Cottage Sugar Bowl		£12-£18	$15-$30	
5672	Tudor Cottage Cream Jug		£12-£18	$15-$30	
5673	Tudor Cottage Butter Dish		£20-£30	$30-$50	
5674	Tudor Cottage Cheese Dish		£20-£30	$30-$50	
5675	Tudor Cottage Preserve Pot		£20-£30	$30-$50	
5676	Tudor Cottage Salt & Pepper		£12-£18	$15-$30	

Toiletry Accessories

Model No	Model	Size Inches	Market Value		Notes
359	Dish		£5-£8	$5-$15	
484	Shaving Mug	4¼	£40-£60	$60-$100	
523	Tray for Dressing Table	13L	£12-£18	$15-$30	
642	Shaving Mug	3¼	£25-£50	$35-$80	
673	Dish		£5-£8	$5-$15	
694	Dressing Table Set		£20-£30	$30-$50	
802	Dressing Table Tray	17¾	£20-£30	$30-$50	
811	Wild Duck Toilet Set	10	£50-£80	$75-$130	
1654	Dish	5D	£10-£15	$15-$25	
1877	Shaving Mug	3¼	£30-£50	$45-$80	
1894	Dish	6L	£8-£12	$10-$20	
1898	Dish	5D	£8-£12	$10-$20	
1968	Dish	5D	£10-£15	$15-$25	
2225	Dish	5¼	£8-£12	$10-$20	
2261	Dish	7½D	£8-£12	$10-$20	
2326	Dish	7¼	£5-£8	$5-$15	
3085	Dish	10L	£5-£10	$5-$15	
3478	Shaving Mug	4¼	£10-£15	$15-$25	
3911	Dish		£5-£8	$5-$15	

Model No	Model	Size Inches	Market Value		Notes
4511	Dinner Plate		£5-£8	$5-$15	
4792	Moustache Cup		£8-£12	$10-$20	
4794	Moustache Cup		£8-£12	$10-$20	
4913	Bath Salt Bowl		£5-£8	$5-$15	
4916	Fish Shaped Soap Dish		£8-£12	$10-$20	
4917	Toilet Roll Holder		£5-£8	$5-$15	
4918	Talcum Powder Holder		£5-£8	$5-$15	
4919	Fish Shaped Tooth Brush Holder		£5-£8	$5-$15	
4924	Shaving Tankard		£6-£10	$10-$15	
4925	Shaving Tankard		£6-£10	$10-$15	
4926	Shaving Tankard		£6-£10	$10-$15	
4927	Shaving Tankard		£6-£10	$10-$15	
4964	Shaving Mug	4¾	£8-£12	$10-$20	
4965	Mosaic Denture Holder	3	£8-£12	$10-$20	
4966	Mosaic Bath Salt Holder		£8-£12	$10-$20	
4968	Mosaic Soap Tray		£8-£12	$10-$20	
4969	Mosaic Toilet Roll Holder		£8-£12	$10-$20	
4970	Mosaic Tooth Brush Holder		£8-£12	$10-$20	
4971	Mosaic Shaving Mug	4	£8-£12	$10-$20	
5099	Moustache Tankard	4¾	£8-£12	$10-$20	
5401	Bath Salts Jar (Made For Boots)		£8-£12	$10-$20	
5439	Soap Dish		£5-£8	$5-$15	
5564	Toilet Roll Holder		£5-£8	$5-$15	
5565	Bath Salt Jar & Cover		£8-£12	$10-$20	
5566	Tooth Brush Holder		£8-£12	$10-$20	
5567	Denture Bowl		£5-£8	$5-$15	
5584	Milady Trinket Box		£8-£12	$10-$20	
5585	Milady Ring Stand		£5-£8	$5-$15	
5587	Milady Tray	10L	£5-£8	$5-$15	
5595	Milady Specimen Vase	7¾	£8-£12	$10-$20	

Vases

2	Vase		£30-£50	$45-$80	
16	Vase		£20-£30	$30-$50	
75	Vase	9	£20-£30	$30-$50	
138	Vase	11¾	£20-£40	$30-$65	
152	Swan Posy Vase		£100-£200	$150-$330	
170	Vase		£15-£20	$20-$35	
178	Vase	4	£10-£20	$15-$35	
192	Falcon Vase		£20-£30	$30-$50	
220	Misty Morn Vase		£20-£30	$30-$50	
221	Misty Morn/Rosslyn Vase	15	£20-£30	$30-$50	
223	Misty Morn Vase	7	£20-£30	$30-$50	
225	Sanora Vase		£10-£20	$15-$35	
226	Misty Morn/Sanora Vase	6	£10-£20	$15-$35	
228	Misty Morn Vase		£10-£20	$15-$35	
229	Vase		£8-£12	$10-$20	
230	Twin Handled Vase		£8-£12	$10-$20	
233	Twin Handled Vase		£8-£12	$10-$20	
236	Sanora/Dovedale Vase	8	£20-£40	$30-$65	
237	Falcon Ware Vase		£12-£18	$15-$30	
238	Falcon Ware Vase		£12-£18	$15-$30	
239	Falcon Ware Vase		£12-£18	$15-$30	
240	Falcon Ware Vase		£12-£18	$15-$30	
246	Sanora Vase		£10-£20	$15-$35	
249	Misty Morn Vase	7¾	£10-£20	$15-$35	
255	Vase	14¾	£15-£20	$20-$35	
258	Rosslyn Vase	10	£10-£20	$15-$35	
265	Vase		£8-£12	$10-$20	
270	Vase		£15-£20	$20-$35	
273	Holborn Vase	9	£20-£30	$30-$50	
275	Springbok Vase		£20-£30	$30-$50	
276	Springbok Vase		£20-£30	$30-$50	

Vases

Model No	Model	Size Inches	Market Value		Notes
282	Hat Vase	8	£20-£40	$30-$65	
283	Hat Vase	6	£15-£30	$20-$50	
291	Vase		£5-£8	$5-$15	
310	Sugar Bowl/Vase		£10-£20	$15-$35	
311	Straw Hat Vase		£10-£15	$15-$25	
316	Vase		£8-£12	$10-$20	
318	Vase		£8-£12	$10-$20	
335	Vase	10	£10-£20	$15-$35	
336	Vase	7	£10-£20	$15-$35	
337	Vase	12	£10-£20	$15-$35	
338	Vase	13	£15-£20	$20-$35	
347	Vase	9	£10-£20	$15-$35	
348	Vase		£5-£8	$5-$15	
349	Handbag Shaped Vase	5	£20-£30	$30-$50	
354	Holborn Vase	16	£80-£120	$120-$200	
355	Vase	6	£10-£20	$15-$35	
359	Vase	10¾	£10-£20	$15-$35	
366	Vase	12	£25-£30	$35-$50	
367	Vase	10	£20-£30	$30-$50	
370	Vase		£8-£12	$10-$20	
371	Vase	10	£30-£50	$45-$80	
374	Vase	12	£10-£20	$15-$35	
375	Vase	12	£20-£30	$30-$50	
379	Vase		£15-£20	$20-$35	
380	Rosslyn Vase	5	£15-£20	$20-$35	
382	Ribbon Wall Vase		£20-£30	$30-$50	
383	Sanora Vase		£15-£20	$20-$35	
384	Galleon Vase		£15-£20	$20-$35	
385	Vase	8	£10-£20	$15-$35	
387	Twin-Handled Vase	11	£30-£50	$45-$80	
389	Vase		£8-£12	$10-$20	
416	Vase	10	£15-£20	$20-$35	
417	Octagonal Vase		£12-£18	$15-$30	
418	Vase		£10-£15	$15-$25	
419	Flower Vase	12¾	£20-£30	$30-$50	
420	Vase	11	£20-£30	$30-$50	
421	Vase	7	£20-£30	$30-$50	
422	Vase	8	£20-£30	$30-$50	
424	Vase		£20-£30	$30-$50	
425	Vase	9	£15-£20	$20-$35	
426	Vase	8	£15-£20	$20-$35	
431	Vase	8¼	£10-£20	$15-$35	
432	Vase	7¼	£10-£20	$15-$35	
434	Vase	9	£10-£20	$15-$35	
435	Vase (with Budgie)	9¾	£10-£20	$15-$35	
439	Vase	7	£20-£30	$30-$50	
443	Vase	6	£10-£20	$15-$35	
446	Vase	8	£12-£18	$15-$30	
475	Vase With Stork Handle	3	£30-£40	$45-$65	
476	Hollyock Vase	3	£20-£30	$30-$50	
477	Hat With Cat On Rim Vase	3	£12-£18	$15-$30	
481	Diamond Posy Vase		£5-£8	$5-$15	
483	Vase	5¾	£12-£18	$15-$30	
495	Vase	11	£10-£20	$15-$35	
496	Vase	11	£25-£50	$35-$80	
509	Vase	10	£25-£50	$35-$80	
511	Vase	11	£18-£25	$25-$40	
515	Vase		£8-£12	$10-$20	
517	Vase		£8-£12	$10-$20	
521	Vase	12	£12-£18	$15-$30	
522	Vase	12	£25-£30	$35-$50	
524	Sydney Wall Vase		£10-£20	$15-$35	
528	Vase	13	£30-£50	$45-$80	
533	Vase	7	£15-£20	$20-$35	

Model No	Model	Size Inches	Market Value		Notes
539	Squirrel with Acorn Vase		£30-£50	$45-$80	
539	Slymcraft Range Vase	8	£15-£20	$20-$35	
540	Slymcraft Range Vase	8	£15-£20	$20-$35	
541	Slymcraft Range Vase	11	£20-£30	$30-$50	
543	Vase	6	£15-£25	$20-$40	
546	Vase	8	£15-£20	$20-$35	
548	Vase	11¼	£20-£30	$30-$50	
548	Vase	11¼	£20-£30	$30-$50	
549	Duotone Vase		£10-£15	$15-$25	
556	Vase		£10-£20	$15-$35	
558	Vase		£10-£15	$15-$25	
561	Vase	7	£15-£20	$20-$35	
562	Vase	14	£20-£30	$30-$50	
565	Vase	11	£20-£40	$30-$65	
567	Wild Duck Vase	11	£20-£30	$30-$50	
570	Vase	8¼	£10-£20	$15-$35	
576	Vase	11	£20-£30	$30-$50	
577	Vase		£15-£20	$20-$35	
578	Vase	7¾	£10-£20	$15-$35	
581	Vase	10¾	£15-£20	$20-$35	
582	Vase	11	£25-£50	$35-$80	
583	Vase	14¾	£40-£60	$60-$100	
585	Vase		£20-£25	$30-$40	
587	Vase	9	£15-£20	$20-$35	
588	Squirrel On Cone Vase		£50-£100	$75-$165	
599	Duotone Vase		£10-£15	$15-$25	
600	Vase	9	£15-£20	$20-$35	
606	Heart Shaped Vase	7	£30-£50	$45-$80	
607	Vase		£8-£12	$10-$20	
609	Heart Shaped Vase	10¾	£30-£50	$45-$80	
610	Vase	7	£15-£20	$20-$35	
611	Vase	12¾	£18-£25	$25-$40	
613	Vase	8	£15-£20	$20-$35	
614	Vase	10¾	£18-£25	$25-$40	
620	Flower Pot	6¼	£10-£20	$15-$35	
621	Vase	13	£20-£30	$30-$50	
622	Vase	14	£12-£18	$15-$30	
623	Vase		£8-£12	$10-$20	
624	Vase		£8-£12	$10-$20	
625	Fish Vase		£10-£15	$15-$25	
626	Vase	8¾	£10-£20	$15-$35	
627	Vase	10	£12-£18	$15-$30	
628	Classic Range Vase	8	£12-£18	$15-$30	
629	Classic Range Vase	9	£15-£20	$20-$35	
629	Vase	11	£20-£30	$30-$50	
630	Classic Range Vase	6	£10-£20	$15-$35	
630	Classic Range Vase	6	£10-£20	$15-$35	
632	Classic Range Vase	10	£20-£30	$30-$50	
634	Vase	6	£15-£25	$20-$40	
635	Vase		£20-£30	$30-$50	
636	Vase	8	£15-£20	$20-$35	
637	Vase	12	£20-£30	$30-$50	
641	Vase		£8-£12	$10-$20	
644	Vase		£8-£12	$10-$20	
648	Vase Gothic Style	10	£30-£50	$45-$80	
648	Vase Gothic Style	10	£30-£50	$45-$80	
650	Vase (To Match 649)	8	£20-£40	$30-$65	
652	Vase (To Match 651)	8	£20-£30	$30-$50	
656	Vase		£8-£12	$10-$20	
658	Vase		£8-£12	$10-$20	
659	Scello Ware Vase	9	£10-£15	$15-$25	
663	Vase	12	£20-£30	$30-$50	
669	Vase	11	£20-£30	$30-$50	
676	Vase		£20-£25	$30-$40	

Vases

Model No	Model	Size Inches	Market Value		Notes
677	Vase		£8-£12	$10-$20	
678	Vase	10	£15-£20	$20-$35	
679	Vase	11	£18-£25	$25-$40	
682	Vase		£12-£18	$15-$30	
682	Vase		£12-£18	$15-$30	
683	Vase		£8-£12	$10-$20	
684	Vase	5	£10-£20	$15-$35	
696	Vase (to match 696 Clock)	8	£15-£20	$20-$35	
697	Vase with Couple in Garden		£10-£20	$15-$35	
698	Vase with Couple in Garden	10¾	£15-£20	$20-$35	
699	Vase with Couple in Garden	11	£20-£30	$30-$50	
703	Vase	10	£20-£30	$30-$50	
709	Vase Decorated with Balcony Scene	10	£18-£25	$25-$40	
710	Fish Vase		£20-£30	$30-$50	
725	Fish Vase		£20-£30	$30-$50	
727	Sydney Harbour Bridge Vase	4	£50-£80	$75-$130	
729	Vase		£8-£12	$10-$20	
730	Vase		£8-£12	$10-$20	
731	Vase		£8-£12	$10-$20	
732	Tribly Hat Wall Vase	4	£25-£50	$35-$80	
734	Vase		£8-£12	$10-$20	
739	Vase		£8-£12	$10-$20	
740	Vase		£8-£12	$10-$20	
741	Vase		£8-£12	$10-$20	
745	Vase		£8-£12	$10-$20	
746	Vase		£8-£12	$10-$20	
748	Vase		£12-£18	$15-$30	
749	Vase	6	£15-£20	$20-$35	
750	Vase		£8-£12	$10-$20	
751	Vase		£8-£12	$10-$20	
752	Vase	10¼	£15-£20	$20-$35	
753	Nautilus Range Vase	9	£30-£50	$45-$80	
755	Vase		£8-£12	$10-$20	
763	Owl Vase	8	£20-£40	$30-$65	
774	Vase	12	£30-£50	$45-$80	
776	Fan Shaped Vase	8W	£15-£20	$20-$35	
778	Basket Vase	10¼	£12-£18	$15-$30	
780	Vase	5	£12-£18	$15-$30	
781	Spill Vase	4	£10-£15	$15-$25	
782	Vase with Couple in Garden		£12-£18	$15-$30	
784	Wild Duck Vase	8¾	£20-£30	$30-$50	
785	Wild Duck Vase	5¼	£15-£20	$20-$35	
790	Wild Duck Vase	6¾	£15-£20	$20-$35	
799	Wild Duck Vase	9	£25-£40	$35-$65	
801	Wild Duck Vase	10	£20-£30	$30-$50	
823	Tree Stump & Lion on Base Vase	5	£30-£50	$45-$80	
824	Tree Stump & Lion On Base Vase	5	£30-£50	$45-$80	
828	Greek Urn Vase	8	£20-£30	$30-$50	
848	Harvest Poppy Vase	6¾	£15-£20	$20-$35	
858	Tree Trunk Flower Vase	5	£15-£20	$20-$35	
861	Vase	8¾	£15-£20	$20-$35	
873	Story Time Vase	12	£20-£30	$30-$50	
882	Vase		£20-£30	$30-$50	
883	Vase		£20-£25	$30-$40	
884	Vase		£20-£30	$30-$50	
898	Diamond Shaped Vase	5	£30-£50	$45-$80	
904	Harvest Poppy Vase	7¼	£20-£35	$30-$55	
905	Harvest Poppy Vase	9¾	£15-£20	$20-$35	
907	Vase	5	£15-£20	$20-$35	
908	Harvest Poppy Vase	7	£20-£30	$30-$50	
927	Cornflower Vase		£10-£15	$15-$25	
944	Palestine Beaker Vase	6	£20-£30	$30-$50	
957	Vase with Poppy Design		£15-£20	$20-$35	
966	Cornflower Vase	6	£10-£20	$15-$35	

Vases

Model No	Model	Size Inches	Market Value		Notes
967	Cornflower Vase	8	£20-£30	$30-$50	
974	Cornflower Oval Vase		£20-£30	$30-$50	
975	Vase		£10-£20	$15-$35	
976	Cornflower Vase		£20-£30	$30-$50	
977	Cornflower Vase		£20-£30	$30-$50	
979	Cornflower Vase	8	£20-£30	$30-$50	
987	Cornflower Vase	11	£20-£30	$30-$50	
1002	Vase	8	£20-£30	$30-$50	
1004	Tree Trunk & Owl Vase	6	£50-£80	$75-$130	
1005	Spill Vase	6	£15-£20	$20-$35	
1006	Vase	8	£20-£30	$30-$50	
1007	Vase	5	£10-£20	$15-$35	
1008	Vase	8	£20-£30	$30-$50	
1011	Vase	8¼	£20-£30	$30-$50	
1014	Globular Vase		£15-£20	$20-$35	
1017	Vase	8¼	£20-£30	$30-$50	
1025	Odeon Vase	7	£20-£30	$30-$50	
1032	Vase	7	£10-£15	$15-$25	
1039	Kingfisher Vase	6	£20-£30	$30-$50	
1040	Vase		£10-£15	$15-$25	
1061	Vase		£10-£15	$15-$25	
1075	Vase	6	£15-£20	$20-$35	
1076	Vase on Square Base	7	£15-£20	$20-$35	
1077	Vase	9¾	£20-£30	$30-$50	
1109	Vase with Sunray Design	7	£30-£50	$45-$80	
1110	Bacchanti Vase	7	£20-£30	$30-$50	
1113	Bacchanti Oval Vase	6¾	£30-£50	$45-$80	
1126	Bacchanti Vase	9¾	£30-£50	$45-$80	
1148	Deco Vase	7	£30-£40	$45-$65	
1149	Vase	8¾	£20-£40	$30-$65	
1153	Elephant Vase	3	£20-£30	$30-$50	
1165	Vase	16	£30-£50	$45-$80	
1166	Vase	17¾	£30-£50	$45-$80	
1173	Vase	7	£20-£30	$30-$50	
1174	Vase	10	£30-£50	$45-$80	
1175	Pilgrim Shaped Vase	6	£15-£20	$20-$35	
1176	Vase	7	£10-£20	$15-$35	
1177	Vase	9¾	£15-£20	$20-$35	
1187	Spill Vase	4¼	£10-£20	$15-$35	
1190	Monkey Nut Flower Vase	7¼	£50-£100	$75-$165	
1201	Vase	5	£5-£10	$5-$15	
1210	Vase	7	£10-£15	$15-$25	
1240	Bunny Vase	6	£100-£150	$150-$245	
1257	Round Vase	8¾	£10-£15	$15-$25	
1271	Spill Vase	5	£12-£18	$15-$30	
1272	Shell Vase	7¼	£25-£30	$35-$50	
1275	Shell Vase	6	£20-£30	$30-$50	
1280	Shell Vase	8	£25-£35	$35-$55	
1306	Rope Vase	5	£20-£30	$30-$50	
1307	Rope Vase	8	£25-£50	$35-$80	
1308	Rope Vase	5	£15-£20	$20-$35	
1309	Rope Vase	8¾	£20-£25	$30-$40	
1321	George VI Commemorative Vase	6¼	£20-£30	$30-$50	
1327	Figurine Vase	9¾	£50-£80	$75-$130	
1327	Animal Vase (various designs)	9¾	£20-£40	$30-$65	
1341	Vase	5¼	£20-£40	$30-$65	
1343	Deco Vase	9	£20-£30	$30-$50	
1345	Vase	9	£15-£20	$20-$35	
1346	Vase	10	£15-£20	$20-$35	
1347	Vase		£10-£20	$15-$35	
1355	Autumn Vase	7	£20-£30	$30-$50	
1403	Seal Vase		£40-£60	$60-$100	
1407	Serpent Vase	8	£15-£20	$20-$35	
1408	Serpent Vase		£15-£20	$20-$35	

Vases

Model No	Model	Size Inches	Market Value		Notes
1413	Tree Trunks Vase	4	£20-£30	$30-$50	
1429	Vase	9	£20-£30	$30-$50	
1478	Twin Vase	3¼	£10-£15	$15-$25	
1489	Vase		£15-£20	$20-$35	
1490	Vase	5¾	£10-£15	$15-$25	
1491	Vase	5¾	£10-£15	$15-$25	
1495	Vase		£15-£20	$20-$35	
1538	Vase	3	£10-£15	$15-$25	
1540	Stag Posy Vase	5	£100-£150	$150-$245	
1549	Vase		£10-£20	$15-$35	
1550	Vase		£10-£20	$15-$35	
1562	Vase	8	£8-£12	$10-$20	
1563	Vase	10	£10-£15	$15-$25	
1564	Vase	12¾	£12-£18	$15-$30	
1566	Vase	5¾	£15-£20	$20-$35	
1568	Vase	5	£10-£15	$15-$25	
1569	Vase	7	£10-£20	$15-$35	
1570	Vase	7	£10-£20	$15-$35	
1571	Vase	10	£12-£15	$15-$25	
1575	Vase	6	£10-£15	$15-$25	
1578	Vase	8	£12-£18	$15-$30	
1597	Dahlia Vase	4	£10-£15	$15-$25	
1607	Dahlia Vase	9	£15-£20	$20-$35	
1615	Vase		£10-£15	$15-$25	
1620	Vase		£8-£12	$10-$20	
1627	Vase	6	£10-£20	$15-$35	
1628	Vase		£5-£10	$5-$15	
1637	Vase		£10-£15	$15-$25	
1644	Dahlia Vase	8	£15-£20	$20-$35	
1645	Vase		£10-£20	$15-$35	
1651	Vase	7¼	£10-£20	$15-$35	
1652	Dahlia Vase	6¾	£15-£20	$20-$35	
1686	Vase		£10-£15	$15-$25	
1701	Flower Vase		£10-£15	$15-$25	
1719	Vase	5	£10-£15	$15-$25	
1731	Vase		£10-£15	$15-$25	
1732	Vase	9	£15-£20	$20-$35	
1757	Wave Patterned Vase	6	£10-£15	$15-$25	
1758	Vase	6	£10-£15	$15-$25	
1763	Vase		£8-£12	$10-$20	
1781	Vase		£10-£20	$15-$35	
1784	Deco Vase	6¼	£15-£20	$20-$35	
1786	Vase	4	£10-£15	$15-$25	
1787	Twin Handled Vase	4¼	£8-£12	$10-$20	
1803	Vase		£10-£15	$15-$25	
1807	Vase	10¾	£10-£20	$15-$35	
1808	Dovedale Vase	8	£15-£30	$20-$50	
1817	Vase		£8-£12	$10-$20	
1831	Vase with Leaf Handles	6	£12-£18	$15-$30	
1832	Twin Handled Vase	8	£12-£18	$15-$30	
1833	Twin Handled Vase	8	£12-£18	$15-$30	
1834	Vase	8	£12-£15	$15-$25	
1835	Twin Handled Vase	8	£12-£18	$15-$30	
1836	Vase	8	£12-£18	$15-$30	
1837	Vase	8	£12-£18	$15-$30	
1853	Wild Duck Vase	6	£12-£18	$15-$30	
1856	Wild Duck Vase	5	£12-£18	$15-$30	
1857	Wild Duck Vase	8	£20-£30	$30-$50	
1858	Wild Duck Vase	8	£20-£30	$30-$50	
1859	Wild Duck Dond Shape Vase	5	£12-£18	$15-$30	
1883	Vase		£10-£15	$15-$25	
1896	Hawthorn Tree & Bird		£40-£60	$60-$100	
1901	Vase		£10-£15	$15-$25	
1922	Vase	2	£5-£8	$5-$15	

Model No	Model	Size Inches	Market Value		Notes
1961	Duck Spill Vase	3	£10-£15	$15-$25	
1963	Heart Shaped Pixie Vase		£20-£30	$30-$50	
1964	Crescent Shaped Posy Vase	6L	£8-£12	$10-$20	
2024	Sealyham Dog Posy Vase	7L	£20-£30	$30-$50	
2029	Vase		£10-£15	$15-$25	
2031	Chrys Vase	4	£10-£15	$15-$25	
2044	Ivyleaf Vase	7L	£12-£18	$15-$30	
2061	Squirrel Vase	11L	£20-£30	$30-$50	
2062	Tree Stump & Animal Vase	7¼D	£50-£80	$75-$130	
2070	Ivyleaf Vase	6	£10-£15	$15-$25	
2075	Ivyleaf Squirrel Vase	6L	£20-£30	$30-$50	
2081	Vase		£8-£12	$10-$20	
2082	Vase		£8-£12	$10-$20	
2113	Seagull Vase	8½W	£30-£50	$45-$80	
2116	Autumn Vase	8½L	£20-£30	$30-$50	
2117	Vase		£8-£12	$10-$20	
2118	Chrys Vase	6½	£15-£20	$20-$35	
2124	Ivyleaf Vase	9½	£20-£30	$30-$50	
2125	Vase		£10-£20	$15-$35	
2130	Rope Vase		£8-£12	$10-$20	
2136	Vase	6½	£8-£12	$10-$20	
2137	Vase		£8-£12	$10-$20	
2139	Vase	8¼	£8-£10	$10-$15	
2144	Vase	11	£10-£12	$15-$20	
2147	Vase		£5-£8	$5-$15	
2152	Autumn Vase		£15-£20	$20-$35	
2155	Vase		£8-£12	$10-$20	
2159	Autumn Vase	14	£30-£50	$45-$80	
2161	Rope Vase	3	£5-£8	$5-$15	
2162	Rope Vase	6	£8-£12	$10-$20	
2163	Rope Vase	7	£12-£18	$15-$30	
2164	Vase		£5-£8	$5-$15	
2173	Vase	5	£5-£8	$5-$15	
2175	Vase		£10-£20	$15-$35	
2176	Raphique Vase		£12-£18	$15-$30	
2180	Raphique Vase		£5-£8	$5-$15	
2187	Rope Posy Vase	15L	£8-£12	$10-$20	
2189	Raphique Vase		£8-£12	$10-$20	
2192	Raphique Vase		£10-£12	$15-$20	
2194	Vase		£8-£12	$10-$20	
2198	Raphique Vase	5¼	£8-£12	$10-$20	
2199	Raphique Vase		£8-£12	$10-$20	
2205	Fish Vase		£20-£30	$30-$50	
2212	Lace Vase	5¼	£8-£12	$10-$20	
2217	Vase		£5-£10	$5-$15	
2218	Trumpet Shaped Vase		£12-£18	$15-$30	
2219	Vase		£8-£12	$10-$20	
2220	Vase with Circle Design		£15-£20	$20-$35	
2224	Oak Wood Vase	5	£18-£25	$25-$40	
2227	Rope Vase	12L	£12-£18	$15-$30	
2231	Vase		£5-£8	$5-$15	
2232	Vase		£5-£8	$5-$15	
2233	Vase		£5-£8	$5-$15	
2237	Vase		£5-£8	$5-$15	
2238	Rope Vase	8	£8-£12	$10-$20	
2243	Vase		£5-£8	$5-$15	
2246	Cactus Vase	6	£20-£30	$30-$50	
2250	Vase		£5-£8	$5-$15	
2251	Cactus Vase		£12-£18	$15-$30	
2252	Cactus Vase	8	£20-£30	$30-$50	
2254	Cactus Vase	7	£20-£30	$30-$50	
2255	Lace Vase	6	£10-£15	$15-$25	
2258	Vase		£8-£12	$10-$20	
2260	Floral Vase		£15-£20	$20-$35	

Vases

Model No	Model	Size Inches	Market Value		Notes
2264	Rope Range Vase	14L	£12-£18	$15-$30	
2265	Rope Vase	5	£8-£12	$10-$20	
2266	Rope Vase	8	£10-£15	$15-$25	
2267	Floral Vase	5¼	£12-£18	$15-$30	
2268	Lace Vase	7¾	£10-£15	$15-$25	
2272	Vase		£8-£12	$10-$20	
2280	Rope Vase	12L	£10-£15	$15-$25	
2281	Vase	7	£8-£12	$10-$20	
2282	Vase	7	£8-£12	$10-$20	
2284	Lace Posy Vase	8½	£5-£8	$5-$15	
2286	Vase	6	£10-£20	$15-$35	
2287	Vase		£8-£12	$10-$20	
2288	Vase	7	£8-£12	$10-$20	
2291	Vase		£5-£8	$5-$15	
2296	Cactus Vase		£5-£8	$5-$15	
2297	Lace Posy Vase		£5-£8	$5-$15	
2300	Lace Vase	12D	£8-£12	$10-$20	
2302	Vase		£5-£10	$5-$15	
2303	Vase		£5-£10	$5-$15	
2304	Vase		£5-£10	$5-$15	
2305	Cactus Vase	8½	£20-£30	$30-$50	
2308	Cactus Vase		£10-£15	$15-$25	
2309	Lace Posy Vase	5½	£8-£12	$10-$20	
2312	Floral Vase	5	£12-£18	$15-$30	
2314	Privet Tree Vase	5¾	£15-£20	$20-$35	
2320	Rope Vase	7D	£10-£15	$15-$25	
2321	Hyacinth Vase	7	£8-£12	$10-$20	
2338	Vase		£5-£8	$5-$15	
2339	Vase	5	£8-£12	$10-$20	
2330	Vase		£5-£8	$5-$15	
2334	Nuleef Vase	6½	£10-£20	$15-$35	
2337	Vase	10¼	£10-£20	$15-$35	
2338	Vase		£5-£10	$5-$15	
2340	Lace Vase	8¼	£8-£12	$10-$20	
2345	Plume Vase	7	£12-£18	$15-$30	
2352	Vase	6	£8-£12	$10-$20	
2364	Nuleef Posy Vase		£8-£12	$10-$20	
2368	Nuleef Vase	6	£12-£18	$15-$30	
2379	Twin Handled Vase	8L	£8-£12	$10-$20	
2383	Vase		£5-£8	$5-$15	
2384	Vase		£5-£8	$5-$15	
2385	Plume Posy Vase		£8-£12	$10-$20	
2390	Vase		£5-£8	$5-$15	
2391	Vase		£8-£12	$10-$20	
2392	Vase		£8-£15	$10-$25	
2401	Plume Vase		£10-£15	$15-$25	
2404	Plume Vase	6¼	£8-£12	$10-$20	
2406	Plume Twin Handled Vase	9½L	£10-£15	$15-$25	
2407	Plume Vase		£8-£12	$10-$20	
2408	Plume Vase	6½	£10-£12	$15-$20	
2418	Vase		£8-£12	$10-$20	
2419	Nuleef Vase		£10-£15	$15-$25	
2420	Nuleef Vase	8¼	£8-£12	$10-$20	
2430	Palm Tree Vase	4	£18-£25	$25-$40	
2439	Nautilus Vase	6	£12-£18	$15-$30	
2440	Nautilus Vase	7½	£15-£20	$20-$35	
2441	Nautilus Vase	10	£18-£25	$25-$40	
2442	Vase		£8-£12	$10-$20	
2445	Vase		£5-£8	$5-$15	
2446	Vase		£5-£8	$5-$15	
2447	Vase	6	£8-£12	$10-$20	
2448	Vase		£5-£8	$5-$15	
2449	Nautilus Vase	8	£12-£18	$15-$30	
2452	Hyacinth Vase	9¼	£8-£12	$10-$20	

Model No	Model	Size Inches	Market Value		Notes
2453	Hyacinth Vase	11¼	£10-£15	$15-$25	
2456	Hyacinth Vase	10	£15-£20	$20-$35	
2457	Squirrel Vase	6¾	£15-£25	$20-$40	
2459	Double Squirrel Vase	6¾	£15-£25	$20-$40	
2460	Vase		£8-£12	$10-$20	
2463	Classical Vase	8¼	£8-£12	$10-$20	
2464	Vase		£5-£8	$5-$15	
2467	Vase	7L	£8-£12	$10-$20	
2468	Squirrel Vase	6¾	£12-£18	$15-$30	
2472	Lilac Vase	5	£10-£15	$15-$25	
2476	Lilac Vase	5	£12-£18	$15-$30	
2478	Hyacinth	14¼	£10-£15	$15-$25	
2484	Hyacinth Twin Handled Vase	13L	£18-£25	$25-$40	
2486	Hyacinth Posy Vase	8L	£5-£8	$5-$15	
2488	Hyacinth Twin Handled Vase	8¼	£10-£15	$15-$25	
2494	Classical Vase	6¼	£5-£8	$5-$15	
2495	Classical Vase	10¼	£15-£20	$20-$35	
2505	Deco Vase	15	£25-£30	$35-$50	
2506	Vase		£8-£12	$10-$20	
2514	Classical Vase	7¼	£12-£18	$15-$30	
2515	Vase		£8-£12	$10-$20	
2531	Long Vase		£8-£12	$10-$20	
2543	Vase		£8-£12	$10-$20	
2544	Vase		£8-£12	$10-$20	
2548	Moselle Vase		£20-£30	$30-$50	
2550	Vase		£8-£12	$10-$20	
2553	Vase		£8-£12	$10-$20	
2564	Moselle Vase	9½	£30-£50	$45-$80	
2565	Heirlooms Urn Shaped Vase		£8-£12	$10-$20	
2598	Squirrel Vase	14L	£12-£18	$15-$30	
2599	Vase		£5-£8	$5-$15	
2608	Laronde Vase	8¾	£5-£10	$5-$15	
2609	Laronde Vase	7	£8-£12	$10-$20	
2614	Laronde Vase	11½L	£8-£12	$10-$20	
2616	Laronde Vase	10	£10-£15	$15-$25	
2617	Laronde Vase	8	£5-£8	$5-$15	
2618	Laronde Vase	6	£5-£8	$5-$15	
2626	Moselle Horn & Cherub Vase	9¾	£60-£80	$90-$130	
2631	Vase		£8-£12	$10-$20	
2632	Vase		£8-£12	$10-$20	
2639	Vase		£5-£8	$5-$15	
2643	Vase		£5-£8	$5-$15	
2645	Ivyleaf Vase	10	£30-£50	$45-$80	
2646	Ivyleaf Vase	8½	£20-£30	$30-$50	
2647	Ivyleaf Vase	15L	£12-£18	$15-$30	
2648	Ivyleaf Vase/Ashtray	7D	£10-£15	$15-$25	
2649	Ivyleaf Vase	12L	£12-£18	$15-$30	
2651	Ivyleaf Vase	7	£8-£12	$10-$20	
2652	Ivyleaf Vase	8¼	£20-£30	$30-$50	
2653	Ivyleaf Vase	6¼	£20-£30	$30-$50	
2655	Vase with Dog/Lamb/Bear	5	£20-£30	$30-$50	
2656	Vase with Dog /Lamb/Bear	5	£20-£30	$30-$50	
2658	Vase with Dog/Lamb/Bear	5	£20-£30	$30-$50	
2659	Vase		£8-£12	$10-$20	
2660	Vase with Dog/Lamb/Bear	5	£20-£30	$30-$50	
2661	Ivy Crescent Vase		£5-£8	$5-$15	
2676	Vase		£8-£12	$10-$20	
2678	Vase	10L	£20-£30	$30-$50	
2680	Vase		£8-£12	$10-$20	
2683	Moselle Cherub & Shell Vase	6½	£12-£18	$15-$30	
2692	Vase		£5-£8	$5-$15	
2694	Vase	6	£8-£12	$10-$20	
2695	Vase	6	£8-£12	$10-$20	
2699	Swan Vase	7¼L	£20-£30	$30-$50	

Vases

Model No	Model	Size Inches	Market Value		Notes
2705	Jewel Vase	6½	£8-£12	$10-$20	
2706	Jewel Vase	8	£10-£15	$15-$25	
2709	Jewel Vase	7¼	£10-£20	$15-$35	
2710	Jewel Twin Handled Vase	11½L	£20-£30	$30-$50	
2711	Jewel Posy Vase	8	£8-£12	$10-$20	
2712	Jewel Vase	10	£8-£12	$10-$20	
2713	Jewel Vase	6	£8-£12	$10-$20	
2718	Bamboo Twin Vase		£8-£12	$10-$20	
2724	Vase		£8-£12	$10-$20	
2727	Swan Vase	9¼	£30-£50	$45-$80	
2732	Bamboo Vase	7	£10-£15	$15-$25	
2739	Twin Handled Vase		£8-£12	$10-$20	
2743	Bamboo Vase	9½	£10-£15	$15-$25	
2746	Vase		£8-£12	$10-$20	
2748	Double Vase		£8-£12	$10-$20	
2749	Bamboo Vase	6¼	£5-£8	$5-$15	
2750	Bamboo Vase	9½	£8-£12	$10-$20	
2751	Vase		£8-£12	$10-$20	
2752	Bamboo Vase		£5-£8	$5-$15	
2753	Vase		£8-£12	$10-$20	
2754	Vase		£8-£12	$10-$20	
2766	Bamboo Vase	6¼	£10-£15	$15-$25	
2770	Vase	8¼	£8-£12	$10-$20	
2772	Vase		£5-£8	$5-$15	
2773	Trellis Vase	9½	£10-£20	$15-$35	
2774	Fan Shaped Vase	6½	£10-£20	$15-$35	
2776	Vase		£5-£8	$5-$15	
2777	Bamboo Vase	6¼	£5-£8	$5-$15	
2779	Vase		£8-£12	$10-$20	
2780	Fan Shaped Vase	7	£10-£20	$15-$35	
2781	Vase		£5-£8	$5-$15	
2786	Vase		£5-£8	$5-$15	
2791	Vase		£8-£12	$10-$20	
2792	Vase	6¼	£5-£8	$5-$15	
2801	Trellis Vase	6½	£8-£12	$10-$20	
2803	Vase		£8-£12	$10-$20	
2806	Vase	6¼	£8-£12	$10-$20	
2811	Vase		£8-£12	$10-$20	
2816	Bamboo Vase	4¼	£8-£12	$10-$20	
2817	Trellis Vase	6¼	£8-£12	$10-$20	
2819	Corinthus Vase		£8-£12	$10-$20	
2820	Vase		£5-£8	$5-$15	
2821	Trellis Vase	10	£10-£20	$15-$35	
2827	Corinthus Vase	8	£12-£18	$15-$30	
2831	Cone Vase	7	£8-£12	$10-$20	
2832	Cone Vase		£8-£12	$10-$20	
2833	Cone Vase		£8-£12	$10-$20	
2834	Cone Vase		£8-£12	$10-$20	
2836	Cone Vase		£8-£12	$10-$20	
2840	Vase		£8-£12	$10-$20	
2841	Scholars Head Book Vase	6	£40-£60	$60-$100	
2844	Vase		£5-£8	$5-$15	
2846	Oakwood Vase	6	£12-£18	$15-$30	
2847	Vase		£5-£8	$5-$15	
2848	Vase		£5-£8	$5-$15	
2852	Vase		£5-£8	$5-$15	
2860	Vase	8¼	£8-£12	$10-$20	
2861	Vase		£8-£12	$10-$20	
2864	Goblet Vase	7	£8-£12	$10-$20	
2867	Shell Vase		£8-£12	$10-$20	
2868	Shell Vase		£8-£12	$10-$20	
2869	Shell Vase		£8-£12	$10-$20	
2870	Apple Blossom Vase	8¼	£12-£18	$15-$30	
2872	Apple Blossom Vase	11½	£20-£30	$30-$50	

Model No	Model	Size Inches	Market Value		Notes
2874	Apple Blossom Vase	7L	£15-£20	$20-$35	
2875	Apple Blossom Vase	8¾	£12-£18	$15-$30	
2876	Apple Blossom Vase	6¼	£12-£18	$15-$30	
2879	Vase		£8-£12	$10-$20	
2893	Bracken Vase		£10-£20	$15-$35	
2894	Bracken Vase		£10-£20	$15-$35	
2896	Vase	6	£8-£12	$10-$20	
2900	Vase		£8-£12	$10-$20	
2901	Oriental Style Vase		£8-£12	$10-$20	
2902	Vase		£8-£12	$10-$20	
2904	Bracken Vase	4¼	£8-£12	$10-$20	
2907	Jewel Vase	4¾	£8-£12	$10-$20	
2914	Vase		£8-£12	$10-$20	
2915	Vase		£8-£12	$10-$20	
2920	Vase		£8-£12	$10-$20	
2925	Oakwood Vase	11L	£12-£18	$15-$30	
2926	Oakwood Vase	10	£12-£18	$15-$30	
2927	Oakwood Vase	8	£12-£18	$15-$30	
2930	Oakwood Vase		£12-£18	$15-$30	
2931	Oakwood Vase	7½	£12-£18	$15-$30	
2932	Oakwood Vase		£12-£18	$15-$30	
2934	Vase		£8-£12	$10-$20	
2935	Vase		£8-£12	$10-$20	
2936	Vase		£8-£12	$10-$20	
2937	Apple Blossom Vase	10	£40-£60	$60-$100	
2942	Vase		£5-£8	$5-$15	
2949	Vase		£8-£12	$10-$20	
2954	Magnolia Vase	9L	£40-£60	$60-$100	
2963	Shell Vase	3½	£8-£12	$10-$20	
2964	Shell Vase		£8-£12	$10-$20	
2972	Vase		£5-£8	$5-$15	
2975	Vase		£8-£12	$10-$20	
2979	Vase	8	£10-£15	$15-$25	
2981	Magnolia Vase	9	£40-£60	$60-$100	
2983	Vase	9	£8-£12	$10-$20	
2991	Oakwood Vase	5	£12-£18	$15-$30	
2992	Magnolia Vase	6¼	£12-£18	$15-$30	
2993	Magnolia Vase	7¾L	£12-£18	$15-$30	
2997	Wyka Vase	11½	£12-£18	$15-$30	
3006	Wyka Vase	13½	£18-£25	$25-$40	
3011	Wyka Vase	8½	£12-£18	$15-$30	
3015	Oakleaf Vase	8L	£12-£18	$15-$30	
3023	Bracken Vase	8¼L	£10-£15	$15-$25	
3025	Symcraft Vase	6¼	£5-£8	$5-$15	
3026	Vase		£5-£8	$5-$15	
3027	Vase		£5-£8	$5-$15	
3028	Vase		£5-£8	$5-$15	
3029	Slymcraft Vase	12	£12-£18	$15-$30	
3030	Slymcraft Vase	8½	£5-£10	$5-$15	
3031	Chesterfield Vase	6	£5-£8	$5-$15	
3032	Slymcraft Vase	9¾	£8-£12	$10-$20	
3033	Vase		£5-£8	$5-$15	
3034	Vase		£5-£8	$5-$15	
3035	Vase		£5-£8	$5-$15	
3036	Slymcraft Vase	8¾	£8-£12	$10-$20	
3037	Slymcraft Vase	10¾	£8-£12	$10-$20	
3038	Slymcraft Vase	10½	£8-£12	$10-$20	
3039	Slymcraft Vase		£5-£8	$5-$15	
3040	Slymcraft Vase	4¾	£5-£8	$5-$15	
3041	Vase		£5-£8	$5-$15	
3042	Slymcraft Vase	8¾	£8-£12	$10-$20	
3043	Slymcraft Vase	5¾	£5-£8	$5-$15	
3044	Slymcraft Vase	8½	£5-£8	$5-$15	
3045	Vase		£5-£8	$5-$15	

Vases

Model No	Model	Size Inches	Market Value		Notes
3046	Slymcraft Vase	8½	£5-£10	$5-$15	
3047	Slymcraft Vase	10½	£8-£12	$10-$20	
3048	Slymcraft Vase	8¾	£5-£10	$5-$15	
3049	Slymcraft Vase	12	£8-£12	$10-$20	
3050	Cylindrical Vase	3	£5-£8	$5-$15	
3051	Slymcraft Vase	8½	£8-£12	$10-$20	
3052	Slymcraft Vase	7½	£5-£10	$5-$15	
3053	Chesterfield Vase	10¼	£12-£18	$15-$30	
3054	Chesterfield Vase	8¼	£8-£12	$10-$20	
3055	Slymcraft Vase	10½	£8-£12	$10-$20	
3056	Slymcraft Vase	10½	£8-£12	$10-$20	
3059	Slymcraft Vase	8¾	£5-£10	$5-$15	
3060	Vase		£5-£8	$5-$15	
3061	Slymcraft Vase	10¾	£8-£12	$10-$20	
3062	Slymcraft Vase	8½	£5-£10	$5-$15	
3063	Slymcraft Vase	6½	£5-£8	$5-$15	
3064	Slymcraft Vase	10	£8-£12	$10-$20	
3065	Slymcraft Vase	4½	£5-£8	$5-$15	
3066	Slymcraft Vase	6½	£5-£8	$5-$15	
3067	Slymcraft Vase	10	£10-£15	$15-$25	
3069	Vase	9L	£5-£8	$5-$15	
3070	Vase		£5-£8	$5-$15	
3072	Vase	7½	£3-£5	$5-$10	
3073	Vase		£5-£8	$5-$15	
3082	Vase		£5-£8	$5-$15	
3084	Vase		£8-£12	$10-$20	
3089	Vase		£8-£12	$10-$20	
3098	Lily Vase	7½L	£30-£50	$45-$80	
3104	Vase		£8-£12	$10-$20	
3107	Vase		£5-£8	$5-$15	
3189	Slymcraft Vase	15½L	£8-£12	$10-$20	
3192	Vase		£8-£12	$10-$20	
3210	Trellis Vase	8½L	£8-£12	$10-$20	
3211	Vase		£8-£12	$10-$20	
3216	Magnolia Vase	10	£40-£60	$60-$100	
3217	Magnolia Vase	8	£30-£50	$45-$80	
3221	Magnolia Twin-Handled Vase	12L	£40-£60	$60-$100	
3223	Log Vase		£8-£12	$10-$20	
3225	Slymcraft Twin-Handled Vase	14L	£12-£18	$15-$30	
3228	Vase		£8-£12	$10-$20	
3230	Fish Shaped Vase	7	£15-£30	$20-$50	
3232	Vase		£8-£12	$10-$20	
3236	Vase		£10-£15	$15-$25	
3247	Lily Vase	10	£40-£60	$60-$100	
3250	Vase		£8-£12	$10-$20	
3252	Vase		£8-£12	$10-$20	
3255	Chesterfield Vase	10	£12-£18	$15-$30	
3256	Chesterfield Vase	8	£12-£18	$15-$30	
3261	Fuchsia Vase		£20-£30	$30-$50	
3263	Fuchsia Vase		£20-£30	$30-$50	
3266	Fuchsia Vase	7¾	£12-£18	$15-$30	
3268	Fuchsia Vase	9	£20-£30	$30-$50	
3269	Fuchsia Vase	8¾	£18-£25	$25-$40	
3272	Fuchsia Vase	12L	£20-£30	$30-$50	
3277	Vase		£8-£12	$10-$20	
3283	Lily Vase	8¼	£40-£60	$60-$100	
3284	Vase		£5-£8	$5-$15	
3285	Lily Vase		£50-£80	$75-$130	
3286	Lily Vase	12	£50-£80	$75-$130	
3290	Lily Vase	12½	£40-£60	$60-$100	
3298	Vase		£5-£8	$5-$15	
3303	Vase		£8-£12	$10-$20	
3305	Vase		£10-£15	$15-$25	
3308	Vase		£8-£12	$10-$20	

Model No	Model	Size Inches	Market Value		Notes
3309	Vase		£8-£12	$10-$20	
3310	Slymcraft Oval Vase		£8-£12	$10-$20	
3312	Vase	7½	£10-£20	$15-$35	
3316	Vase	9½	£8-£12	$10-$20	
3323	Vase	6¼	£10-£15	$15-$25	
3324	Vase	10	£12-£18	$15-$30	
3329	Shell Vase	7	£12-£18	$15-$30	
3330	Vase	8	£10-£15	$15-$25	
3334	Sea Shell Vase	5L	£8-£12	$10-$20	
3341	Opelle Oval Vase		£8-£12	$10-$20	
3342	Vase	7	£8-£12	$10-$20	
3343	Vase	6½	£8-£12	$10-$20	
3344	Vase	5	£8-£12	$10-$20	
3345	Vase		£8-£12	$10-$20	
3347	Fluted Vase	8½	£12-£18	$15-$30	
3348	Vase	11½L	£12-£15	$15-$25	
3349	Pebbles Vase	10L	£12-£18	$15-$30	
3350	Pebbles Vase	7¾	£10-£18	$15-$30	
3358	Pebbles Vase	9	£12-£18	$15-$30	
3362	Vase	5	£8-£12	$10-$20	
3364	Alpine Vase	8	£10-£20	$15-$35	
3368	Pebbles Vase	11¼	£15-£20	$20-$35	
3369	Alpine Rope Vase	8	£10-£15	$15-$25	
3371	Alpine Vase	11	£12-£18	$15-$30	
3373	Vase	3¼	£5-£8	$5-$15	
3374	Etched Vase	6½	£8-£12	$10-$20	
3375	Embossed Vase	6½	£8-£12	$10-$20	
3376	Vase	6½	£8-£12	$10-$20	
3379	Alpine Vase	8	£10-£15	$15-$25	
3380	Alpine Vase	8	£10-£15	$15-$25	
3381	Alpine Vase	11	£12-£18	$15-$30	
3382	Alpine Vase	6	£10-£15	$15-$25	
3385	Alpine Vase	8	£10-£15	$15-$25	
3386	Alpine Vase		£8-£12	$10-$20	
3398	Alpine Vase	9	£20-£30	$30-$50	
3399	Alpine Vase	8	£18-£25	$25-$40	
3400	Alpine Vase	6	£15-£18	$20-$30	
3412	Vase		£5-£8	$5-$15	
3414	Sea Horse Vase	8	£15-£20	$20-$35	
3416	Vase		£5-£8	$5-$15	
3434	Pebbles Vase	14½L	£12-£18	$15-$30	
3441	Vase	6	£5-£8	$5-$15	
3443	Chequers Oval Vase	8	£10-£15	$15-$25	
3444	Chequers Vase		£8-£12	$10-$20	
3448	Vase		£5-£8	$5-$15	
3449	Opelle Vase	6	£5-£8	$5-$15	
3450	Opelle Vase	8	£8-£12	$10-$20	
3451	Opelle Vase	10	£12-£18	$15-$30	
3453	Opelle Posy Vase		£5-£8	$5-$15	
3458	Opelle Vase		£5-£8	$5-$15	
3460	Sea Horse Vase	10	£30-£50	$45-$80	
3466	Opelle Wall Vase		£12-£18	$15-$30	
3470	Sea Horse Posy Vase	8L	£12-£18	$15-$30	
3471	Sea Horse Posy Vase	9½L	£12-£18	$15-$30	
3472	Sea Horse Vase	6	£10-£15	$15-$25	
3473	Sea Horse Vase		£12-£18	$15-$30	
3477	Tudor Vase		£5-£8	$5-$15	
3483	Vase	5	£8-£12	$10-$20	
3487	Panel Fronted Vase	10	£12-£18	$15-$30	
3490	Tudor Vase	6	£8-£12	$10-$20	
3491	Tudor Vase	8	£10-£15	$15-$25	
3492	Tudor Vase	10	£18-£22	$25-$35	
3493	Tudor Vase		£18-£22	$25-$35	
3494	Tudor Vase		£5-£8	$5-$15	

Vases

Model No	Model	Size Inches	Market Value		Notes
3498	Tudor Posy Vase		£5-£10	$5-$15	
3499	Tudor Posy Vase		£5-£8	$5-$15	
3501	Vase	9	£12-£18	$15-$30	
3517	Panel Fronted Vase		£8-£12	$10-$20	
3518	Panel Fronted Vase		£8-£12	$10-$20	
3523	New Shell Vase	8	£10-£20	$15-$35	
3524	New Shell Conch Vase	10	£10-£20	$15-$35	
3525	New Shell Vase		£10-£20	$15-$35	
3526	New Shell Vase	6¾	£8-£12	$10-$20	
3527	New Shell Wall Vase		£12-£18	$15-$30	
3528	New Shell Posy Vase	11L	£10-£15	$15-$25	
3529	New Shell Vase	8½L	£12-£18	$15-$30	
3535	Vase		£5-£8	$5-$15	
3538	Vase	6	£8-£12	$10-$20	
3539	Tudor Vase	6	£8-£12	$10-$20	
3540	Slymcraft Vase	8	£8-£12	$10-$20	
3541	Tudor Vase	8	£8-£12	$10-$20	
3548	Vase	8	£8-£12	$10-$20	
3549	Vase	8¼	£8-£12	$10-$20	
3551	Vase		£5-£8	$5-$15	
3557	Lily Vase	8	£20-£30	$30-$50	
3558	Vase	13	£15-£20	$20-$35	
3572	Twin Handled Vase		£8-£12	$10-$20	
3577	Vase		£5-£8	$5-$15	
3587	Vase	8	£12-£18	$15-$30	
3591	Vase	6	£8-£12	$10-$20	
3595	Vase	8	£8-£12	$10-$20	
3598	Oval Vase		£5-£8	$5-$15	
3602	Embossed Vase		£5-£8	$5-$15	
3603	Embossed Vase		£5-£8	$5-$15	
3618	Vase	11L	£12-£18	$15-$30	
3631	Vase		£5-£8	$5-$15	
3639	Twin Handled Vase	13½	£12-£18	$15-$30	
3643	Stone Wall Vase	9	£12-£18	$15-$30	
3651	Vase	13	£12-£18	$15-$30	
3652	Vase		£8-£12	$10-$20	
3653	Stone Wall Vase		£8-£12	$10-$20	
3654	Vase	11	£12-£18	$15-$30	
3655	Vase	10	£10-£15	$15-$25	
3656	Vase	8	£8-£12	$10-$20	
3657	Vase	6	£5-£8	$5-$15	
3662	Vase	6	£5-£8	$5-$15	
3678	Palm Leaf Vase	8	£12-£18	$15-$30	
3680	New Shell Vase		£12-£18	$15-$30	
3684	Shell Posy Vase	7½	£5-£8	$5-$15	
3689	Vase		£5-£8	$5-$15	
3690	Palm Tree Vase	8	£10-£15	$15-$25	
3692	Chequers Vase		£15-£20	$20-$35	
3693	Chequers Vase		£10-£15	$15-$25	
3694	Chequers Vase	8	£10-£15	$15-$25	
3695	Chequers Vase		£10-£15	$15-$25	
3704	Vase	5½	£5-£8	$5-$15	
3705	Chequers Vase	7½	£8-£12	$10-$20	
3714	Palm Leaf Vase	7¾	£12-£18	$15-$30	
3717	Palm Leaf Slipper Vase		£8-£12	$10-$20	
3720	Palm Leaf Vase	9½L	£8-£12	$10-$20	
3721	Palm Leaf Wall Vase		£8-£12	$10-$20	
3723	Palm Leaf Vase		£8-£12	$10-$20	
3724	Palm Leaf Vase	10	£10-£15	$15-$25	
3725	Palm Leaf Vase	6	£8-£12	$10-$20	
3731	Oslo Vase	10½	£10-£15	$15-$25	
3732	Oslo Vase	8	£10-£15	$15-$25	
3733	Oslo Vase	6	£8-£12	$10-$20	
3739	Oslo Posy Vase		£5-£8	$5-$15	

Model No	Model	Size Inches	Market Value		Notes
3740	Oslo Vase	6¼L	£8-£12	$10-$20	
3741	Oslo Vase	9¼L	£8-£12	$10-$20	
3752	Vase	10	£12-£18	$15-$30	
3769	Vase	11½L	£10-£15	$15-$25	
3792	Vase		£5-£8	$5-$15	
3793	Square Vase		£5-£8	$5-$15	
3794	Round Vase		£10-£15	$15-$25	
3795	Vase		£8-£12	$10-$20	
3796	Vase		£8-£12	$10-$20	
3797	Vase		£8-£12	$10-$20	
3800	Square Vase		£5-£8	$5-$15	
3801	Vase		£5-£8	$5-$15	
3810	Stone Wall Vase	10	£12-£18	$15-$30	
3811	Stone Wall Vase	8	£10-£15	$15-$25	
3812	Stone Wall Vase	6	£8-£12	$10-$20	
3814	Stone Wall Twin Vase	13	£12-£18	$15-$30	
3816	Stone Wall Vase		£5-£8	$5-$15	
3817	Stone Wall Vase	14	£12-£18	$15-$30	
3819	Stone Wall Posy Vase	14L	£10-£15	$15-$25	
3820	Stone Wall Posy Vase		£5-£8	$5-$15	
3824	Privet Vase	5	£12-£18	$15-$30	
3825	Privet Vase	7	£15-£20	$20-$35	
3842	Privet Vase	9½	£10-£15	$15-$25	
3844	Privet Vase	10¼	£15-£20	$20-$35	
3845	Privet Vase	6	£8-£12	$10-$20	
3850	Linton Vase	4	£5-£8	$5-$15	
3851	Linton Vase	6	£5-£8	$5-$15	
3852	Linton Vase	8	£8-£12	$10-$20	
3853	Linton Vase		£10-£12	$15-$20	
3856	Linton Vase		£8-£12	$10-$20	
3857	Linton Vase		£8-£12	$10-$20	
3863	Begonia Vase	4	£5-£8	$5-$15	
3864	Begonia Vase	6	£8-£12	$10-$20	
3865	Begonia Vase	8	£8-£12	$10-$20	
3866	Begonia Vase	10	£10-£15	$15-$25	
3869	Begonia Vase	5½	£5-£8	$5-$15	
3870	Begonia Vase		£8-£12	$10-$20	
3877	Textured Vase	4	£5-£8	$5-$15	
3878	Textured Vase	6	£5-£8	$5-$15	
3879	Textured Vase	8	£8-£12	$10-$20	
3880	Textured Vase	10	£12-£18	$15-$30	
3883	Textured Vase		£5-£8	$5-$15	
3884	Textured Vase		£8-£12	$10-$20	
3898	Coral Vase		£20-£30	$30-$50	
3900	Privet Posy Vase		£5-£8	$5-$15	
3901	Coral Vase	8	£15-£20	$20-$35	
3903	Privet Vase	11½D	£12-£18	$15-$30	
3904	Coral Vase	10	£10-£15	$15-$25	
3905	Coral Vase		£10-£15	$15-$25	
3907	Coral Vase	16½D	£15-£20	$20-$35	
3916	Vase		£5-£8	$5-$15	
3917	Vase		£5-£8	$5-$15	
3924	Vase	10	£12-£18	$15-$30	
3929	Tree Vase with Rabbits		£20-£30	$30-$50	
3932	Vase	12	£8-£12	$10-$20	
3938	Manhattan Vase	6¼	£5-£8	$5-$15	
3939	Manhattan Vase	8	£8-£12	$10-$20	
3944	Manhattan Vase	7L	£5-£8	$5-$15	
3946	Manhattan Vase	8	£8-£12	$10-$20	
3947	Manhattan Vase	11½	£10-£15	$15-$25	
3956	Manhattan Vase	12½L	£8-£12	$10-$20	
3964	Wild Pigs Vase	10	£10-£20	$15-$35	
3965	Embossed Vase	14L	£8-£12	$10-$20	
3966	Vase	9	£8-£12	$10-$20	

Vases

Model No	Model	Size Inches	Market Value		Notes
3967	Vase on Stand		£10-£15	$15-$25	
3969	Vase		£5-£8	$5-$15	
3970	Embossed Vase	10¾	£12-£18	$15-$30	
3971	Horse Shoe Wall Vase		£20-£30	$30-$50	
3972	Vase	4	£5-£8	$5-$15	
3974	Vase	5	£5-£8	$5-$15	
3980	Vase		£5-£8	$5-$15	
3983	Long Vase		£5-£8	$5-$15	
3992	Vase		£5-£8	$5-$15	
3993	Vase	6	£5-£8	$5-$15	
3994	Olympus Vase	4½	£5-£8	$5-$15	
3995	Maple Vase	10¼	£10-£15	$15-$25	
3997	Vase	8	£10-£15	$15-$25	
3999	Embossed Vase	10	£15-£20	$20-$35	
4000	Olympus Vase	6	£8-£12	$10-$20	
4001	Maple Vase	10L	£8-£12	$10-$20	
4008	Maple Vase	7L	£8-£12	$10-$20	
4010	Maple Vase	6	£5-£8	$5-$15	
4011	Maple Vase	8	£8-£12	$10-$20	
4012	Manhattan Vase	9L	£10-£15	$15-$25	
4023	Maple Posy Vase		£5-£8	$5-$15	
4063	Nouveau Vase		£8-£12	$10-$20	
4064	Nouveau Vase		£8-£12	$10-$20	
4068	Acorn & Squirrel Vase	9½	£30-£50	$45-$80	
4069	Stork Vase	10	£30-£50	$45-$80	
4079	Urn Vase		£5-£8	$5-$15	
4091	Vase	8	£10-£15	$15-$25	
4092	Vase	10	£12-£18	$15-$30	
4093	Olympus Vase	8	£10-£15	$15-$25	
4096	Vase	5	£5-£8	$5-$15	
4098	Olympus Vase	10	£12-£18	$15-$30	
4100	Vase	12	£12-£18	$15-$30	
4103	Olympus Vase	5	£8-£12	$10-$20	
4105	Olympus Vase	12	£15-£20	$20-$35	
4110	Horse & Shamrock Vase	5¾	£8-£12	$10-$20	
4114	Vase	8	£10-£15	$15-$25	
4116	Seaweed & Shells Vase	8	£10-£15	$15-$25	
4117	Floral Vase	8	£10-£15	$15-$25	
4119	Vase	8	£8-£12	$10-$20	
4121	Cornflower Vase	8	£10-£15	$15-$25	
4126	Vase	8½	£8-£12	$10-$20	
4127	Sycamore Vase	6	£5-£8	$5-$15	
4128	Sycamore Vase	7½	£5-£8	$5-$15	
4138	Vase	6	£5-£8	$5-$15	
4152	Marina Vase	8	£8-£12	$10-$20	
4157	Marina Vase	6¼	£8-£12	$10-$20	
4160	Marina Vase		£8-£12	$10-$20	
4162	Marina Vase		£8-£12	$10-$20	
4163	Marina Vase	5	£8-£12	$10-$20	
4164	Flora Vase	8	£8-£12	$10-$20	
4165	Flora Vase	6	£8-£12	$10-$20	
4166	Flora Vase	10½L	£8-£12	$10-$20	
4168	Flora Vase		£10-£15	$15-$25	
4174	Flora Vase	10	£10-£15	$15-$25	
4181	Knib Vase		£5-£8	$5-$15	
4199	Crazy Paving Vase	9½	£8-£12	$10-$20	
4203	Vase		£5-£8	$5-$15	
4206	Sycamore Vase	8	£8-£12	$10-$20	
4207	Sycamore Vase		£8-£12	$10-$20	
4208	Sycamore Vase	10	£10-£15	$15-$25	
4209	Sycamore Vase		£10-£15	$15-$25	
4215	Sycamore Vase	6	£8-£12	$10-$20	
4226	Welsh Lady & Horseshoe Vase		£8-£12	$10-$20	
4228	Devon Horseshoe Vase		£8-£12	$10-$20	

Model No	Model	Size Inches	Market Value		Notes
4229	Cornwall Horseshoe Vase		£8-£12	$10-$20	
4230	Somerset Horseshoe Vase		£8-£12	$10-$20	
4232	Embossed Vase		£5-£8	$5-$15	
4233	Woodland with Squirrel Tree Vase		£8-£12	$10-$20	
4236	Cheddar Horse Shoe Vase		£8-£12	$10-$20	
4241	Woodland Squirrel Tree Vase		£10-£15	$15-$25	
4242	Woodland Rabbit Tree Vase		£12-£18	$15-$30	
4243	Woodland Rabbit Twin Tree Vase		£12-£18	$15-$30	
4258	Vase		£5-£8	$5-$15	
4263	Vase		£5-£8	$5-$15	
4264	Autumn Chintz Vase	6	£10-£15	$15-$25	
4266	Oak Leaves Vase	8	£8-£12	$10-$20	
4277	Vase	11	£12-£18	$15-$30	
4284	Collon No:1 Vase		£20-£30	$30-$50	
4285	Collon No:2 Vase		£20-£30	$30-$50	
4286	York Vase		£20-£30	$30-$50	
4290	Woodland Twin Tree Vase with Deer		£8-£12	$10-$20	
4297	Embossed Pixie & Horseshoe Vase		£5-£8	$5-$15	
4299	Harmony Vase	8	£8-£12	$10-$20	
4301	Harmony Vase	10	£8-£12	$10-$20	
4304	Harmony Vase		£8-£12	$10-$20	
4305	Harmony Vase		£5-£8	$5-$15	
4306	Harmony Vase		£10-£15	$15-$25	
4307	Harmony Vase		£10-£15	$15-$25	
4319	Aurora Vase	8	£12-£18	$15-$30	
4320	Vase	8	£10-£15	$15-$25	
4321	Vase	8	£8-£12	$10-$20	
4322	Vase	8	£8-£12	$10-$20	
4327	Aurora Vase	6	£8-£12	$10-$20	
4328	Aurora Vase	10	£10-£15	$15-$25	
4329	Aurora Vase	4	£8-£12	$10-$20	
4330	Aurora Oval Vase		£10-£15	$15-$25	
4331	Aurora Oval Vase		£10-£15	$15-$25	
4340	Harmony Vase	8	£8-£12	$10-$20	
4346	Embossed Vase		£5-£8	$5-$15	
4347	Vase		£5-£8	$5-$15	
4364	Vase	6	£5-£8	$5-$15	
4365	Vase	6	£5-£8	$5-$15	
4366	Vase	6	£5-£8	$5-$15	
4367	Vase	8	£10-£15	$15-$25	
4371	Vase	4	£5-£8	$5-$15	
4373	Vase		£5-£8	$5-$15	
4374	Embossed Vase		£5-£8	$5-$15	
4375	Riverside Vase	8	£12-£18	$15-$30	
4375	Riverside Vase	8	£12-£18	$15-$30	
4377	Riverside Vase	6	£10-£15	$15-$25	
4379	Vase of Various Design		£5-£8	$5-$15	
4385	Riverside Vase	4	£10-£15	$15-$25	
4393	Riverside Twin Vase	4½	£10-£15	$15-$25	
4523	Rose Vase	6	£8-£12	$10-$20	
4528	Figural Vase	9¾	£12-£18	$15-$30	
4529	Gossamer Vase	7	£12-£18	$15-$30	
4532	Vase		£5-£8	$5-$15	
4534	Vase	10	£8-£12	$10-$20	
4535	Privet Vase	5	£8-£12	$10-$20	
4537	Privet Vase	4	£5-£8	$5-$15	
4540	Privet Vase	7	£10-£15	$15-$25	
4542	Adam & Eve Vase	10	£20-£30	$30-$50	
4548	Vase	8	£20-£30	$30-$50	
4550	Tristan Vase	6	£8-£12	$10-$20	
4552	Vase	6	£8-£12	$10-$20	
4554	Rhapsody Vase	8¼	£10-£15	$15-$25	
4555	Autumn Chintz Oval Vase		£10-£15	$15-$25	
4556	Autumn Chintz Vase	10	£12-£18	$15-$30	

Vases

Model No	Model	Size Inches	Market Value		Notes
4557	Autumn Chintz Vase	8	£10-£15	$15-$25	
4558	Autumn Chintz Vase	6	£8-£12	$10-$20	
4559	Autumn Chintz Vase	10D	£12-£18	$15-$30	
4563	Tristan Vase	8	£8-£12	$10-$20	
4564	Tristan Vase		£5-£8	$5-$15	
4568	Evening Fantasy Vase	8	£8-£12	$10-$20	
4573	Assyria Vase	8	£8-£12	$10-$20	
4581	Tristan Vase	10	£15-£20	$20-$35	
4586	Tristan Vase	6	£5-£8	$5-$15	
4588	Tristan Vase	6	£8-£12	$10-$20	
4592	Vase	6	£5-£8	$5-$15	
4593	Tristan Vase		£10-£15	$15-$25	
4594	Gossamer Vase	9	£12-£18	$15-$30	
4595	Tristan Vase		£5-£8	$5-$15	
4597	Tristan Vase		£8-£12	$10-$20	
4599	Gossamer Vase	5	£5-£8	$5-$15	
4602	Vase	10	£12-£18	$15-$30	
4603	Gossamer Vase	10½	£12-£18	$15-$30	
4606	Gossamer Vase		£5-£8	$5-$15	
4607	Oval Vase		£5-£8	$5-$15	
4608	Rhapsody Vase	6	£5-£8	$5-$15	
4609	Vase		£5-£8	$5-$15	
4610	Vase	10	£8-£12	$10-$20	
4614	Rhapsody Oval Vase		£8-£12	$10-$20	
4615	Rhapsody Vase		£8-£12	$10-$20	
4617	Vase	10	£12-£18	$15-$30	
4618	Vase	6	£8-£12	$10-$20	
4619	Vase	8	£8-£12	$10-$20	
4625	Vase	6	£8-£12	$10-$20	
4626	Vase	7	£8-£12	$10-$20	
4629	Hollyberry Vase	6	£12-£18	$15-$30	
4630	Vase	6	£12-£18	$15-$30	
4631	Spectrum Vase	6	£10-£15	$15-$25	
4636	Spectrum Vase	10	£8-£12	$10-$20	
4638	Rhapsody Vase	10	£12-£18	$15-$30	
4643	Spectrum Vase	7½L	£5-£8	$5-$15	
4646	Hollyberry Vase	8½D	£12-£18	$15-$30	
4648	Spectrum Vase	10D	£12-£18	$15-$30	
4651	Spectrum Vase	5¾	£8-£12	$10-$20	
4654	Vase	6	£5-£8	$5-$15	
4655	Vase	6	£5-£8	$5-$15	
4656	Vase	6	£5-£8	$5-$15	
4657	Vase	6	£5-£8	$5-$15	
4658	Vase	6	£5-£8	$5-$15	
4659	Vase	6	£5-£8	$5-$15	
4660	Vase		£5-£8	$5-$15	
4661	Vase	10	£12-£18	$15-$30	
4662	Vase	10	£12-£18	$15-$30	
4663	Vase	8	£10-£15	$15-$25	
4689	Vase	8	£8-£12	$10-$20	
4692	Vase	7½	£8-£12	$10-$20	
4693	Assyria Vase	6¼	£5-£8	$5-$15	
4694	Vase	7½	£8-£12	$10-$20	
4695	Vase	7½	£8-£12	$10-$20	
4701	Vase	7	£8-£12	$10-$20	
4702	Etruscan Vase	8	£8-£12	$10-$20	
4704	Assyria Vase		£5-£8	$5-$15	
4772	Etruscan Vase	6	£8-£12	$10-$20	
4773	Etruscan Vase	5	£8-£12	$10-$20	
4775	Etruscan Vase	4	£5-£8	$5-$15	
4784	Rhapsody Vase	3¾	£8-£12	$10-$20	
4786	Vase	3	£5-£8	$5-$15	
4787	Vase	3	£5-£8	$5-$15	
4789	House in the Glen Vase	8	£10-£20	$15-$35	

Model No	Model	Size Inches	Market Value		Notes
4790	House in the Glen Twin Vase		£10-£20	$15-$35	
4791	House in the Glen Vase	6	£8-£12	$10-$20	
4796	Vase	10	£12-£18	$15-$30	
4799	Vase		£5-£8	$5-$15	
4800	Bamboo Vase	8	£8-£12	$10-$20	
4803	Vase	6	£5-£8	$5-$15	
4804	Dolphin Vase		£12-£18	$15-$30	
4805	Vase	8	£10-£15	$15-$25	
4808	Bamboo Vase		£8-£12	$10-$20	
4824	Fleur Oval Vase		£5-£8	$5-$15	
4826	Fleur Oval Vase		£12-£18	$15-$30	
4827	Fleur Vase	7	£10-£15	$15-$25	
4828	Fleur Vase	5	£8-£12	$10-$20	
4829	Fleur Vase	9	£10-£15	$15-$25	
4835	Vase with Figure & Leaf		£10-£15	$15-$25	
4840	Privet Vase with Figure		£10-£15	$15-$25	
4842	Vase		£5-£8	$5-$15	
4845	Vase	6	£10-£15	$15-$25	
4854	Rock Shaped Vase		£5-£8	$5-$15	
4855	Medway Vase	5	£8-£12	$10-$20	
4856	Medway Vase	5	£8-£12	$10-$20	
4857	Medway Vase	5	£8-£12	$10-$20	
4858	Medway Vase	7	£10-£15	$15-$25	
4859	Medway Vase	7	£10-£15	$15-$25	
4860	Medway Vase	9	£12-£18	$15-$30	
4861	Medway Vase	6	£8-£12	$10-$20	
4862	Medway Vase	10	£10-£15	$15-$25	
4863	Medway Vase	7	£8-£12	$10-$20	
4884	Vase	7	£8-£12	$10-$20	
4885	Blue Tit Log Vase		£20-£30	$30-$50	
4932	Vase		£8-£12	$10-$20	
4933	Mushroom Vase		£8-£12	$10-$20	
4934	Mushroom Vase	5	£8-£12	$10-$20	
4935	Mushroom Vase	7½	£10-£15	$15-$25	
4936	Vase		£5-£8	$5-$15	
4946	Vase	5	£5-£8	$5-$15	
4947	Vase		£5-£8	$5-$15	
4948	Vase	10	£8-£12	$10-$20	
4950	Vase	7	£8-£12	$10-$20	
4951	Floral Basket		£8-£12	$10-$20	
4952	Etched Vase		£8-£12	$10-$20	
4979	Embossed Basket Vase		£8-£12	$10-$20	
4993	Florence Vase	5¾	£8-£12	$10-$20	
4994	Florence Vase	5¾	£8-£12	$10-$20	
4995	Florence Grapevine Vase	5¾	£10-£15	$15-$25	
4996	Florence Twin-Handled Vase		£8-£12	$10-$20	
4997	Florence Vase	5¾	£8-£12	$10-$20	
4998	Florence Cottage Vase	5¾	£8-£12	$10-$20	
5003	Churnet Vase	8	£8-£12	$10-$20	
5004	Churnet Vase	6	£8-£12	$10-$20	
5007	Churnet Vase	10	£10-£15	$15-$25	
5015	Milton Vase	8	£10-£15	$15-$25	
5026	Vase	6½	£8-£12	$10-$20	
5051	Etched Vase	6	£5-£8	$5-$15	
5066	Trentham Vase	5	£5-£8	$5-$15	
5067	Trentham Vase	8	£8-£12	$10-$20	
5068	Trentham Vase	5¼	£5-£8	$5-$15	
5071	Trentham Vase	8¾	£8-£12	$10-$20	
5075	Trentham Vase	4¼	£5-£8	$5-$15	
5132	Florence Vase	8½	£8-£12	$10-$20	
5133	Florence Vase	3¾	£5-£8	$5-$15	
5134	Florence Vase	9	£8-£12	$10-$20	
5186	Dolphin Vase	4	£8-£12	$10-$20	
5188	Dolphin Vase	6¾	£8-£12	$10-$20	

Vases

Model No	Model	Size Inches	Market Value		Notes
5190	Dolphin Posy Vase		£8-£12	$10-$20	
5192	Dolphin Twin Vase	3¼	£8-£12	$10-$20	
5196	Vase		£5-£8	$5-$15	
5223	Embossed Vase	8	£8-£12	$10-$20	
5224	Embossed Vase	8	£8-£12	$10-$20	
5225	Vase	8	£8-£12	$10-$20	
5226	Vase	10	£8-£12	$10-$20	
5227	Vase	7	£8-£12	$10-$20	
5228	Vase	6	£8-£12	$10-$20	
5247	Harvest Time Twin Vase	6	£12-£18	$15-$30	
5250	Harvest Time Oval Vase		£18-£25	$25-$40	
5256	Vase	6	£8-£12	$10-$20	
5267	Vase	6½	£8-£12	$10-$20	
5268	Etched Vase	7	£8-£12	$10-$20	
5269	Etched Vase	7½	£8-£12	$10-$20	
5278	Vintage Vase	7	£8-£12	$10-$20	
5279	Bamboo Vase		£5-£8	$5-$15	
5370	Bamboo Vase	8¾	£10-£15	$15-$25	
5372	Bamboo Vase	10	£12-£15	$15-$25	
5373	Bamboo Vase	12	£12-£18	$15-$30	
5374	Bamboo Vase	6	£10-£15	$15-$25	
5387	Lincoln Vase	8	£5-£8	$5-$15	
5391	Lincoln Vase	10	£10-£15	$15-$25	
5392	Vase	8	£8-£12	$10-$20	
5485	High Tide Vase	8¾	£12-£18	$15-$30	
5486	High Tide Vase	5½	£10-£15	$15-$25	
5490	Acorn Vase		£5-£10	$5-$15	
5491	Vase		£5-£8	$5-$15	
5492	Vase		£5-£8	$5-$15	
5493	Vase		£5-£8	$5-$15	
5494	Vase		£5-£8	$5-$15	
5499	Autumn Leaves Vase	6	£5-£8	$5-$15	
5502	Autumn Leaves Vase	10	£10-£15	$15-$25	
5504	Autumn Leaves Vase	11L	£8-£12	$10-$20	
5510	Specimen Vase		£5-£8	$5-$15	
5511	Specimen Vase		£5-£8	$5-$15	
5512	Solo Specimen Vase	4¼	£5-£8	$5-$15	
5513	Solo Specimen Vase	6¼	£8-£12	$10-$20	
5514	Solo Specimen Vase	4	£5-£8	$5-$15	
5515	Solo Specimen Vase	6¼	£8-£12	$10-$20	
5516	Solo Corn Cob Specimen Vase		£8-£12	$10-$20	
5572	Giant Panda Twin Vase	6¼	£20-£30	$30-$50	
5592	Milady Vase	8	£12-£18	$15-$30	
5593	Milady Vase	6	£10-£15	$15-$25	
5596	1904 Vase	9½	£8-£12	$10-$20	
5598	1904 Vase	10½	£8-£12	$10-$20	
5599	1904 Vase	9¼	£8-£12	$10-$20	
5600	1904 Vase	9	£8-£12	$10-$20	
5606	Belgravia Vase	8¼	£10-£15	$15-$25	
5607	Belgravia Vase	7¾	£8-£12	$10-$20	
5608	Belgravia Vase	6	£8-£12	$10-$20	
5609	Belgravia Vase	6¼	£8-£12	$10-$20	

Wall Pockets, Wall Plates & Wall Vases

No	Model	Size	Market Value		Notes
24	Bird Wall Plaque		£60-£100	$90-$165	
88	Spaniel Dog Wall Plaque		£120-£180	$180-$295	
90	Terrier Dog Wall Plaque	4	£120-£180	$180-$295	
128	Wall Vase		£15-£20	$20-$35	
139	Wall Plaque		£20-£30	$30-$50	
153	Wall Vase		£20-£30	$30-$50	
156	Wall Vase		£20-£30	$30-$50	
319	Wall Vase		£8-£12	$10-$20	
321	Wall Vase	9	£15-£20	$20-$35	

Model No	Model	Size Inches	Market Value		Notes
381	Wall Vase		£12-£18	$15-$30	
472	Vine Patterned Wall Vase	8	£10-£20	$15-$35	
645	Classic Range Wall Vase	9	£15-£30	$20-$50	
653	Wall Vase	5	£20-£30	$30-$50	
668	Wall Vase		£12-£18	$15-$30	
675	Wall Plate	12¾	£40-£60	$60-$100	
687	Coconut & Blue Tit Wall Vase	6	£40-£60	$60-$100	
688	Treetrunk & Blue Tit Wall Vase	7	£50-£80	$75-$130	
713	Wall Vase		£8-£12	$10-$20	
718	Wall Vase		£12-£18	$15-$30	
721	Wall Vase		£12-£18	$15-$30	
733	Straw Boater Wall Vase	4	£25-£50	$35-$80	
1226	Clown Wall Plaque	9	£100-£200	$150-$330	
1381	Wall Pocket	7¼	£30-£50	$45-$80	
1384	Sun Ray Wall Pocket	7¼	£70-£100	$105-$165	
1385	Wall Pocket		£30-£50	$45-$80	
1395	Flower Wall Pocket	6¼	£40-£60	$60-$100	
1395	Flower Wall Pocket (Without Flowers)	6¼	£20-£30	$30-$50	
1401	Duck Wall Plaque	6L	£30-£50	$45-$80	
1402	Duck Wall Plaque	9L	£60-£100	$90-$165	
1403	Duck Wall Plaque	5L	£30-£50	$45-$80	
1543	Seagull Wall Plaque	4L	£40-£60	$60-$100	
1544	Seagull Wall Plaque	7¼L	£60-£100	$90-$165	
1545	Seagull Wall Plaque	8L	£80-£120	$120-$200	
1608	Kissing Bunnies Wall Plaque		£150-£200	$220-$330	
1611	Wall Pocket		£8-£12	$10-$20	
1613	Dahlia Wall Vase	4	£20-£30	$30-$50	
1956	Budgie Wall Pocket (Blue)	8	£70-£100	$105-$165	
1956	Budgie Wall Pocket (Green)	8	£70-£100	$105-$165	
1956	Fan Shaped Wall Pocket	6¾	£20-£30	$30-$50	
1956	Swallow Wall Pocket	8	£80-£120	$120-$200	
1972	Wall Pocket		£20-£30	$30-$50	
2050	Ivyleaf Wall Pocket	7	£25-£50	$35-$80	
2052	Ivyleaf Wall Vase	5	£20-£30	$30-$50	
2079	Seagull Wall Pocket	6¼	£40-£60	$60-$100	
2083	Floral Wall Pocket	6	£40-£60	$60-$100	
2084	Floral Wall Pocket	6	£30-£50	$45-$80	
2091	Chrys Wall Pocket	5¼	£25-£35	$35-$55	
2092	Chrys Wall Pocket	9	£30-£50	$45-$80	
2110	Wall Pocket		£20-£30	$30-$50	
2140	Shield Shaped Wall Pocket		£12-£18	$15-$30	
2151	Rope Wall Pocket	9½	£12-£18	$15-$30	
2154	Floral Bow Wall Pocket		£12-£18	$15-$30	
2156	Autumn Wall Pocket		£15-£20	$20-$35	
2181	Raphique Wall Pocket		£20-£30	$30-$50	
2193	Wall Pocket		£20-£30	$30-$50	
2195	Wall Pocket		£20-£30	$30-$50	
2208	Floral Wall Pocket	7	£50-£80	$75-$130	
2222	Wall Pocket		£12-£18	$15-$30	
2235	Wall Pocket	7	£10-£15	$15-$25	
2247	Cactus Wall Pocket		£30-£50	$45-$80	
2262	Cactus Wall Pocket	7½	£30-£50	$45-$80	
2263	Cactus Wall Pocket	5¼	£30-£50	$45-$80	
2269	Lace Wall Pocket		£15-£25	$20-$40	
2274	Lace Wall Pocket	7¼	£15-£20	$20-$35	
2293	Cactus Wall Pocket		£15-£25	$20-$40	
2306	Wall Pocket		£20-£30	$30-$50	
2310	Wall Pocket		£12-£18	$15-$30	
2322	Wall Pocket		£10-£15	$15-$25	
2366	Nuleef Wall Pocket		£15-£20	$20-$35	
2372	Lily Wall Pocket		£12-£18	$15-$30	
2386	Plume Wall Pocket		£15-£20	$20-$35	
2480	Wall Pocket		£12-£18	$15-$30	
2487	Hyacinth Wall Pocket	9	£20-£30	$30-$50	

Wall Pockets, Wall Plates & Wall Vases

Model No	Model	Size Inches	Market Value		Notes
2593	Squirrel Wall Pocket		£20-£30	$30-$50	
2607	Laronde Wall Pocket	6¼	£10-£15	$15-$25	
2720	Wall Pocket	10½	£20-£30	$30-$50	
2741	Bamboo Wall Pocket		£12-£18	$15-$30	
2771	Wall Pocket		£20-£30	$30-$50	
2775	Wall Pocket		£15-£20	$20-$35	
2838	Wall Pocket		£20-£30	$30-$50	
2917	Wall Pocket		£20-£30	$30-$50	
3156	Swallow Wall Plaque	7½	£30-£50	$45-$80	
3157	Swallow Wall Plaque	5L	£20-£30	$30-$50	
3158	Swallow Wall Plaque	5½L	£18-£25	$25-$40	
5327	New Cavalier Wall Plaque		£20-£30	$30-$50	
5559	Miniature Wall Plaque	4¼D	£8-£12	$10-$20	
5560	Miniature Wall Plaque	4½D	£8-£12	$10-$20	
5580	Small Plaque		£5-£8	$5-$15	
5582	Three Martingale Plaques on Leather		£20-£30	$30-$50	
5583	Three Martingale Plaques on Leather		£20-£30	$30-$50	

Wild Animals

1	Deer		£40-£60	$60-$100	
17	Brown Bison		£50-£100	$75-$165	
33	Lizard		£50-£80	$75-$130	
40	Rhino		£60-£100	$90-$165	
41	Elephant		£60-£100	$90-$165	
48	Rhino		£50-£80	$75-$130	
49	Lion		£50-£80	$75-$130	
50	Camel		£50-£80	$75-$130	
53	Wolf/Bison		£50-£80	$75-$130	
56	Buffalo Lamp Base		£80-£120	$120-$200	
62	Lion		£40-£60	$60-$100	
63	Giraffe		£50-£80	$75-$130	
66	Sealion		£40-£60	$60-$100	
68	Grey Elephant	9	£50-£80	$75-$130	
69	Bear		£40-£60	$60-$100	
85	Tiger		£40-£60	$60-$100	
92	Elephant	4	£50-£100	$75-$165	
93	Lion	7½L	£200-£300	$295-$495	
94	Bull		£30-£50	$45-$80	
96	Brown Chimpanzee	7	£100-£200	$150-$330	
97	Brown Chimpanzee	5½	£70-£150	$105-$245	
98	Brown Chimpanzee	4	£60-£120	$90-$200	
105	Mouse		£15-£20	$20-$35	
106	Mouse		£15-£20	$20-$35	
108	Brown Foal		£15-£20	$20-$35	
109	Giraffe		£30-£50	$45-$80	
133	Hippo		£30-£50	$45-$80	
134	Bear		£30-£50	$45-$80	
159	Elephant		£30-£50	$45-$80	
172	Bear		£30-£50	$45-$80	
173	Bear		£30-£50	$45-$80	
174	Bear		£30-£50	$45-$80	
175	Bear		£30-£50	$45-$80	
538	Bear		£20-£30	$30-$50	
538	Bear		£20-£30	$30-$50	
766	Camel with Saddlebags	5	£30-£50	$45-$80	
767	Camel with Saddlebags on Base	5	£30-£50	$45-$80	
772	Camel with Howdah	7	£35-£70	$50-$115	
779	Cheetah		£30-£60	$45-$100	
815	Elephant	4	£15-£20	$20-$35	
816	Elephant		£15-£20	$20-$35	
817	Lion	5¾	£30-£50	$45-$80	
818	Lion	4	£30-£50	$45-$80	
819	Lion	7¾	£50-£80	$75-$130	

Model No	Model	Size Inches	Market Value		Notes
820	Lion on Base	7¾	£60-£100	$90-$165	
821	Lion on Base	8¾	£50-£80	$75-$130	
822	Lion on Base	8¾	£70-£100	$105-$165	
825	Lion On Base with Vase	8¾	£30-£50	$45-$80	
846	Panther with Howdah	6	£40-£60	$60-$100	
991	Lion	4¾	£30-£50	$45-$80	
1142	Squirrel	5¼	£25-£50	$35-$80	
1143	Squirrel	7¾	£30-£60	$45-$100	
1144	Squirrel	8¾	£40-£80	$60-$130	
1146	Squirrel	10¾	£150-£200	$220-$330	
1265	Harry the Hare Figure	3	£20-£30	$30-$50	
1298	Harry the Hare	6¾	£50-£80	$75-$130	
1299	Harry the Hare	8¾	£120-£180	$180-$295	
1300	Harry the Hare	9	£200-£300	$295-$495	
1372	Polar Bear	3¾	£30-£50	$45-$80	
1390	Koala Bear on Log	4	£40-£60	$60-$100	
1391	Koala Bear on Log	6	£50-£80	$75-$130	
1399	Crouching Frog	2	£70-£100	$105-$165	
1423	Bear	3	£50-£80	$75-$130	
1424	Crouching Fox	2¼	£30-£50	$45-$80	
1425	Hippo	3	£60-£100	$90-$165	
1426	Bear/Panda	3¼	£40-£60	$60-$100	
1451	Stag	5¼	£40-£60	$60-$100	
1458	Leopard	9	£220-£320	$325-$530	
1464	Tortoise	2	£80-£120	$120-$200	
1465	Alligator		£80-£120	$120-$200	
1467	Lizard	7¼	£80-£120	$120-$200	
1493	Kangaroo		£100-£200	$150-$330	
1494	Squirrel	4	£40-£60	$60-$100	
1500	Panda	4	£60-£80	$90-$130	
1506	Panda	5	£50-£80	$75-$130	
1517	Squirrel Ashtray		£30-£50	$45-$80	
1518	Squirrel Holding Nut	3	£30-£50	$45-$80	
1519	Stag on Rock	5¾	£80-£120	$120-$200	
1520	Bear	2¼	£30-£50	$45-$80	
1521	Bear on Back	1	£30-£50	$45-$80	
1522	Bear on all Fours	2¾	£30-£50	$45-$80	
1527	Elephant	3	£80-£120	$120-$200	
2428	Giraffe		£80-£120	$120-$200	
2429	Elephant		£80-£120	$120-$200	
2523	Squirrel		£18-£25	$25-$40	
2529	Squirrel		£12-£18	$15-$30	
2572	Seal		£20-£30	$30-$50	
2667	Fawn (not sold separately)		Not known		
2757	Seal		£20-£30	$30-$50	
2912	Giraffe	6½	£30-£50	$45-$80	
2933	Giraffe	6	£40-£60	$60-$100	
2946	Zebra		£40-£60	$60-$100	
3088	Zebra		£20-£30	$30-$50	
3120	Hare	4	£20-£30	$30-$50	
3147	Amused Donkey		£50-£80	$75-$130	
3152	Horse or Zebra	10	£50-£100	$75-$165	
3153	Tiger	6½	£30-£50	$45-$80	
3154	Stag	7½	£30-£50	$45-$80	
3459	Otter with Fish Prestige Figure	10½L	£100-£150	$150-$245	
3568	Giraffe	10	£30-£50	$45-$80	
3575	Hare	7	£30-£50	$45-$80	
3612	Mouse	4	£20-£30	$30-$50	
3912	Squirrel		£20-£30	$30-$50	
3918	Fox		£30-£50	$45-$80	
3925	Bambi Fawn		£30-£50	$45-$80	
3957	Fox		£20-£30	$30-$50	
4250	Squirrel		£20-£30	$30-$50	
4531	Dolphin	8	£30-£50	$45-$80	

Wild Animals

Model No	Model	Size Inches	Market Value		Notes
4650	Badger	4	£30-£50	$45-$80	
4732	Bison	8L	£40-£60	$60-$100	
4733	Buffalo	10½L	£50-£80	$75-$130	
5152	Elephant	5L	£30-£50	$45-$80	
5166	Rhinoceros	11½	£100-£150	$150-$245	
5209	Prestige Fox	11½	£50-£100	$75-$165	
5210	Modus Gazelle	10½L	£30-£60	$45-$100	
5211	Prestige Squirrel	7L	£50-£100	$75-$165	
5212	Modus Cheetah	10L	£30-£60	$45-$100	
5216	Badger And Rock	5	£25-£35	$35-$55	
5229	Hippopotamus	6L	£12-£18	$15-$30	
5230	Camel	5L	£20-£30	$30-$50	
5231	Bear	6L	£30-£50	$45-$80	
5233	Lion	6¼	£20-£30	$30-$50	
5234	Giraffe	5	£20-£30	$30-$50	
5238	Modus Polar Bear	7	£30-£50	$45-$80	
5239	Badger	6½	£20-£30	$30-$50	
5251	Mouse (used for ornaments)		Not known		
5252	Mouse (used for ornaments)		Not known		
5254	Mouse (used for ornaments)		Not known		
5255	Fox (used for ornaments)		Not known		
5578	Giant Panda Sitting	2¼	£20-£30	$30-$50	
5579	Giant Panda Standing	2½	£20-£30	$30-$50